THE IDEAS BEHIND

THE CHESS OPENINGS

THE IDEAS BEHIND
THE CHESS OPENINGS

By

REUBEN FINE

AUTHOR OF

Practical Chess Openings
Chess the Easy Way
Basic Chess Endings

DAVID M^{c}KAY COMPANY, INC.

NEW YORK

PREFACE TO THE FIRST EDITION

It has been said that ideas are weapons. That is certainly as true in chess as in any other field. A mastery of a little theory which conveys real understanding of the game is infinitely more valuable than a carefully memorized compilation of endless moves. Paradoxically, a thorough grasp of the ideas behind the openings, which are relatively few in number, is a royal road to knowledge which eliminates much of the drudgery associated with remembering a long series of variations. My object in this work is to present the necessary "ideology" as concisely as possible.

The present work grew out of some articles which I wrote for the CHESS CORRESPONDENT about two years ago. Because so many encouraging letters came to me from so many enthusiastic readers it was a real pleasure to expand the previous short sketches into a full-length book.

As usual, the finished product is about twice as long as was anticipated, but it did not seem advisable to compress the material any further.

I feel confident that the book can be read with profit without reference to any compilation of moves. However, those who have a copy of MODERN CHESS OPENINGS, 6th edition, will be well advised to use the two treatments together. Ideas and moves are complementary, not mutually exclusive.

I wish to acknowledge a debt of gratitude to Mr. Walter F. James for the original suggestion which led to these pages. My thanks are also due Miss Nora L. Keesing for her kind assistance in typing a major portion of the manuscript.

REUBEN FINE

Washington, D. C.
May 5, 1943.

PREFACE TO SECOND EDITION

This edition has been revised to conform to PRACTICAL CHESS OPENINGS. As before, this book may be read independently, but ideas are most useful in conjunction with variations, and the reader would do best to use the two books together.

REUBEN FINE

New York, N. Y.
Dec. 12, 1948.

CONTENTS

THE IDEAS BEHIND

THE CHESS OPENINGS

Chapter I

GENERAL PRINCIPLES

It is always true, though not always clear, that moves in the chess openings are based on certain definite ideas. These ideas form the background and foundation, while the moves themselves represent actual construction.

In every field the man who can merely do things without knowing why is at a disadvantage to the one who can not only build but also tell you just why he is building in that way. This is especially noticeable when the prescribed cycle does not obey the laws it is supposed to: then the laborer must sit by with folded hands while the mechanic or engineer comes in and adjusts the delicate mechanism.

All this holds true in chess, just as it holds true in every field which is a combination of theory and action. And since action or moves in chess are much less standardized than, say, the construction of a house, theory as represented by *ideas* is so much more important.

An apt illustration occurs in deviations from "book." A game begins with 1 P—K4, P—KB3? The reply is bad, so bad in fact that it will not be found in any collection of standard opening moves. What to do about it? The man who has memorized oodles and oodles of moves without understanding them is at a loss; he will not even be able to give a good reason why the move is bad. But the man who knows that Black has neglected the center, deprived his KKt of its best square, and weakened his King position will find it a simple matter to refute his opponent's faulty play.

It is perhaps not generally realized that opening theory in

1

chess proceeds on certain definite assumptions. They are simple enough and once learned they will never be forgotten. They are:

1. In the initial position White, because of the extra move, has a slight advantage. Consequently:

2. White's problem in the opening is to secure the better position, while

3. Black's problem is to secure equality.

The elaboration of these questions in each individual case is what is meant by "the theory of the openings." Once either question 2 or 3 is clearly answered, the "theory" is satisfied and the rest is left to mortal man.

As yet, however, nobody has found a method of determining values which is superior to that of good master practise. That is, by sticking to well-established rules and principles we get to a position where there are pros and cons for both sides. In that event a game between two experts is the most important clue that we can possibly have. This is one of the chief reasons for quoting games. We shall return to this question a little later but suffice it to say for the time being that in many examples "theory" is nothing but "good practise."

Throughout PRACTICAL CHESS OPENINGS and other similar treatises there is continual mention of "normal" moves and "normal" positions. This "normalcy" arises in the following manner.

There are two fundamental concepts in the opening: development and the center. Development is getting the pieces out. The center consists of the four squares in the geometrical center of the board. The basic principle is that it is essential in the opening to develop all the pieces harmoniously and in such a way as to secure the most favorable position possible in the center.

More elaborately, there are ten practical rules which are usually worth sticking to, though the more expert player will be aware of the many exceptions. These rules are:

1. Open with either the King's Pawn or the Queen's Pawn.

2. Wherever possible, make a good developing move which threatens something.

3. Develop Knights before Bishops.

4. Pick the most suitable square for a piece and develop it there once and for all.

5. Make one or two Pawn moves in the opening, not more.

6. Do not bring your Queen out early.

7. Castle as soon as possible, preferably on the King's side.

8. Play to get control of the center.

9. Always try to maintain at least one Pawn in the center.

10. Do not sacrifice without a clear and adequate reason.

In number 10 we can further specify that for the offer of a Pawn there must be one of four reasons: a) Secure a tangible advantage in development; b) deflect the enemy Queen; c) prevent the enemy from castling, either permanently or for several moves; d) build up a strong attack.

Finally, it is worth remembering that there are two questions which must be answered for each move played:

1. How does it affect the center?

2. How does it fit in with the development of my other pieces and Pawns? [1]

Any move which is in accordance with the basic principle is "normal"; any move which is not is "abnormal." Thus 1 P—K4, which places a Pawn in the center and aids the development of the K-side, is normal, while 1 P—QR4, which helps neither development nor the center, is abnormal. Similarly, after 1 P—K4, P—K4; 2 Kt—KB3, developing and threatening a center Pawn, is normal, while 2 P—QKt3, which develops a relatively unimportant piece, and does not affect the center, is abnormal. The reader will readily think of many similar examples.

Sacrifices and gambits sometimes seem to violate sound opening procedure. This is in a sense true, since every sacrifice requires special justification. However, it is a well-known and

---

[1] The reader who would like to have a more detailed explanation of these ideas is advised to consult R. Fine, Chess The Easy Way, Chapter IV.

easily established fact that under certain circumstances extra material is useless when it is hampered by an immobile position. In such cases sacrifices are likewise perfectly normal.

With gambits, the sacrifice is the essence of it all. Normal procedure must necessarily take that into account and accordingly a third factor is introduced. While this analysis is correct from a purely theoretical point of view, in practise it will be found that the center is relatively of less moment, so that the essential question to be answered by both sides is: Is the advantage in development sufficient compensation for the material given up or not? Normal moves in gambits are those which help to answer this question.

In almost all openings there is a well-defined series of normal moves which leads to what is usually called a "normal position." This normal position is the point of departure for further opening investigations. If it is favorable for White, theory concerns itself with the improvement of Black's defensive possibilities. Conversely, if, as is usually the case, it is even, the problem is to better White's play. Sometimes—as in the Orthodox Defense to the Queen's Gambit Declined—it is theoretically even, but in practise full of pitfalls and difficulties. In that event theory can and does concern itself with an examination for both sides, to give White better winning chances on the one hand, and to make Black's task easier on the other.

An allied pertinent conception which will be used on occasion is that of "ideal positions." An ideal position is one which is reached by a sequence of normal moves for both sides and which represents the maximum positional superiority which one player or the other can secure. It is therefore a worthwhile goal for one man, but something to be avoided for his opponent.

In a number of modern openings—such as Alekhine's Defense and the Catalan System—the play of one side or the other turns out to be highly successful even though it is in apparent contradiction with healthy opening principles. The contradiction can be resolved only by considering the element of *per-*

manency. E.g., in Alekhine's Defense Black allows White to build up a powerful Pawn center not because he believes such a center is bad, but because he is convinced that he will be able to crack it sooner or later. Consequently, among other things in some opening, we must examine how long a given advantage will last.

Another modern nuance is *transposition*, which is quite common in the Queen's Pawn Openings.

It is important to be clear about the question of the evaluation of a position reached in the opening. This must, of course, be based on the general analysis of any position. Such general analysis involves five factors: Material; Pawn structure; Mobility; King safety; Combinations. In most openings (except gambits) only Pawn structure and mobility are really important (the center is a special case of mobility, for the side which has control of the center automatically enjoys more freedom for his pieces).

It will sometimes be observed that the ideas which are said to be at the basis of certain openings are either avoided or entirely absent in practise. That is because ideas are not dictatorial laws but counselling guides. Strategy, the body of ideas, holds only as a framework. Tactics, the individual variations, is what goes into this framework, which is why the result often varies so widely from the original conception. Frequently a line which carries out the basic idea and is therefore strategically sound must be rejected because there is a tactical refutation: it just won't work. Proper timing comes in here. Further, in most openings there are several ideas for each side, not all of which may be realized in a single game.

It is obvious that many of the situations reached in PRACTICAL CHESS OPENINGS are so complicated that cursory analysis of this type will not lead to any conclusive result. That is why games with masters are quoted which continued from those positions. The argument is simple enough. Two experts examined this game and came to the following conclusion. Their opinions have been checked by another expert who finds that both played reasonably well (if not, a comment to that effect will be found). Unless there is some excellent evidence to support the contrary, it is therefore to be assumed that the judgment of the book is to be accepted as substantially correct.

This emphatically does not mean that the book is infallible. Quite the contrary. Chess is, fortunately, not a finished science, but a steadily growing organism. Many corrections and improvements have been found and will continue to be found. Still, all this does not do away with the fact that a person who deliberately deviates from "book" lines should have some good reason for doing so. Uncritical rejection of all theory because it is incomplete and wrong on occasion is foolish and harmful; intelligent criticism of standard material, no matter how long it has been accepted, is sensible and wholesome.

Chapter II

KING PAWN OPENINGS
PART I

OPENINGS WITH 1 P—K4, P—K4

Both White's and Black's initial moves here are perfectly natural and normal: both assist development and affect vital central squares.

As long as Black can retain symmetry, White can lay no claim to an advantage. Consequently the task is to compel the defender to give up his strong center positions, in other words to abandon his P at K4.

White can achieve this aim only by playing P—Q4. If Black then replies with .... P×P he will be left with a Pawn at Q3 (eventually) vs. his opponent's at K4 and our general theory of the game teaches us that such a Pawn structure is favorable for White (*Diagram No. 1*).

The reason why such a Pawn vis-a-vis is better for the man with the center Pawn is twofold: it cramps the enemy's pieces and it creates valuable outposts at Q5, KB5. From this explanation we can see why such a Pawn is not an *absolute* advantage, for if neither of the above conditions holds to an appreciable extent (chiefly in the endgame, where there is nothing to cramp and where the outposts lack real meaning) the center Pawn is not essentially different from any other. If it is exposed to attack then, it may even be a weakness.

Likewise it is clear that when one has such a strong Pawn in the opening or early middle game, it is essential to use it for an *attack*. Otherwise the normal course of exchanges will simply deprive it of its supporting pedestal, from which its

strength is derived. Naturally, White should also avoid unnecessary exchanges, which only help to liberate his opponent.

All this is only another illustration of the general principle
that an advantage in mobility must be exploited energetically
(usually by an assault), otherwise it will be dissipated in short
order.

On the other hand, if Black wishes to keep a Pawn at K4, he
can only do so by .... P—Q3, which cramps his pieces some-

No. 1

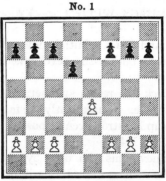

Ideal Pawn skeleton for White in all
openings with 1 P—K4, P—K4.

what. These theoretical considerations suffice to explain why
White so often retains a persistent, if slight, superiority in this
group of openings. They also show how ideal positions arise in
these debuts.

From the above it is clear that there are two types of defense
which Black may adopt in his search for equality. The first is
the *strong point method*, where he retains a Pawn at K4 come
what may. The second is the *counter-attack*, where he re-
linquishes his KP, but compels White to give up his KP as
well, or to weaken his position otherwise. (It is worth noting
that the execution of this plan does not involve hitting at the
KP at every move; it is the set-up as a whole that counts.)

This analysis holds good if White continues "theoretically"
or "according to Hoyle." Against less regular lines Black can

and should do what his opponent has neglected: advance . . . .
P—Q4 and secure the favorable Pawn skeleton (*Diagram No.
1*) for himself. In fact, it may be adopted as a good working
rule that *once Black succeeds in playing . . . . P—Q4 without
any immediate harmful consequences he has equalized.*

These preliminaries should be borne in mind in the course of
what follows.

I. CENTER GAME: 1 P—K4, P—K4; 2 P—Q4

This represents the most direct application of our theories,
for Black is forced to make an immediate decision. It will not
do to defend the Pawn by 2 . . . . P—Q3 because he then ob-
structs his KB and permits 3 Kt—KB3, with transposition to
other openings (e.g., Philidor's Defense) which are favorable for
White. But Black can capture, in which event White must
recapture with the Queen or play a gambit. The gambit will
be considered separately.

The trouble with this opening is, of course, the early development of White's Queen and it is not surprising that Black has
two excellent lines to choose from.

After 2 . . . . P×P; 3 Q×P, Kt—QB3; 4 Q—K3, Kt—B3;
5 Kt—QB3 (*Diagram No. 2*) Black has the choice of two continuations, both direct applications of our basic rule. He can
either play for an early exchange of the White KP by 5 . . . .
B—K2 and 6 . . . . P—Q4, followed by castling on the Q-side,
or he can bring pressure to bear on the White KP by . . . . B—
Kt5, ... O—O, ... R—K1, etc. In both lines all moves are
quite normal.

The first runs as follows: 5 . . . . B—K2; 6 B—Q2, P—Q4;
7 P×P, Kt×P; 8 Kt×Kt, Q×Kt; 9 Kt—K2 (White must
not castle because his QRP is undefended), B—Kt5; 10 Kt—
B4, Q—Q2; 11 P—KB3, O—O—O!; 12 O—O—O, B—KB4 and
Black's development is freer.

The second is equally effective: 5 . . . . B—Kt5; 6 B—Q2,
O—O; 7 O—O—O, R—K1; 8 B—B4, P—Q3; 9 Kt—B3,
B—K3!; 10 B×B, R×B; 11 KKt—Kt5 (note the constant

pressure on the White KP which compels White to adopt radical measures), R—K1, again with a healthier formation for Black.

Attempts to improve upon White's play have been uniformly unsuccessful. Consequently the opening cannot be

No. 2

No. 3

Center Game after White's 5th Move.   Scotch Game: Position in the Normal Line after 14 .... B—K3.

considered adequate for White. It is well, however, to master its variations because it is a clear and uncomplicated illustration of our fundamental principles.

II. SCOTCH GAME: 1 P—K4, P—K4; 2 Kt—KB3, Kt—QB3; 3 P—Q4

Again a perfectly logical idea, for the strong point method (3 .... P—Q3) is once more inapplicable. Unfortunately, as in the previous case the counter-attack against the White KP is quite effective.

The first and most obvious counter-attack begins with 3 .... P×P; 4 Kt×P, Kt—KB3. Then the normal line would run 5 Kt—QB3, B—Kt5; 6 Kt×Kt, KtP×Kt; 7 B—Q3, P—Q4; 8 P×P, P×P, 9 O—O, O—O; 10 B—KKt5, P—B3; 11 Q—B3, B—K2; 12 QR—K1, R—Kt1; 13 Kt—Q1, R—K1; 14 P—KR3, B—K3 (*Diagram No. 3*).

The position reached is approximately even: White has

somewhat more freedom for his pieces, which is counter-balanced by Black's stronger center Pawn. Consequently this is one of those cases where both sides have searched for improvements: White to strengthen his bind, Black to ease the defense.

White's attempts have ended in failure. In the above main line, we find that 7 B—Q2!, O—O; 8 B—Q3, P—Q4; 9 P—B3!? was once tried to maintain the Pawn at K4, but after 9 .... P×P; 10 Kt×P, Kt×Kt; 11 P×Kt, B—QB4! Black's game is excellent.

A more common variant is 5 Kt×Kt (instead of 5 Kt—QB3 in the main line), KtP×Kt; 6 P—K5 (to keep the Pawn in a central position anyhow and thus cramp Black's game), Q—K2; 7 Q—K2, Kt—Q4; 8 Kt—Q2, but here Black can mobilize his forces quickly and attack the enemy KP, thus actually securing a slight advantage. The same holds true if White tries to play P—K5 after adequate or inadequate preparation.

A simplification of Black's problem in the main line is to be found with 8 .... Q—K2ch! (instead of 8 .... P×P), for then 9 Q—K2 is forced, when the exchange of Queens and minor pieces leads to a drawn ending. It is worth remembering that in all such openings as the Scotch, where White hopes to engineer an attack against the enemy King, the exchange of Queens has the effect of a wet blanket.

There are also other simplifications available for Black.

A more subtle—and more promising—counter-attack is that which begins with 4 .... B—B4. Then the normal line would be 5 B—K3, Q—B3; 6 P—B3, KKt—K2; 7 Kt—B2, B×B; 8 Kt×B, O—O; 9 B—K2, P—Q3 (he must work up to .... P—Q4); 10 O—O, B—K3; 11 Kt—Q2, P—Q4 and Black's game is a trifle freer.

Attempts at improvement (based chiefly on the fact that Black's QBP is temporarily undefended) are thus to be expected from White. Perhaps the most valuable is 7 Q—Q2, P—Q4; 8 Kt—Kt5, B×B; 9 Q×B, O—O; 10 Kt—Q2, P×P; 11 Kt×KP, Q—K4; 12 O—O—O with fair opportunities for both sides. Note here that White cannot afford to take the proffered Pawns because his development is too backward. Other tries are much less likely to succeed.

There are several interesting features in the two openings just discussed which merit attention if one would like to penetrate beneath the surface.

It cannot be maintained that White committed any theoretical error: his principal objective in all openings with 1 P—K4, P—K4 is to get rid of the enemy KP and in both cases he proceeded to do so with exemplary dispatch. Yet Black equalizes faster than his opponent can set the pieces up. Is our theory wrong?

No, we need not reject the lessons of logic and experience, if we bear in mind that it is always essential to strike a balance. Yes, White's major goal is to exchange the enemy KP for his own QP. Why? Because by doing so he sets up the Pawn structure in *Diagram No. 1*, where his plus is derived from the fact that the powerful KP in the center yields him greater mobility. Thus the basic factor is not the abstract rigidity of merely having a foot soldier in the middle: it is, instead, the living fact that his total mobility is greater because of that Pawn.

But mobility is, after all, a fragile weapon that must be handled with finesse. What if in the process of setting up the better Pawn there are such sacrifices of time and distortion of the careers of other pieces that Black is allowed to develop his men freely? Then the Pawn in the center loses its reason for being; White's advantage is dissipated. Most often White is so badly harassed that he is compelled to exchange his KP for Black's QP in turn, when it is all too clear that his alleged advantage rests on sand.

We should not be blind to a more general conclusion which experience with these and other "old-fashioned" openings points to. There are valid rules in chess, but they must never be applied mechanically. In any given situation there are a number of questions to be considered; the complexity and the artistry of the game derive from our skill in balancing them to pick out the most significant at any given stage.

Since P—Q4 at a very early stage evidently leads to nothing of value for White because of Black counter-attacks, the lines where he postpones this advance until several pieces have been developed become so much more important. The two openings which follow—Giuoco Piano (and variants) and Ruy Lopez are indeed the chief ones in this chapter because they hold out most hope of an advantage.

III. GIUOCO PIANO: 1 P—K4, P—K4; 2 Kt—KB3, Kt—QB3; 3 B—B4, B—B4

Here White takes a somewhat different tack: he will defer the advance of his QP until it is supported by his QBP, so that he will always be able to retain a Pawn at Q4.

Against extremely negligent defense the two center Pawns will be a crushing steamroller. E.g., 4 P—B3, Kt—B3; 5 P—Q4, P×P; 6 P×P, B—Kt3?; 7 P—Q5, Kt—QKt1; 8 P—K5, Kt—Kt1; 9 O—O, Kt—K2; 10 P—Q6, Kt—Kt3; 11 Kt—Kt5, O—O; 12 Q—R5 and Black will soon have to give up his Queen to avoid mate.

But even reasonably plausible moves will not suffice to give Black an adequate position if he plays too passively. Thus after 4 P—B3, P—Q3?; 5 P—Q4, P×P; 6 P×P, B—Kt3; 7 Kt—B3, Kt—B3?; 8 Q—Q3, B—Kt5; 9 B—K3, O—O; 10 P—QR3, R—K1; 11 B—R2, Q—Q2; 12 Kt—Q2, R—K2; 13 P—B3, B—R4; 14 O—O White has a permanent, though small advantage. (*Diagram No. 4.*)

To avert such eventualities Black must have recourse to one of the two old standbys—counter-attack, or strong point defense. The more promising of these is the counter-attack.

First we must note that the normal line 4 P—B3, Kt—B3; 5 P—Q4, P×P; 6 P×P, B—Kt5ch; 7 B—Q2, B×Bch; 8 QKt×B, P—Q4! breaks up the center and thereby equalizes immediately. White must therefore resort to a Pawn sacrifice, which branches off into two main lines at an early stage. This runs: 4 P—B3, Kt—B3!; 5 P—Q4, P×P; 6 P×P, B—Kt5ch!; 7 Kt—B3!, Kt×KP; 8 O—O. Black can now pursue one of two policies: return the extra material quickly and be content with a draw (a common procedure against gambits) or retain the extra Pawn at the cost of allowing White a strong attack.

The first of these is exemplified in the Greco line: 8 .... Kt×Kt; 9 P×Kt, B×P. Here the new move 10 B—R3! completely destroys Black's plan, the main line running 10 .... Kt—K2; 11 Q—Kt3!, P—Q4; 12 Q×B, P×B; 13 KR—K1, B—K3; 14 B×Kt, K×B; 15 P—Q5!, Q×P; 16 QR—Q1, Q—QB4; 17 R—K5, Q—Kt3; 18 R×Bch!! and wins for if 18 .... P×R; 19 Q×Pch.

No. 4

Ideal position for White in the Giuoco Piano.

Hence the only playable line here is 8 .... B×Kt (instead of 8 .... Kt×Kt); 9 P—Q5! (on 9 P×B the normal 9 .... P—Q4 is wholly adequate), Kt—K4!; 10 P×B, Kt×B; 11 Q—Q4, P—KB4; 12 Q×Kt(B4), P—Q3. This is a normal position: White's development is virtually ideal, but Black is a Pawn ahead, with a solid position. Consequently, we again have a case where both sides search for improvements.

The branch 9 .... B—B3 (instead of 9 .... Kt—K4) leads to a draw, though an exceedingly complicated one, after 10

R—K1, Kt—K2; 11 R×Kt, P—Q3; 12 B—Kt5, B×B; 13 Kt×B, O—O; 14 Kt×RP!, K×Kt; 15 Q—R5ch, K—Kt1; 16 R—R4, P—KB4! etc.

Nothing better has ever been found for Black than any of the above lines. White's most important endeavor to strengthen the bind is 7 K—B1! (instead of 7 Kt—B3). One negative merit of this variant is that it is little known. On the normal 7 .... Kt×KP; 8 P—Q5, Kt—K2; 9 Q—Q4 White evidently secures tangible pressure for the Pawn.

It is interesting to observe that the refusal on Black's part to accept the sacrifice (in the main lines) is bad. Thus after 4 P—B3, Kt—B3; 5 P—Q4, P×P; 6 P×P, B—Kt5ch; 7 Kt—B3, the normal 7 .... P—Q4 is refuted by 8 P×P, Kt(KB3)× P; 9 O—O, B×Kt; 10 P×B, B—K3; 11 R—K1, O—O; 12 Kt—KKt5 etc. This is a striking example of the fact that strategically sound conceptions may be utterly ruined by accidental tactical interpositions.

One general tip worth remembering is that on P—K5 by White .... P—Q4 is almost always the proper reaction, to prevent White from forming a steamroller in the center. E.g., after 4 P—B3, Kt—B3; 5 P—Q4, P×P; 6 P—K5, 6 .... Kt—K5? would be met by 7 B—Q5, P—KB4; 8 P×P, while 6 .... Kt—KKt1?; 7 P×P, B—Kt3?; 8 P—Q5 is also obviously bad. But 6 .... P—Q4!; 7 B—QKt5, Kt—K5 leads to equality.

While the balance in the counter-attack is in theory quite adequate for Black, some players often prefer a more quiet line, in the conviction that White's attack will rebound. This quiet line is the *strong point defense*.

The strategical notion of holding the bomb-proof anchor at K4 is not in itself sufficient to determine the right moves. For after 4 P—B3 the normal 4 .... P—Q3; 5 P—Q4, B—Kt3? loses a Pawn by 6 P×P, P×P; 7 Q×Qch etc. Likewise moves such as 4 .... P—B3 or 4 .... B—Q3 would be unnatural, so that we get to 4 P—B3, B—Kt3; 5 P—Q4, Q—K2 by elimination.

To be sure, White can get rid of the enemy KP by 6 P×P,

Kt×P; 7 Kt×Kt, Q×Kt; 8 O—O but he thereby merely exposes himself to an attack against his King position: 8 ....
Kt—B3; 9 Q—K2, P—Q3; 10 Kt—Q2, O—O; 11 Kt—B3,
Q—R4 etc.

In view of this variation (typical for the opening) White must base his strategy on one of two ideas:

1. weakening the defenses of the Black KP, in the hope that the exchange will eventually be forced, or

2. maneuvering his Kt to Q5 or KB5 (strong outposts defended by the KP).

The difficulty with the latter is that the White center Pawns are constantly menaced, so that the former is the only really suitable plan. It is nevertheless worth remembering that the Kt maneuver is an idea which comes into prominence later, *after* the threat to the White center has been removed.

The most accessible of the supporters of the KP is the QKt. So we go after him first. We repeat the previous moves for the sake of clarity: 4 P—B3, B—Kt3; 5 P—Q4, Q—K2 and now 6 O—O (development must be completed first—a basic principle), Kt—B3; 7 R—K1 (it is almost never advisable for White to give up the KP), P—Q3; 8 P—QR4, P—QR3; 9 P—R3 (there is no hurry; meanwhile the pin of the White KKt which might prove very annoying is prevented), O—O; 10 P—QKt4, P—KR3; 11 B—R3, Kt—Q2 (note that Black is compelled to adopt this unnatural move in order to hold his anchor); 12 P—Kt5, Kt—Q1; 13 QKt—Q2 and *now* the shifting of the Kt to B1—K3—Q5 or KB5 will be a most effective prosecution of the initial ideas. Black has managed to maintain the KP, but only at the cost of blocking his development. White consequently has slightly the better of it.

It is clear that both counter-attack and strong point systems have their pros and cons. From a rigidly objective point of view, the counter-attack is better, but players who prefer a solid positional type of game are well advised to choose the other.

The lines where White does not try to secure a Pawn at Q4

are, with one exception, easy to meet and consequently of little importance. Symmetrical development is the indicated counter for Black and if he takes care to prevent P—Q4 by White as long as possible and threaten to prepare it on his own hook he will have little to fear.

The exception is the Canal Variation, which has led to some striking successes. This runs 4 P—Q3, Kt—B3; 5 Kt—B3, P—Q3; 6 B—KKt5. Now the customary reply had always been 6 .... P—KR3, when Canal showed that 7 B×Kt! has a good deal of merit. After 7 .... Q×B; 8 Kt—Q5, Q—Q1; 9 P—B3 we see the idea: Pawns are to be set up at Q4 and K4. From the theoretical point of view there are two objections to this plan: White has conceded his opponent the two Bishops, and so many pieces have been exchanged that the value of the strong Pawn center is dissipated.

Black's counter in accordance with the discussion must consist of offering exchanges. Thus either 9 .... Kt—K2, or 9 .... Kt—QR4. Both are adequate, though Black must be careful about possible tactical consequences of some exchanges. White always manages to secure a somewhat freer position, but it is of little use against a ruthlessly consistent swapping policy.

Finally it is well to bear in mind that there are two excellent and simple alternatives to the provocative 6 .... P—KR3: 6 .... B—K3 and 6 .... Kt—QR4.

TWO KNIGHTS' DEFENSE: 1 P—K4, P—K4; 2 Kt—KB3, Kt—QB3; 3 B—B4, Kt—B3

There is no variation of the Giuoco Piano where White does not secure and retain the initiative for quite a while, though in some cases he must give up a Pawn to do so. To avoid this and other bad features Black may develop his Kt first.

Though it is not usually classed as such, this opening is in reality a gambit. However, it differs from the more conventional gambits in that Black sacrifices a Pawn in order to have a greater say in the course of events and lead into a more comfortable position than would otherwise be the case.

To secure an advantage White must take the offer by 4 Kt—Kt5, P—Q4; 5 P×P (*Diagram No. 5*). In fact, a good working rule to adopt for all openings is Steinitz's old maxim that "the way to refute a sacrifice is to accept it."

Strategically, the normal reply for Black is 5 .... Kt×P, and Pinkus has recently shown that it is playable. However,

No. 5

Position in the Two Knights' Defense
after 5 P×P.

this line is full of pitfalls, and the defender must be thoroughly familiar with the published analysis if he wishes to try it.

The most usual variation begins with 5 .... Kt—QR4, when White in turn has two different ways of holding on to the Pawn. However, the procedure of holding on to the material with a tight grip does not work out well here. That is, on a simple move such as 6 P—Q3, P—KR3; 7 Kt—KB3, P—K5; 8 Q—K2, Kt×B; 9 P×Kt, B—QB4! gives Black more than enough for the Pawn. Nor can White advantageously give back the extra material at any point above.

Since the Black Kt is out of play at QR4, the natural alternative to the above unsatisfactory line is 6 B—Kt5ch, P—B3; 7 P×P, P×P; 8 B—K2, P—KR3 (Black chases the Kt before it can return to the excellent square K4); 9 Kt—KB3, P—K5; 10 Kt—K5, B—Q3.

So far everything has been virtually forced for both sides.

But now White must stop to think. Shall he move the Kt to B4, or shall he defend it, and if he does defend it, shall it be with the QP or with the BP?

Before he can answer this question, he must first decide whether he is going to try to hold on to the Pawn at all costs. If he is, then either 11 Kt—B4 or 11 P—Q4 is called for. On 11 Kt—B4, Kt×Kt; 12 B×Kt, O—O, he still cannot castle (because of the common sacrifice 13 .... B×RPch), while 13 P—Q3, P×P, followed by .... R—K1ch and .... Kt—Kt5 only leads to further difficult problems. Likewise 11 P—Q4, P×P e.p. (best); 12 Kt×QP, Q—B2!; 13 Kt—R3, B—R3!; 14 P—KKt3, O—O, etc. is in Black's favor.

It follows that White cannot afford to hold on to the Pawn. Before continuing the analysis it will be well to recall two vital principles:

1. The gambit player in the opening furthers his attack by preventing his opponent from developing normally.

2. The defender against a gambit can often secure the better position by returning the extra material at an opportune moment.

Examination of the last variation shows that all White's difficulties arise from his inability to get his pieces out in a reasonable manner. First the Kt is misplaced at Q3, then he cannot castle, then he must weaken his Pawns, etc. But if he chooses 11 P—KB4! instead of 11 P—Q4, and prepares to give back the extra Pawn, he can secure a clear superiority. For now 11 .... P×Pe.p.; 12 Kt×P(KB3) leaves the Kt on its natural square, while after 11 .... O—O; 12 Kt—QB3, Q—B2; 13 O—O!, B×Kt; 14 P×B, Q×P; 15 P—Q4, P×P e.p.; 16 Q×P! Black's Pawn position is ruined, his QKt is out of play and his opponent has the advantage of two Bishops in an open game—a crushing handicap.

One comment is in order here: if he cannot distort White's development, Black's attacking chances derive from the strong point at K5. It follows that White in defending must concentrate on the removal of this Pawn.

In view of the strengthening of White's game by this line, theoreticians began to look for improvements for Black. The most promising is 5 .... Kt×P, revived by Pinkus, which was discussed above (see p. 18). Ulvestad's 5 .... P—QKt4 is refuted by 6 B—B1!, Kt×P; 7 B×P, B—Kt2; 8 P—Q4, while Fritz's move, 5 .... Kt—Q5, is defeated by 6 P—QB3!

It may be said that the strategy underlying the Two Knights' is simple, but that the tactical execution if always complicated. There is a constant see-saw of improvements for both sides with the balance usually in White's favor. However, it is by no means inconceivable that some time-honored variations may be upset here.

MAXLANGE: 1 P—K4, P—K4; 2 Kt—KB3; Kt—QB3; 3 B—B4, B—B4; 4 O—O, Kt—B3; 5 P—Q4

Another gambit idea, this time by White. The main varia‹ tion of the opening is important chiefly because it may arise by transposition from a number of others (e.g., from the Two Knights': 1 P—K4, P—K4; 2 Kt—KB3, Kt—QB3; 3 B—B4, Kt—B3; 4 P—Q4, P×P; 5 O—O, B—B4; 6 P—K5, P—Q4, etc.).

After 5 .... P×P (5 .... B×P is better, but, as mentioned, the position may arise from a different order of moves) 6 P— K5, P—Q4 (a normal reaction); 7 P×Kt, P×B; 8 R—K1ch, B—K3; 9 Kt—Kt5, Q—Q4; 10 Kt—QB3, Q—B4; 11 QKt— K4, O—O—O; 12 Kt×QB, P×Kt; 13 P—KKt4, Q—K4; 14 P×P, KR—Kt1; 15 B—R6! Black can get the better of it with either 15 .... B—Kt5! or 15 .... P—Q6!, when analysis indicates that Black's resources are greater than commonly seen. White's attack is based on the exposed position of the Black KB and later on his passed KKtP; Black's counterchances are based on an attack against the enemy King. Strategy is relatively unimportant here; it is purely a question of who can press his advantage home first. Interestingly the new move 15 .... B—Kt5! was discovered independently in Los Angeles and Budapest.

RUY LOPEZ: 1 P—K4, P—K4; 2 Kt—KB3, Kt—QB3; 3 B—Kt5

Since White's only trump is the initiative or the extra move, he is the first who can attack anything. Consequently, to force the game into favorable channels he must use threats. 2 Kt—KB3 fits in, because it menaces the KP. And 3 B—Kt5 is the most logical continuation because it attacks the defender of the KP and thus continues the series of threats. It is

No. 6

Ideal position for White in the Ruy Lopez.

no surprise that of all the openings in this chapter the Ruy Lopez is hardest for Black to meet.

One reason why the Ruy Lopez is so strong is that the most natural sequence of moves leads to an ideal position for White. Thus: 3 .... P—Q3; 4 P—Q4, B—Q2; 5 Kt—B3, Kt—B3; 6 O—O, B—K2; 7 R—K1, P×P (forced); 8 Kt×P, O—O; 9 B—B1! White has the better Pawn center and Black's position is badly cramped. (*Diagram No. 6.*)

It took quite a while for experts to appreciate the strength of this and similar lines. The two main older defenses—which are now the buffalo of the KP openings—dominated the stage right up to the twenties, but then gradually disappeared.

If he does not choose the modern waiting move, 3 .... P—QR3, Black must adopt one of the usual two defensive systems: strong point or counter-attack. It should be noted that the only alternative which does not yield White a marked advantage is 3 .... B—B4, the Classical Defense, but that it is inadequate because White secures stronger center Pawns at an early stage.

The strong point line is the Steinitz Defense, 3 .... P—Q3. Only the opening defeats its purpose because Black cannot avoid the exchange .... KP×QP (as he can in other lines). As a result he must submit to an inferiority in the center which, if coupled with a cramped position, will spell his downfall sooner or later. His only hope then is a series of exchanges. For, as we know, the value of the superior center Pawn is that it keeps the opponent's position congested. With many pieces on the board, Black's game is bound to be cramped because he disposes of less terrain, but once a number have gone into the woodpile Black has more room and the enemy center Pawn has lost most of its strength.

This theoretical discussion explains virtually everything in the Steinitz. White's first task is to compel .... P×P (which is done easily enough). Then he avoids exchanges and seeks to build up an attack. Black on the other hand must exchange as much as possible in order to free himself. If successful, he has excellent drawing chances, but the fight is always uphill. The whole defense, incidentally, is a classic illustration of the fundamental principle that a cramped position is freed by exchanges, but exploited by an attack.

The first main line runs 3 .... P—Q3; 4 P—Q4, B—Q2; 5 Kt—B3, Kt—B3; 6 O—O, B—K2; 7 R—K1. So far, so good: everything has been normal development for both sides. But now Black discovers that he cannot castle because of the trap: 7 .... O—O?; 8 B×Kt, B×B; 9 P×P, P×P; 10 Q×Q, QR×Q; 11 Kt×P, B×P; 12 Kt×B, Kt×Kt; 13 Kt—Q3, P—KB4; 14 P—B3, B—B4ch; 15 Kt×B, Kt×Kt; 16 B—Kt5, R—Q4; 17 B—K7, R—B2; 18 P—QB4 and wins.

So 7 .... P×P (instead of 7 .... O—O) is forced. Now we find a striking illustration of the principle enunciated above: the more pieces exchanged, the better Black's game becomes. Thus where three pieces go from each camp, White's advantage is so small that Black can draw without much trouble: 7 .... P×P; 8 Kt×P, Kt×Kt; 9 Q×Kt, B×B!; 10 Kt×B, P—QR3!; 11 Kt—B3, O—O; 12 B—Kt5, Kt—Q2, etc. With fewer exchanges, White secures a slight, but unmistakable superiority.

Still, if this were the best that White could do, the defense would be sufficient for a draw with exact play. This fact led to a search for improvements for White, and they were found. First of all, White reasons that since he cannot avoid all exchanges, he had better concentrate on finding the one which will be most effective. This turns out to be B×Kt at an early stage: 3 .... P—Q3; 4 P—Q4, B—Q2; 5 Kt—B3, Kt—B3; 6 B×Kt! (the point to the immediate capture is that White reserves the possibility of castling on the Q-side, which is of great value in some lines), B×B (forced); 7 Q—Q3! Now the Black KP is attacked, and after the normal 7 .... P×P; 8 Kt×P, B—Q2; 9 B—Kt5, B—K2; 10 O—O—O!, O—O; 11 P—B4 White has a powerful attack (the *attack* is the way to exploit a congested position).

Perhaps the decisive reason why this defense has gone out of fashion is not so much that Black must lose by force (such a claim would be exaggerated) but that the best he can possibly do, and that only in a few cases, is draw after a long uphill fight.

On the other hand, the immediate counter-attack 3 .... Kt—KB3 involves a good deal of tricky play, and is not theoretically refuted, but Black's game remains slightly uncomfortable in all variations. The line which practically banished 3 .... Kt—KB3 from tournament play involves developing quickly and taking advantage of the exposed position of Black's KKt: 3 .... Kt—KB3; 4 O—O, Kt×P; 5 P—Q4, B—K2; 6 Q—K2!, Kt—Q3; 7 B×Kt, KtP×B; 8

P×P, Kt—Kt2 (forced); 9 Kt—B3, O—O and now either 10 Kt—Q4! or 10 R—K1 prevents the liberating .... P—Q4 for a while and assures White a tangible advantage because of Black's development. The central idea for White throughout is to restrain the enemy center Pawns and thus prevent Black from developing normally. If Black can advance his center Pawns successfully he will be all right, but against best play he cannot do so.

Instead of 5 .... B—K2, however, Black can still save himself with either 5 .... P—QR3 (which would transpose into Morphy Defense lines) or 5 .... Kt—Q3, e.g., 6 P×P!, Kt×B; 7 P—QR4, P—Q3; 8 P—K6, P×P! and Black can survive the storm.

Other lines would transpose into some defense already discussed and seen to be inferior, such as the Steinitz or Classical. However, one point is worth noting. The strongest line against the Steinitz is that with B×Kt and Q—Q3 before castling. So after 4 O—O, if Black transposes into the Steinitz the advantage that White secures will not be so crushing. This is why anyone who chooses this system should begin with 3 .... Kt—KB3, rather than the Steinitz directly.

That Black never really does well is clear enough, but the reason is a bit harder to ferret out. It may have been noticed that in virtually all cases Black's QKt was chained to its post until castling was completed. Nor was there ever time to free the Kt. Consequently, if some move could be found which would infuse more life into this chunk of wood in the opening stages Black's game would be bound to improve.

Such a move is 3 .... P—QR3!, the indispensable prelude to all good defenses. It is possible only because White's threat of 4 B×Kt, QP×B; 5 Kt×P cannot be carried out immediately in view of the reply 5 .... Q—Q5! which regains the Pawn with an excellent game.

Just how great a difference the interpolation of the Pawn move makes is well illustrated by a comparison of two sets of variations.

Without 3 .... P—QR3		With 3 .... P—QR3	
A. 3	P—Q3	**3 ....**	P—QR3
4 P—Q4	B—Q2	**4** B—R4	P—Q3
5 Kt—B3	Kt—B3	**5** P—Q4?	*P—QKt4!*
6 B×Kt	B×B	**6** B—Kt3	Kt×P
7 Q—Q3	P×P	**7** Kt×Kt	P×Kt
8 Kt×P	B—Q2	**8** B—Q5!	R—Kt1
9 B—Kt5		**9** B—B6ch	B—Q2

White has much the better of it because of his powerful center.

Even game because all the exchanges have weakened White's position and liberated Black's pieces.

B. 3	Kt—B3	**3 ....**	P—QR3
4 O—O	Kt×P	**4** B—R4	Kt—B3
5 P—Q4	B—K2	**5** O—O	Kt×P
6 Q—K2	Kt—Q3	**6** P—Q4	*P—QKt4*
7 B×Kt	KtP×B	**7** B—Kt3	P—Q4
8 P×P	Kt—Kt2	**8** P×P	B—K3
9 Kt—B3		**9** P—B3	

White has a marked advantage because Black's Kt has had to move so often.

Even game because Black has been able to maintain his Kt at K5 and develop quickly.

After 3 .... P—QR3; 4 B—R4, Kt—B3! (it is always advisable to play energetically; alternatives will be discussed later); 5 O—O the defender is again at the parting of the ways and has the usual two directions to choose from—strong point and counter-attack.

While the strong point system is perfectly sound, it requires oodles of patience and knowledge of positional motifs. The immediate continuation for both sides is dictated by four considerations: a) development; b) holding the Pawns at K4; c) (for White only) avoiding the exchange of the KB; d) (for Black only) the advance of the QBP to QB4 in order to free the

QKt. With this in mind, the moves are easy enough to understand.

(*Diagram No. 7*): 5 .... B—K2; 6 R—K1, P—QKt4; 7 B—Kt3, P—Q3; 8 P—B3 (else the B will be exchanged by .... Kt—QR4), Kt—QR4; 9 B—B2, P—B4; 10 P—Q4, Q—B2 (*Diagram No. 8*). (This will be referred to as the *main line*.) So far, so good.

Both sides have achieved their main objectives: White has a favorable Pawn phalanx in the center (P's at Q4, K4 vs. P's at Q3, K4), while Black has held his strong point and is battering White's QP. For the further continuation, the new ideas which come into play are the following:

1. White will pursue the task of bringing pressure to bear on Black's center, especially the center Pawns; he will try to maneuver his Kt to Q5 or KB5.

2. In view of the fact that Black's position is still somewhat cramped, White will attempt to build up an attack against the Black King.

3. Black first must concentrate on closing the center (i.e., compelling either P×P or P—Q5). The effect will be the solidification of his strong point K4, which in turn frees his pieces for action elsewhere. Under no circumstances must he undertake any action before the center situation is clarified. This point is far more important for Black than for White because the defender is still striving for complete equality.

4. Black's eventual counter-chances lie on the Q-side. He must never allow the Pawn position there to be blocked in such a way that he cannot secure an open file.

The *crucial line* has been tried time and again: 11 P—KR3 (the pin is annoying in some cases), O—O; 12 QKt—Q2, Kt—B3; 13 P—Q5, Kt—Q1; 14 P—QR4, R—Kt1; 15 P—B4!, P—Kt5; 16 Kt—B1, Kt—K1; 17 P—Kt4, P—Kt3; 18 Kt—Kt3, Kt—KKt2; 19 K—R2, P—B3; 20 R—KKt1, Kt—B2; 21 P—Kt3, R—Kt2; 22 B—Q2, K—R1; 23 Q—K2, B—Q1, etc.

This line confers a minimal advantage upon White, because

Black has been deprived of his counter-chances on the Q-side. However, it is probable that the game is drawn with exact defense.

The other variations are elaborations, either for better or for worse, of this main one. The attempt to get the QKt to Q5 or KB5 without locking the center is unsound because Black can accept the Pawn: 13 Kt—B1 (instead of 13 P—Q5), BP× P; 14 P×P, P×P; 15 B—Kt5, P—KR3, etc.

On P—QR4, Black *must avoid* .... *P—Kt5* as long as possible. His best reply is usually .... R—QKt1, sometimes .... B—Q2, or .... R—R2. An example of the bad effect of a premature .... P—Kt5 is 14 .... P—Kt5 (in the crucial line above, instead of 14 .... R—Kt1); 15 Kt—B4, Kt—Kt2; 16 P×P, P×P; 17 P—QKt3 with advantage to White.

Improvements for White always involve keeping the center open. E.g., 11 QKt—Q2 (instead of 11 P—KR3), O—O; 12 Kt—B1, B—Kt5; 13 Kt—K3, B×Kt; 14 Q×B, BP×P; 15 P×P, P×P; 16 Kt—B5 with a promising game, or here 11 .... Kt—B3 (instead of 11 .... O—O); 12 P—QR4!, R—QKt1; 13 RP×P, RP×P; 14 P×KP, P×P; 15 Kt—B1, B—K3; 16 Kt—K3 etc.

Improvements for Black may take various forms. Where White does not choose the strongest line, after the center is locked, he should continue with .... P—B5, ... Kt—QKt2, ... Kt—B4, ... P—QR4, ... P—Kt5 etc. with play on the Q-side. Or if the QR file is opened, he should maneuver there. Another idea is to keep the QB file open, e.g., 12 .... BP×P (instead of 12 .... Kt—B3 in the crucial line); 13 P×P, Kt—B3; 14 P—Q5, Kt—QKt5; 15 B—Kt1, P—QR4; 16 P—QR3. Though here too White has a little the better of it, Black at any rate retains more play.

There are two interesting alternatives for Black at an earlier stage. One involves setting up a majority of Pawns on the Q-side: 8 .... O—O (instead of 8 .... Kt—QR4 in the main line); 9 P—Q4, B—Kt5; 10 B—K3, P×P; 11 P×P, Kt—QR4; 12 B—B2, Kt—B5; 13 B—B1, P—B4; 14 P—QKt3, Kt—QR4;

15 QKt—Q2, Kt—B3 with free play for the pieces, though Black has not equalized.

The other is the Marshall sacrifice, which prefers quick and speculative development to a sound but cramped position: 7 .... O—O (instead of 7 .... P—Q3 in the main line); 8 P—B3, P—Q4!; 9 P×P, Kt×P; 10 Kt×P, Kt×Kt; 11 R×

No. 7

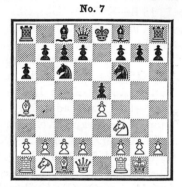

Best defense for Black against the
Ruy Lopez. Position after 5 O—O.

Kt, P—QB3! (Marshall's latest improvement) and White's game is none too easy.

Since the Rook at K1 does nothing but defend the KP, the idea of dispensing with the move suggests itself. The Worrall Attack is the most powerful effort to realize this idea: (*Diagram No. 7*) 5 .... B—K2; 6 Q—K2. Soon the Rook will go to Q1 and the Black center will be attacked at an earlier stage. The variations where White allows .... P—QKt4, ... Kt—QR4, ... P—B4, ... Q—B2 are much the same as those with R—K1. Important differences arise where White takes advantage of the fact that his Queen is aimed at the QKtP and plays P—QR4 at an early stage: 6 Q—K2, P—QKt4; 7 B—Kt3, P—Q3; 8 P—QR4. Here White is motivated by the thought that he can open the QR file and exert continuous pressure on the Black QKtP. E.g., 8 .... R—QKt1; 9 P×P,

P×P; 10 P—B3, B—Kt5; 11 R—Q1 (note how the Q move vacates a good square for the Rook and thus expedites White's set-up), O—O; 12 P—Q4, R—R1; 13 R×R, Q×R; 14 P—Q5! and the QKtP is artificially isolated and weak.

To avoid such a crippling of his Pawn position Black should resort to the more energetic reply 8 .... B—Kt5 (instead of 8 .... R—QKt1 above); 9 P—B3, O—O! because accepting

No. 8

Position after 10 .... Q—B2 in the Strong Point Defense.

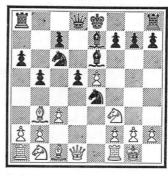

No. 9

Position after 9 .... B—K2 in the Counter-Attack Defense.

the sacrifice with 10 P×P, P×P; 11 R×R, Q×R; 12 Q×P? is refuted by 12 .... Kt—R2, when White can at best draw. However, here too 10 R—Q1 is not easy for Black.

Since Black's game is not entirely satisfactory in either of the above lines, the sacrificial continuation 7 .... O—O (instead of 7 .... P—Q3) is worth consideration: if 8 P—B3, P—Q4; 9 P×P, B—Kt5! strengthens Black's attack considerably, e.g., 10 P—KR3, B×Kt; 11 Q×B, P—K5; 12 Q—K2, Kt—QR4; 13 B—B2, Q×P with equality. On 10 P×Kt, P—K5, the free maneuverability of Black's minor pieces is undoubtedly sufficient compensation for the Pawns.

The Steinitz Defense Deferred and Fianchetto Defense likewise use the strong point idea; they will be considered below.

The counter-attack idea in *Diagram No. 7* has recently returned to popularity after a long period of disfavor. Again the first few moves are forced: 5 .... Kt×P; 6 P—Q4, P—QKt4; 7 B—Kt3, P—Q4; 8 P×P, B—K3; 9 P—B3, B—K2 (*Diagram No. 9*).

Here the leading ideas have been: For White, preservation of the KB and securing a strong Pawn at K5; for Black, maintenance of the Kt at K5 and securing a strong Pawn at Q4, adequate development of the KB without cramping the other pieces.

The ideas here are relatively easier than in the other variation, but the tactical execution is more complicated.

First of all we notice that the position has a number of striking features: Black has not yet completed his development, and some of his pieces, particularly the QKt and QB, are or may turn out to be in vulnerable spots. Further, White has a majority of Pawns on the K-side, Black on the Q-side.

Essentially, the long-range plans for both sides boil down to two vital points:

1. White will try to utilize the rather loose position of the Black pieces to secure a K-side attack or a permanent bind on the Q-side. (Such a bind is usually brought about by playing Kt—Q4, when Black exchanges .... Kt×Kt, P×Kt, opening the QB file and leaving Black with a backward Pawn (QBP) on an open file.)

2. Black will try to get his QKt out of the way and start his Pawns rolling.

The lines which begin with 10 QKt—Q2 (*Diagram No. 9*) are chiefly designed to secure a bind on the Q-side, though attacking possibilities are not entirely absent. After the normal reply 10 .... O—O White's first thought is to get rid of the troublesome enemy Kt at K5: thus 11 Q—K2 or 11 R—K1 or 11 B—B2. On the first two Black can gain a tempo by 11 .... Kt—B4, for then if the B moves, ... P—Q5! compels exchanges favorable for Black (they free his Q-side). After 11

Q—K2, Kt—B4; 12 Kt—Q4 prevents .... P—QB4 longest: 12 .... Kt×B!; 13 QKt×Kt, Q—Q2; 14 Kt×Kt, Q×Kt; 15 B—K3, but Black still secures equality by advancing his Q-side—the point is that there is no *permanent* bind.

On 11 B—B2, Black cannot gain the tempo, so that 11 .... Kt—B4; 12 Kt—Q4! does force a favorable Pawn structure on the Q-side. But 11 .... P—B4 maintains the Kt (note that on 11 R—K1 or 11 Q—K2 this advance is bad because of the capture en passant) and after 12 Kt—Kt3 (on 12 Kt—Q4, Q—Q2 is in order and if then 13 P—KB4, QKt×Kt; 14 P×Kt, P—QB4!—the QBP should not be left backward), Q—Q2; 13 KKt—Q4, Kt×Kt; 14 Kt×Kt (on the alternative 14 P×Kt Black will soon force .... P—QB4 under favorable circumstances), P—B4; 15 Kt—K2, QR—Q1; 16 Kt—B4, Q—B3; 17 Q—R5, B—B1; 18 P—QR4 does exert some pressure on the Black Q-side Pawns, but in view of Black's excellent development the chances are about even.

Somewhat more promising for White are the lines which are based on the attack idea. Here there are five different continuations from *Diagram No. 9*, each with distinct opportunities and dangers. In all cases White is going to continue with Kt—Q4 and an advance of Pawns on the K-side at an early stage; the differences concern the details of preparation and execution.

I. 10 B—KB4 defends the KP, so that Kt—Q4 can follow immediately. Black can defend by allowing White to carry out his plan and then breaking up the White center by .... P—KB3! at the appropriate moment. A fascinating alternative is the counter-attack 10 .... P—Kt4; 11 B—K3, P—Kt5!; 12 KKt—Q2, R—KKt1!, which has not been refuted despite its unprepossessing appearance.

II. 10 B—K3 strengthens the point Q4 (thus preventing a possible break .... P—Q5) and envisages giving up a Pawn in the chief variation. After the normal 10 .... O—O; 11 QKt—Q2, Kt×Kt is best (note that on 11 .... Kt—B4; 12 B—B2 is good in contrast to the position after 10 QKt—Q2, O—O; 11 Q—K2, Kt—B4, when 12 B—B2? is refuted by 12 .... P—

Q5!), when 12 Q×Kt, Kt—R4; 13 B—B2 carries out the chief ideas of both sides. Black's part in this drama has recently been reenforced: 13 .... Kt—B5; 14 Q—Q3, P—Kt3; 15 B—R6, Kt×KtP; 16 Q—K2, R—K1; 17 Kt—Q4, B—KB1! when the defense is more than adequate. Once more we see that strategical considerations cannot be divorced from tactics.

III. 10 R—K1 defends the KP indirectly and thus again makes Kt—Q4 next move possible. The idea would be irrefutable were it not for the fact that Black can turn the tables by a counter-sacrifice: 10 .... O—O; 11 Kt—Q4, Kt×KP!; 12 P—B3, B—Q3!; 13 P×Kt, B—KKt5; 14 Q—Q2, Q—R5! and best analysis available says that the result should be a draw.

IV. 10 Kt—Q4 gives up the KP at once for the attack. Black should accept and then has the choice of offering to return it with a slight positional plus (a counter which is peculiarly effective against an attacker) or of holding on for all he is worth, i.e., accepting a cramped position for the sake of a Pawn. The first is 10 .... Kt×KP; 11 P—B3, Kt—KB3!; 12 Q—K2, Kt—B5. The second is 10 .... Kt×KP; 11 P—B3, Kt—B4; 12 B—B2, B—Q2; 13 P—QKt4, Kt—R5. Both lines are adequate; which one is chosen is up to the temperament and mood of the player.

V. 10 P—QR4 prepares the sacrifice by weakening Black's Q-side. 10 .... P—Kt5 is forced, when 11 Kt—Q4, Kt×KP; 12 P—KB4 yields a strong attack which is best met by returning the extra material: 12 .... B—Kt5!; 13 Q—B2, P—QB4!; 14 P×Kt, P×Kt; 15 P×QP. It is worth mentioning that in a recent game it was shown that Black is by no means out of the woods here, so that the whole line may well be full of promise for White.

There is no way for either side to strengthen the play before the ninth move. E.g., in the main line 8 P—QR4 (instead of 8 P×P), which is strong if Black replies 8 .... R—QKt1; 9 P×RP, RP×P, yielding the open R file, is refuted by 8 ....

QKt×P!; 9 Kt×Kt, P×Kt; 10 P×P, B—QB4!; 11 P—QB3, O—O; 12 BP×P, B—Kt3 with an even game.

One idea well worth remembering is that in all cases where White does not advance the QP and QBP in time his prospects for an advantage are doomed by the exchange of his KB. E.g., 6 R—K1 (after 5 .... Kt×P from *Diagram No. 7*), Kt—B4; 7 B×Kt, QP×B; 8 P—Q4, Kt—K3; 9 Kt×P, B—K2 etc. with complete equality.

The only other alternative for Black on his 5th move (*Diagram No. 7*) is the attempt to get the B out to QB4 immediately, but this allows White too strong a center: 5 .... B—QB4; 6 P—B3, B—R2; 7 P—Q4, Kt×KP; 8 R—K1!, P—B4; 9 QKt—Q2, O—O; 10 Kt×Kt, P×Kt; 11 B—KKt5, Q—K1; 12 R×P and White should win.

Inferior alternatives for White prior to his fifth move are usually to be met by the early development of the Black KB. When, as is common, White's move is poor because it does not threaten the center, Black develops satisfactorily and has a good center, so that his theoretical difficulties are as good as gone. One example should suffice: 5 P—Q3, P—QKt4; 6 B—Kt3, B—B4; 7 B—K3, P—Q3; 8 QKt—Q2, B—K3 and the game is already even.

Poor continuations for Black are, of course, punished by the formation of a powerful Pawn center and the preparation of an attack. Numerous examples may be found above. What might be called "local" refutations are also found against specific mistakes. E.g., in the Worrall Attack, on P—QR4, if Black replies .... P—QKt5 before castling, Q—B4! is ruinous, while if he tries it after castling, P—R5! splits the Black Q-side Pawns.

We come now to another variant of the strong point system: the Steinitz Defense Deferred: 3 .... P—QR3; 4 B—R4, P—Q3 (*Diagram No. 10*).

The theoretical considerations which underlie the defense here are relatively simple:

1. Black holds the strong point K4, but without advancing on the Q-side. On the one hand he thereby avoids any weakening of that wing, but on the other hand he also deprives himself of any counterplay there.

2. White can build up long-range plans in a variety of ways. The most common is locking the center, followed by an advance against the Pawn chain base. (Black P's at Q3, K4, White P's at Q5, K4—the Black base is Q3, the White one is K4.)

3. Black wishes to have the center locked, when he can build up counterplay by .... P—KB4 (again attacking the base of a Pawn chain). In this connection the fianchetto of his KB (playing .... P—KKt3 and .... B—Kt2) is frequently useful because it backs up the KBP with the KKtP and further solidifies the center.

Proceeding from *Diagram No. 10*, the normal variation is 5 P—B3, B—Q2; 6 P—Q4, Kt—B3; 7 Q—K2, B—K2; 8 O—O, O—O; 9 P—Q5, Kt—Kt1; 10 B—B2, P—QR4; 11 P—B4, Kt—R3; 12 Kt—B3, Kt—B4; 13 B—K3 and White has a slight plus, though Black's chances are by no means to be underestimated. The ideas in this type of position will be more fully elucidated in connection with the Indian Defenses in the QP opening (pages 160 ff.). Suffice it to say that White should proceed by an advance on the Q-side (P—QR3, P—QKt4, eventually P—B5) while Black maneuvers on the K-side (.... P—KKt3, ... P—KB4). (See also the second point above.)

Where Black plays too passively and omits the attempt to secure counter-action on the K-side, his game is virtually hopeless. A horrible example is the famous Lasker-Steinitz encounter at Hastings, 1895: 5 P—B3, B—Q2; 6 O—O, KKt—K2; 7 P—Q4, Kt—Kt3; 8 R—K1, B—K2; 9 QKt—Q2, O—O; 10 Kt—B1, Q—K1; 11 B—B2, K—R1; 12 Kt—Kt3, B—Kt5; 13 P—Q5, Kt—QKt1; 14 P—KR3 ..... Poor Steinitz just choked to death.

As in previous Lopez lines, both sides can use improvements.

One of the first thoughts that come to mind for Black is the King fianchetto, coupled with .... KKt—K2. Then locking the center would be premature because Black's counter-attack begins immediately, while White's requires at least five or six moves to get under way. E.g., 5 P—B3, B—Q2; 6 O—O, P—KKt3; 7 P—Q4, B—Kt2; 8 B—K3, KKt—K2; 9 P—Q5, Kt—QKt1; 10 B—B2, O—O; 11 P—B4, P—KB4 and Black stands well.

No. 10

Steinitz Defense Deferred.

The chief trouble is that White is not compelled to lock the center. He may, if he wishes, keep it mobile for quite a while, in which case Black's counterplay is fraught with danger because of his loose Pawns. Or he may exchange P×P, which blocks the Black KB, and takes the sting out of an eventual .... P—KB4, to which the answer would be P×P, when Black's KP and KBP are exceedingly weak.

An instance of the former is 5 P—B3, B—Q2; 6 P—Q4, P—KKt3; 7 O—O, B—Kt2; 8 B—K3, KKt—K2; 9 P—B4! when Black has nothing better than 9 .... P×P; 10 Kt×P, O—O; 11 Kt—QB3, Kt×Kt; 12 B×Kt with the better Pawn position and the better ending.

An example of the latter is 5 P—B3, B—Q2; 6 P—Q4, P—KKt3; 7 O—O, B—Kt2; 8 P×P, P×P (or 8 .... Kt×P; 9

Kt×Kt, P×Kt; 10 P—B4! and White has a good attack); 9 B—KKt5, KKt—K2; 10 Q—Q3, P—KR3; 11 B—K3, B—Kt5; 12 Q—K2, O—O; 13 B—B5 and Black's game is difficult.

Again, as in so many other variations of the leading openings, neither side is satisfied. Black does not secure complete equality, while White is often anxious to secure a shattering advantage.

In *Diagram No. 10* there are four feasible alternatives for White. In view of the fact that none yields any lasting plus, the choice is largely a matter of taste.

I. 5 B×Ktch is theoretically good, since White secures the better Pawn structure, but Black's two Bishops and open QKt file are ample compensation. After 5 .... P×B; 6 P—Q4, the defender can again resort to either strong point or counterattack (opportunity knocks twice in this line!). The strong point is 6 .... P—B3, which has the drawback of giving Black a closed game for his Bishops, which thrive on open lines. The attempt to clear the diagonals and files by an eventual .... P—KB4 is bound to fail as long as White can keep up the pressure on the center. Still, by holding on to the K4 point the defender maintains approximate equality. An illustration of excellent play by both sides is 7 B—K3, P—Kt3; 8 Q—Q2, B—KKt2; 9 Kt—B3, B—Q2; 10 O—O, Kt—K2; 11 P—KR3, O—O; 12 QR—Q1, Q—Kt1; 13 P—QKt3, Q—Kt2; 14 B—R6, etc. White should continue by hammering at the Black KP (Kt—K1, P—KB4), after exchanging the potentially dangerous KB. Black may try to secure counter-play on the K-side, but cannot set up a plan independent of White's continuation.

The counter-attack line is 6 .... P×P (instead of 6 .... P—B3). To this the obvious objection is also the most serious: the abandonment of the center leaves Black without an anchor. All the same, counterplay against the White KP may be built up. One typical possibility is 6 .... P×P; 7 Kt×P, B—Q2; 8 Kt—QB3, Kt—B3; 9 O—O, B—K2; 10 R—K1, O—O; 11 P—QKt3 with about even chances. White has the better center, but Black has play on the semi-open QKt file.

On the whole, this second line is less promising for Black than the first.

II. 5 P—Q4 leads to too much blood-letting after 5 .... P—QKt4; 6 B—Kt3, Kt×P; 7 Kt×Kt, P×Kt; 8 B—Q5 (not 8 Q×P??, P—QB4), R—Kt1; 9 B—B6ch, B—Q2 etc. Interesting here is the sacrifice 8 P—QB3.

III. 5 P—B4 came into the limelight some years ago when Keres used it to score a sensational win against Alekhine. The idea is that by preventing .... P—QKt4 White will be able to secure the good feature of the 5 B×Ktch variation (better Pawn structure) without permitting the bad feature (giving Black two B's and an open QKt file). E.g., if 5 .... Kt—B3; 6 Kt—B3, B—K2; 7 P—Q4, P×P; 8 Kt×P, B—Q2; 9 KKt—K2 White's game is virtually ideal with his powerful KP and QBP making a break .... P—Q4 impossible and thus saddling Black with a permanently weak Pawn structure. All that Black can do is take the sting out of the White cramping maneuver by exchanging (as in the Steinitz Defense proper): 5 .... B—Q2!; 6 P—Q4, (else .... Kt—Q5), P×P; 7 Kt×P, Kt×Kt!; 8 B×Bch, Q×B; 9 Q×Kt, Kt—B3 etc. Black can develop satisfactorily.

Finally, there is the noncommittal

IV. 5 O—O, the main object of which is to transpose into the 5 B×Ktch line, without allowing the preferable defense .... P—B3 (i.e., force .... P×P after P—Q4). If he does not wish to transpose into the more conventional lines by 5 .... B—Q2 Black must try 5 .... Kt—B3; 6 B×Ktch, P×B; 7 P—Q4, Kt×P (again 7 .... P×P goes back to the usual course); 8 R—K1 (8 Q—K2 leads to a minimal positional advantage), P—KB4; 9 P×P, P—Q4; 10 Kt—Q4, Q—R5! or 10 .... B—B4; 11 B—K3, P—B5! both result in wild melees which analysis indicates should end in a draw.

In all this, Black has had to wait upon his adversary. Some enterprising spirits have been dissatisfied with this state of affairs and attempted to take matters into their own hands but with a total lack of success. The most important counter-attack for Black is the Siesta Variation, designed to hammer at White's center from an early stage (it will be recalled that Black usually has to go to much effort to effect .... P—KB4). After 5 P—B3 (*Diagram No. 10*), P—B4!?? is the line. Unfortunately it is refuted, as are many similar attempts, by opening up the game, which aids White because he is ahead in development: 6 P×P!, B×P; 7 P—Q4, P—K5; 8 Kt—Kt5!, B—K2; 9 O—O!, B×Kt; 10 Q—R5ch, B—Kt3; 11 Q×B, Q×Q; 12 B×Q and White has all the play, chiefly because Black cannot prevent the exchange of his only trump, the powerful KP, after 12 .... Kt—K2; 13 Kt—Q2, P—Kt4; 14 B—Kt3, P—Q4; 15 QR—K1, K—Q2; 16 P—B3!

Of the variations which have not been touched upon, only one is worth mentioning: the exchange variation, which occurs after 3 .... P—QR3; 4 B×Kt. Despite the fact that it is unusual, all the remaining defenses which begin with the QRP advance are dependent upon it, for if it could be shown that White could get the better of it by exchanging, they would all automatically become worthless. But as fate or whoever else invented chess would have it, that is far from being the case.

The most customary and best reply is 4 .... QP×B. After 5 P—Q4, P×P; 6 Q×P, Q×Q; 7 Kt×Q the object of White's play becomes clear: he has set up the majority of Pawns on the K-side. Sooner or later he will be able to force a passed Pawn on the K-side, while Black's Pawn majority on the other wing is hopelessly blocked, provided White does not touch the Pawns there. White therefore reasons that he should be able to exchange all or almost all the pieces and then win with his extra passed Pawn.

As is to be expected, there is another side to the story. To carry out his plan White has had to concede to the defender, who must usually cope with a cramped position for at least 10 or 15 moves, the theoretical advantage of the two Bishops and a free and easy development. Further, White does not have a passed Pawn yet; he merely has a Pawn majority and there are many cases known where a minority can hold or even attack a

Pawn phalanx numerically superior. That is done by splitting the Pawns and exposing them, when they can be picked off singly.

Thus the leading ideas for both sides boil down to the following: White heads straight for the endgame. Every time a piece is exchanged he is one step nearer his goal. Black wishes to make his Bishops tell and keep the White steamroller back where it belongs.

One further point: usually both sides castle on the Q-wing. White gets his King over to the left because he wants to defend his Pawns and because he expects the main theater of action to be on the K-side and prefers to have his King out of the way as long as complications may still arise. Black's reasoning is much the same: support his Pawns and clear the way for counter-action.

Theoretically there seems to be little wrong with White's plan, which explains why the line can be held quiescent but never made to disappear completely. But in practise Black almost invariably turns out to have more play with his pieces, especially if he takes care to avoid exchanges. A typical line runs 3 .... P—QR3; 4 B×Kt, QP×B; 5 P—Q4, P×P; 6 Q×P, Q×Q; 7 Kt×Q, B—Q2; 8 B—K3, O—O—O; 9 Kt—Q2, Kt—K2; 10 O—O—O, R—K1; 11 KR—K1, Kt—Kt3; 12 Kt—K2, B—Q3; 13 P—KR3, P—KB4! and Black has all the play. A noteworthy point is that Black delays the development of his KB until White cannot offer to exchange it by B—KB4.

FOUR KNIGHTS' GAME: 1 P—K4, P—K4; 2 Kt—KB3, Kt—QB3; 3 Kt—B3, Kt—B3

In this relatively tame opening White departs from his usual attempt to get the better of it with an early P—Q4 and relies solely on his extra move. Because of the paucity of direct threats Black can content himself with copying his opponent's moves and is therefore faced by no difficult problems at an early stage. Later on, however, he must watch his step because he cannot continue aping the other fellow indefinitely. He can also, if he so desires, try a most promising attack of his own (Rubinstein Defense).

White must threaten something early, for otherwise Black will be able to counter with .... P—Q4 or develop all his pieces without any trouble. So 4 B—Kt5. Now the question for Black all along is: When shall I break the symmetry? After 4 .... B—Kt5; 5 O—O, O—O; 6 P—Q3, P—Q3; 7 B—Kt5, B—Kt5?; 8 Kt—Q5 leads to a won game for White.

No. 11

Position in the Four Knights' Game
after 8 P×B.

So Black must vary earlier. Experience has shown that the sixth or seventh move is best (unless he plays the Rubinstein Line), so 7 .... B×Kt above (instead of 7 .... B—Kt5?); 8 P×B (*Diagram No. 11*). Examination of the diagrammed position reveals several features which must be taken into consideration in deciding upon the continuation.

White has the inferior Pawn position, but the two Bishops and somewhat more freedom for his pieces. Thus he wants an open game and a mobile Pawn center. Black with his Kt's prefers a closed position where he will be able to secure impregnable posts for his horsemen (especially QB4). A locked center is better for him. Further, he notes that White will soon try P—Q4. To close the center he will then have to hammer away with .... P—QB4 (compare Ruy Lopez variations), so that he must get his QKt out of the way.

One obvious idea is to shift the Kt to KKt3 via K2, but this is refuted after 8 .... Kt—K2 by 9 Kt—R4!, Kt—Kt3; 10 Kt×Kt, RP×Kt; 11 P—KB4 and White has an overwhelming position.

An ideal move for Black in *Diagram No. 11* is 8 .... Q—K2, which strengthens the center and clears the way for a regrouping of the pieces. Then a normal line where both sides are partially satisfied is 9 R—K1, Kt—Q1; 10 P—Q4, Kt—K3; 11 B—QB1, P—B4!; 12 P—Kt3, Kt—B2; 13 B—B1, B—Kt5; 14 P—KR3, B—R4; 15 B—KKt2, QR—Q1; 16 P—Q5, Q—Q2 with about even chances. Note here that White delayed closing the center as long as feasible, but that he could not delay it indefinitely.

Black can simplify his problem by compelling the early exchange of the White KB by 9 .... P—QR3 (instead of 9 .... Kt—Q1): 10 B—QB4, Kt—QR4; 11 Kt—Q2, P—R3! (he must be careful not to let the pin become too dangerous), etc. Again, since Kt's are better than B's in closed Pawn positions, Black may reason that he should exchange his QB for the White KKt with .... B—Kt5, but his game remains too cramped: 8 .... P—KR3; 9 B—KR4, B—Kt5 (9 .... P—KKt4; is refuted by the usual Kt×KtP); 10 P—KR3, B×Kt; 11 Q×B, P—Kt4; 12 B—Kt3, Kt—Q2; 13 P—Q4, P—B3; 14 Q—Kt4, K—R1; 15 P—KR4 and White's game remains freer: he can build up a strong attack on the KR file.

A noteworthy improvement for White in the main line is 9 Q—Q2 (instead of 9 R—K1), so that if then 9 .... Kt—Q1; 10 P—Q4, Kt—K3? would lose the KP without adequate compensation. However, Black can then lift the pin by .... P—QR3, ... Kt—QR4, and .... Q—K3 after the exchange of the enemy KB.

It is a natural impulse for Black to try to force the normal .... P—Q4 in view of White's seemingly passive play. But there is a tactical refutation: 4 B—Kt5, B—Kt5; 5 O—O,

O—O; 6 P—Q3, B×Kt; 7 P×B, P—Q4?; 8 B×Kt, P×B; 9 Kt×P, Q—Q3; 10 B—B4, R—K1; 11 P×P!, R×Kt; 12 P—Q4 and White should win.

Of the other deviations for Black at an earlier stage (again excepting the Rubinstein Defense) 7 .... Kt—K2 in the main line (instead of 7 .... B×Kt) is most important. Black's idea is to bolster the center with .... Kt—Kt3, ... P—QB3, and .... P—Q4, eventually releasing the pin by .... Q—Q3. The weakening of the Black K-position by 8 B×Kt, P×B; 9 Kt—KR4 and 10 P—B4 is hard to exploit: there is enough compensation for the defender in his strong center, the open Kt file may even work out to his advantage. Black must, however, avoid allowing his QB to be shut in without securing counterplay in return. Instead of 8 B×Kt, a natural reply is 8 Kt—KR4 (to play P—KB4), P—B3; 9 B—QB4. Now 9 .... P—Q4; 10 B—Kt3, Q—Q3; 11 P—KR3, P—KR3; 12 B×Kt, Q×B; 13 Q—R5! leaves Black's center Pawns weak (this motif of allowing an advance of Pawns in the center and then hammering away at them occurs chiefly in QP openings, but also in KP games on occasion). A better reply for Black is 9 .... Kt—Kt3 (instead of 9 .... P—Q4) and if then 10 Kt×Kt, P×Kt; 11 P—B4, B—B4ch; 12 K—R1, B—K6! and the exchanges free Black's game satisfactorily.

The symmetrical line where White tries 7 Kt—K2 (instead of 7 B—KKt5) offers fewer difficulties because Black can keep on copying longer: 7 .... Kt—K2; 8 P—B3, B—R4; 9 Kt—Kt3, P—B3; 10 B—R4, Kt—Kt3; 11 P—Q4 and now 11 .... P—Q4! liquidates the center problem.

Black must be careful not to allow a favorable transposition into the Ruy Lopez. E.g., on 5 .... P—Q3 (instead of 5 .... O—O); 6 Kt—Q5!, B—QB4; 7 P—Q4!, P×P; 8 Kt×QP is a line similar to the Classical Defense to the Ruy Lopez. The same holds for 4 .... B—B4; 5 O—O, P—Q3; 6 P—Q4. It must not be supposed that because White does not play P—Q4 immediately he will never do so when an opportunity arises.

While White does not secure any noticeable advantage in the above variations, he none the less retains the initiative. Consequently the Four Knights' would undoubtedly be more popular were it not for the speculative but promising

Rubinstein Defense: 4 B—Kt5, Kt—Q5: The thought underlying this gambit is that Black can secure adequate counterplay by developing and hitting at the White center. Despite a great deal of analysis, the sacrifice is still considered sound. The strategic ideas, as in most gambits, are of minor importance: tactics predominates.

First of all we have the most obvious line 5 Kt×P. Then it has been found that Black can equalize with 5 .... Q—K2, for if 6 P—B4, Kt×B; 7 Kt×Kt, P—Q3; 8 Kt—KB3, Q×Pch; 9 K—B2, Kt—Kt5ch; 10 K—Kt3, Q—Kt3! the exposure of the White King will soon lead to an incurable lung disease. Here White pursues the plan of gaining material, while the Black attack is too strong: the best that White can do is content himself with an even game.

Since the direct acceptance fails, the indirect alternatives must be considered. For Black cannot merely offer the Pawn for one move and then call it quits: his object is to secure a good game, and he must not rest before that is done. The chief advantage of the Kt sortie in that connection is that it leaves the way open for the development of the Black KB. (It will be recalled that this is a great problem in many variations of the Ruy Lopez.) Thus after either 5 B—R4, or 5 B—B4 (in reply to 4 .... Kt—Q5), 5 .... B—B4 must be tried. After 5 B—R4, Black profits from the fact that the White diagonal Q1—KR5 cannot be held by the Bishop, so that if he can secure the pin .... B—KKt5 he will have a good bind. Thus 5 B—R4, B—B4; 6 Kt×P, O—O! If now 7 Kt—B3, P—Q4; 8 P—Q3, B—KKt5 White's game is far from easy. Likewise on the normal 7 O—O, P—Q3 (or even 7 .... P—Q4: the point is that White must not be allowed to develop properly); 8 Kt—Q3 (forced, since 8 Kt—B3?, B—KKt5 is disastrous), B—Kt3!; 9 K—R1!, Kt—Kt5!;

10 Kt—Q5, Q—R5; 11 P—KR3, P—KB4 Black's attack is very hard to meet. On other replies Black likewise gets enough play for the Pawn by speedy and pointed development.

Similarly on 5 B—B4, B—B4! can be and should be ventured. Then 6 Kt×P, Q—K2! (now 6 .... O—O is not good because the critical diagonal can be held by the Bishop: 7 O—O, P—Q3; 8 Kt—B3, B—KKt5; 9 B—K2! etc.); and again the normal 7 Kt—B3, P—Q4!; 8 B×P, B—KKt5; 9 P—Q3, P—B3; 10 B—Kt3, Kt—Q2! takes advantage of the weak diagonal.

White may wish to exploit the Kt thrust by concentrating on quick development himself, but this leads to nothing because Black's position is too solid. E.g., on 5 O—O, Kt×B; 6 Kt×Kt, P—B3; 7 Kt—B3, P—Q3; 8 P—Q4, Q—B2 or 5 B—K2, Kt×Ktch; 6 B×Kt, B—B4; 7 O—O, O—O; 8 P—Q3, P—Q3; 9 B—K3, R—K1 Black has little to fear. The point is that the exchange frees his game to such an extent that even if White gets a slightly stronger Pawn center it will be of little avail because there is too little to constrict in the Black camp.

White may if he so desires transpose into the Scotch Game or the Giuoco Piano on his fourth move. On untheoretical lines, the usual rejoinder of .... P—Q4 guarantees equality. E.g., 4 P—KKt3, P—Q4; 5 P×P, Kt×P; 6 B—Kt2, Kt×Kt; 7 KtP×Kt, B—Q3 etc.

It should be noted that when White is anxious to draw no weapon is more effective against a player of equal strength. Against complicated lines he can always simplify by exchanges.

THREE KNIGHTS' GAME: 1 P—K4, P—K4; 2 Kt—KB3, Kt—QB3; 3 Kt—B3, or 1 P—K4, P—K4; 2 Kt—KB3, Kt—KB3; 3 Kt—B3

This is really a generic name to cover all the replies at Black's disposal other than the regular 3 .... Kt—B3.

The most usual line in the first branch is 3 .... B—Kt5, which has the advantage of avoiding the main lines of the

Four Knights', a consideration which is chiefly of psychological value.

Since Black's B is exposed, the most natural reply is 4 Kt—Q5, to continue with P—B3 and P—Q4. But Black can counter with an immediate threat to White's center, so that White's plan cannot be realized: 4 .... Kt—B3! Then after the normal continuation 5 B—B4! O—O (compare the Rubinstein Defense to the Four Knights'); 6 P—B3, B—K2 White has no time to build up a strong center because of his exposed KP. E.g., if 7 Kt×Ktch, B×Kt; 8 P—Q4?, P×P; 9 P×P, R—K1; 10 P—K5, P—Q3 etc. with an excellent position. Thus 8 P—Q3 (instead of 8 P—Q4) is necessary, when 8 .... P—Q3; 9 O—O, O—O and .... B—K3 equalizes. Note that P—Q4 may also be answered by .... P×P followed by .... B—KKt5.

More promising for White—if Black persists in avoiding the Four Knights'—is 4 B—Kt5, so that on 4 .... KKt—K2 (of course 4 .... Kt—B3 is possible); 5 P—Q4!, P×P; 6 Kt×P gives him the better center position.

Alternatives to 3 .... B—Kt5, other than the standard 3 .... Kt—KB3, give Black a cramped game, similar to Philidor's Defense.

In the second branch, after 3 .... B—Kt5, Black is threatening to exchange White's valuable center Pawn, so that the line is far more effective. On the normal 4 B—B4 (or 4 Kt×P, O—O; 5 B—K2, R—K1 when White must return his booty), the simplest equalizing line is 4 .... O—O; 5 P—Q3, P—B3! (to secure strong center Pawns); 6 O—O, P—Q4; 7 B—Kt3, B—Kt5 and Black's game is already wholly satisfactory.

PHILIDOR'S DEFENSE: 1 P—K4, P—K4; 2 Kt—KB3, P—Q3

This is the strong point defense reduced to its essentials. It has the outstanding merit of that type of game—solidity—and it has its outstanding demerit—lack of mobility.

Black must be on his guard against a number of traps, all

based on the weakness of his KB2 and his cramped K position. On the normal course 3 P—Q4, B—Kt5?, e.g., leads to
the loss of a Pawn after 4 P×P, B×Kt; 5 Q×B, P×P;
6 B—QB4, Kt—KB3; 7 Q—QKt3, etc. Likewise on 3 P—Q4,
Kt—Q2; 4 B—QB4, B—K2?; 5 P×P, P×P; 6 Q—Q5 is
immediately disastrous.

But the defender can avoid all the traps and secure a tenable
though passive position with 3 P—Q4, Kt—Q2; 4 B—QB4, P—-
QB3; 5 Kt—B3, B—K2; 6 O—O, KKt—B3; 7 *P—QR4,* O—O;
8 Q—K2, P—KR3; 9 B—Kt3, Q—B2; 10 *P—R3,* K—R2;
11 B—K3, P—KKt3; 12 QR—Q1.

The two prophylactic moves 7 P—QR4 and 10 P—R3 have
been stressed because they illustrate the all-important principle that by depriving the enemy of counterplay, a cramped
but sound position such as Black's here has all the life taken
out of it and is reduced to pure passivity.

Black may follow one of two lines to get some counterplay:
after due preparation .... P×P and pressure on the White
KP, or maneuver his Kt to KB5. White can proceed by opening some lines (especially with P—KB4) and securing an
attack. All told, such positions offer the defender little promise
against a person equipped with modern technique.

One of the chief merits of the defense is that it is rather
difficult for White to form a good plan right after the opening
in view of Black's lack of obvious weaknesses. One worthwhile idea is the fianchetto of the QB, in order to hammer
away at the QP. Another, as mentioned, is playing P—KB4
early.

The abandonment of the center with 3 .... P×P is sometimes seen, but nevertheless bad, since Black gets nothing in
return. White can recapture with either Kt or Q and secures
an ideal development.

Finally, it should be noted that if White does not harass the
Black center with 3 P—Q4, the second player can secure good
counter-chances with the natural 3 .... P—KB4. On 3
P—Q4, however, 3 .... P—KB4? is shown to be premature

by 4 Kt—B3!, Kt—KB3; 5 P×KP, Kt×P; 6 Kt×Kt, P×Kt; 7 Kt—Kt5, P—Q4; 8 P—K6, B—QB4; 9 Kt×KP!

PETROFF'S DEFENSE: 1 P—K4, P—K4; 2 Kt—KB3, Kt—KB3

Here we have the counter-attack in its most elemental form. Again the usual advantages and disadvantages appear: Black develops quickly, but at the cost of a rather loose position.

Omitting transpositions into other openings (e.g., 3 Kt—B3, Kt—QB3; or 3 Kt—B3, B—Kt5), there are only two possibilities for White if he is to try to secure an advantage: 3 Kt×P and 3 P—Q4, both designed to gain the upper hand in the center immediately.

After 3 Kt×P, Kt×P? costs Black a Pawn because of 4 Q—K2, Q—K2; 5 Q×Kt, P—Q3; 6 P—Q4. Instead, the normal sequence is 3 Kt×P, P—Q3; 4 Kt—KB3, Kt×P; 5 P—Q4, P—Q4, when further play revolves around the position of the Black Kt at K5. White undermines its position by B—Q3, P—B4 and R—K1, eventually Kt—B3. Black, on the other hand, maintains the strongly centralized horseman until he has no further choice in the matter. The natural continuation is 6 B—Q3, B—Q3; 7 O—O, O—O; 8 Kt—B3 (or 8 P—B4), Kt×Kt; 9 P×Kt, B—KKt5; 10 R—Kt1, P—QKt3; 11 P—B4 with about even prospects. Black can also vary with 6 .... B—K2 (instead of 6 .... B—Q3) in order to have the QP defended. With a simple line such as P—QB4, R—K1, Kt—B3, eventually Kt—K5, White retains control of slightly more terrain.

The alternative 5 Q—K2 on White's 5th move is designed to exploit the extra move in an endgame. So slight a superiority, however, is too little to win against modern technique. A typical line is 5 Q—K2, Q—K2; 6 P—Q3, Kt—KB3; 7 B—Kt5, Q×Qch; 8 B×Q, B—K2; 9 Kt—B3, B—Q2; 10 O—O—O, P—KR3!; 11 B—R4, Kt—B3, etc.

The alternative 3 P—Q4 is based on the idea of exploiting the undefended Black center. Thus on 3 .... P×P; 4 P—K5, Kt—K5; 5 Q×P Black apparently has to lose more time.

Still, 5 .... P—Q4! is an adequate reply because the White Queen is too exposed. Black secures a rather cramped position, but since he has no organic weaknesses his game is not too bad.

GRECO COUNTER-GAMBIT: 1 P—K4, P—K4; 2 Kt—KB3, P—KB4

This counter-attack is much more violent than any of the others and consequently more easily refuted. Black hopes to be able to secure play on the open KB file and a strong Pawn center, but if the latter is prevented his game is badly dis-organized. Thus the best is 3 Kt×P, Q—B3!; 4 P—Q4!, P—Q3; 5 Kt—B4! (5 Kt—KB3, P×P; 6 Kt—Kt5, P—Q4; 7 P—QB4! is also good), P×P; 6 Kt—B3, Q—Kt3; 7 B—B4!, Kt—KB3; 8 Kt—K3!, B—K2; 9 B—B4, P—B3; 10 P—Q5! and White has much the better of it. Note that White's strategy revolved around the prevention of .... P—Q4.

QUEEN'S PAWN COUNTER-GAMBIT: 1 P—K4, P—K4; 2 Kt—KB3, P—Q4

Just as violent as the preceding, but even more unsound. After 3 P×P, Q×P; 4 Kt—B3, Q—K3; 5 B—Kt5ch Black is too badly developed, while the sacrifice 3 P×P, P—K5; 4 Q—K2, Q—K2; 5 Kt—Q4 is not sufficient.

This and the Greco are another illustration of the principle that it is far more dangerous for Black to experiment in the openings than it is for White.

PONZIANI'S OPENING: 1 P—K4, P—K4; 2 Kt—KB3, Kt—QB3; 3 P—B3

With his last move White envisages setting up a strong Pawn center. Yet the obvious disadvantages of the move cannot be conjured away: the QKt is deprived of its most natural square and there is nothing to prevent a counter-action by Black in the center.

This counter-action can take one of three forms: 3 .... P—Q4, 3 .... P—B4 or 3 .... Kt—B3.

On *3 .... P—Q4,* 4 Q—R4, the Pawn sacrifice for the sake of speedy development yields Black enough: 4 .... Kt—B3; 5 Kt×P, B—Q3!; 6 Kt×Kt, P×Kt; 7 P—Q3, O—O; 8 B—KKt5, P—KR3; 9 B×Kt, Q×B; 10 Kt—Q2, R—Kt1! etc. 4 .... B—Q2 is also playable, but 4 .... P—B3; 5 B—Kt5, Kt—K2; 6 P×P, Q×P; 7 P—Q4! is inferior because White has all the initiative.

3 .... P—B4 is far more speculative (as is to be expected, since it exposes the King). After 4 P—Q4, BP×P!; 5 Kt×P, Q—B3 is the most promising. Finally, *3 .... Kt—B3* is excellent if followed by the normal break 4 P—Q4, P—Q4! With the center liquidated White has nothing to show for his efforts.

BISHOP'S OPENING: 1 P—K4, P—K4; 2 B—B4

Except for the Center Game, this is the first line discussed so far where White does not attack the center immediately with 2 Kt—KB3. White's thought is that he will be able to ward off any Black counter-attacks and then hit at the center with P—KB4. He may also have a chance to transpose into one of a number of other openings.

It goes almost without saying that Black should react at once against the White center. Most effective is 2 .... Kt—KB3, although 2 .... P—QB3, and the neutral 2 .... B—B4, are also adequate.

After 2 .... Kt—KB3, 3 P—B4? fails against 3 .... Kt×P!; 4 P—Q3, Kt—Q3!; 5 B—Kt3, Kt—B3, etc. More promising is 3 P—Q4 (after 2 .... Kt—KB3) when the Pawn sacrifice is counterbalanced by superior development: 3 .... P×P; 4 Kt—KB3, Kt×P; 5 Q×P, Kt—KB3; 6 B—KKt5, B—K2; 7 Kt—B3, Kt—B3; etc.: an excellent illustration of a position where the attacking chances are just about good enough to compensate for the loss of a Pawn.

Somewhat more logical on 2 .... Kt—KB3 is 3 P—Q3. If then 3 .... B—B4; 4 Kt—B3, Kt—B3; 5 P—B4, P—Q3; 6 Kt—B3, we have transposed into a variation of the King's

Gambit Declined which is not too easy for Black to handle. But the defender can improve upon this line by 3 .... P—B3 (after 3 P—Q3). Then the establishment of a good Pawn center will at least equalize. On 4 P—B4, P×P!; 5 B×P, P—Q4; 6 P×P, Kt×P liquidates the center Pawns and gives Black a little the better of it.

There is one danger in this latter variation: the center Pawns may become weak. E.g., 2 .... Kt—KB3; 3 P—Q3, P—B3; 4 Kt—KB3!, P—Q4; 5 P×P, P×P; 6 B—Kt3, B—Q3; 7 O—O, Kt—B3; 8 B—KKt5, B—K3; 9 Kt—B3 and Black can no longer keep his Pawns intact. To avoid such a weakness he should play 6 .... B—Kt5ch! in the above variation (instead of 6 .... B—Q3), for on 7 P—B3, B—Q3 White's QKt is deprived of its best square and the Black center cannot be molested.

VIENNA GAME: 1 P—K4, P—K4; 2 Kt—QB3

Again the road is left clear for the advance of the KBP—this explains why the Vienna Game, Bishop's Opening and King's Gambit Declined are so intimately connected.

As usual, the most effective counter for Black is 2 .... Kt—KB3, threatening .... P—Q4. If he wishes to get the better of it, White must try either 3 P—B4 or 3 B—B4; otherwise 3 .... P—Q4 (e.g., on 3 P—KKt3) equalizes without any trouble.

On 3 P—B4, the timid 3 .... P—Q3? would be weak: it shuts in the KB and permanently abandons the fight for equality in the center. Instead 3 .... P—Q4! is indicated and strong. Then the obvious 4 BP×P (on Steinitz's 4 P—Q3, played with a view to maintaining a Pawn in the center, 4 .... P×BP!; 5 P×P, B—QKt5 gives Black the freer game), Kt× P; 5 Kt—B3 leads to *Diagram No. 12.*

From the diagram it can be seen that the central ideas are simple enough. White wishes to drive the Black Kt away (preferably by P—Q3) and set up a strong Pawn center (P's at Q4, K5). Black's chief trump for the moment is his Kt at K5:

he would like to keep it there as long as possible. Further he must either prevent White from maintaining a Pawn center or break it up as soon as it is formed. Another goal that he may pursue is the artificial isolation of the White KP by .... P—QB4, ... Kt—QB3, eventually .... P—Q5 if necessary.

For the realization of his objectives Black may choose one of five moves:

I. 5 .... B—QKt5 is obviously meant to prevent P—Q3. If White tries to develop normally with 6 B—K2, O—O; 7

No. 12

Position after 5 Kt—B3 in the Vienna Game.

O—O, Kt—QB3!, he does get the worst of it, since he must resort to artificial measures to get his B out. But instead 6 Q—K2! compels Black to get rid of his Kt, when 6 .... Kt×Kt; 7 QP×Kt, B—K2; 8 B—B4, P—QB4; 9 O—O—O! gives White good attacking possibilities. The advantage of castling on opposite sides is that the Pawns may be advanced without exposing one's own King. Further, White's King has an extra Pawn for protection here.

II. 5 .... B—QB4 is designed to secure the position of the Kt at K5. 6 P—Q4, however, strengthens White's center, so that after the normal sequence 6 .... B—QKt5; 7 Q—Q3, P—QB4 (he must not give his opponent time to consolidate); 8

P×P, Kt×P; 9 Q—K3, Kt—B3; 10 B—Kt5 the chances are about even.

III. 5 . . . . B—K2 is simplest, but not the most promising. Then since 6 P—Q3, Kt×Kt; 7 P×Kt, O—O would have to be followed by 8 P—Q4, White plays 6 P—Q4 immediately. After the natural 6 . . . . O—O; 7 B—Q3, P—KB4! White must either let the intruder stay there indefinitely or give up his center. On 8 P×P e.p., there is a finesse: 8 . . . . B×P! which yields Black immediate equality, since he can develop without any trouble.

IV. 5 . . . . B—KKt5 is played with a view to undermining the support of the White center Pawns. On 6 P—Q3, Kt×Kt; 7 P×Kt, P—QB4; 8 B—K2, Kt—B3 he has already created a threat: the White center is none too secure. Likewise on 6 Q—K2, Kt×Kt; 7 KtP×Kt, P—QB4 Black gets a satisfactory game if he challenges the White center early.

V. 5 . . . . Kt—QB3 is a promising counter-attacking line. Here again Black may artificially isolate the KP after 6 P—Q3, Kt×Kt; 7 P×Kt, P—Q5. And on 6 Q—K2?, B—KB4!; 7 Q—Kt5, P—QR3! gives Black strong counterplay for the Pawn.

On the whole, Black has a variety of good defenses to choose from.

For White the chief alternative worth considering is 3 B—B4 (instead of 3 P—B4). True, ... P—Q4 is thus prevented, but instead 3 . . . . Kt×P! liquidates the center satisfactorily: 4 Q—R5!, Kt—Q3!; 5 B—Kt3, Kt—B3!; 6 Kt—Kt5, P—KKt3; 7 Q—B3, P—B4; 8 Q—Q5, Q—K2; 9 Kt×Pch, K—Q1; 10 Kt×R, P—Kt3; 11 P—Q3, B—QKt2 and Black has a very strong attack, easily worth the exchange, e.g., 12 P—KR4, P—B5!; 13 Q—B3, Kt—Q5; 14 Q—R3, B—KR3 and so on.

Other lines often transpose into the King's Gambit Declined.

Recapitulation: We have passed in rapid review a number of openings and it is well to pause for a moment on the lessons to be learned.

Although the differences are at times great, all the openings with 1 P—K4, P—K4 are closely related. It is an historical accident that they are all set off with different names. In the Queen's Pawn Game and Queen's Gambit Declined, on the other hand, the connections are clearer because the different lines are called variations. Center Game and Ponziani's Opening are no more alike and no more different than Tarrasch's Defense and the Manhattan Variation.

We have stressed the similarities, but it is helpful to put them ᴧown again for convenient reference. Likewise the differences are understood best as variations from a common beginning and approaches towards analogous goals.

First, we know that there is one and only one way in which White can secure an advantage: by playing P—Q4. Yet it would do him no good to play it right away. That may seem a paradox, but it is true of many chess openings.

Leaving the Gambits to one side, there are two openings where White takes a different tack: the Vienna and the Bishop's. In both his immediate objective is a favorable P—KB4, though at a later stage he might well play P—Q4 too. Black's reply is based on his .... P—Q4, the move which, wherever possible, blasts all hopes of a plus for White.

In the Center Game, White tries to carry out the basic idea immediately. He fails because of the time lost with his Queen.

In the search for White superiority, we have now come to the point where it is seen that the most direct methods fail. To strengthen the attack, White must threaten something. Hence 2 Kt—KB3 emerges as the strongest continuation.

With 2 Kt—KB3, White, however, does not *abandon* the idea of P—Q4, he merely *postpones* it to a more favorable moment. Black's thoughts must always be directed to the problem of how he will reply to the inevitable P—Q4. And he can be sure that it will come relatively early.

Once P—Q4 is adopted, Black can either capture or maintain his own Pawn at K4. If he captures, he must adopt some action against the White KP. Otherwise the Pawn structure will be White's ideal, illustrated in *Diagram No. 1.* That is why the choice narrows down to what we have called the *counter-attack* and the *strong point* methods. There is no other way to equalize.

In general, the counter-attack yields a free game, but the Pawn position is disunited, while in the strong point lines the Pawn structure is satisfactory, but the pieces are cramped. Black's problem is to strike the proper balance.

Of the many counter-attacks available on Black's second turn the best is Petroff's Defense (2 .... Kt—KB3), which is theoretically enough for an even game. The Greco (2 .... P—KB4) and the QP Counter-Gambit (2 .... P—Q4) are both too violent and unsound against best play. It is always more dangerous for Black to attack than it is for White. But even though the immediate counter-attack is none too good for Black, the idea is indispensable: it may be applied with good results at many other stages.

The strong point systems are likewise many in number, but only one is of real value. Philidor's Defense (2 .... P—Q3), the most immediate, is by no means the best. For after 3 P—Q4 Black can no longer get his pieces posted freely; in particular, his KB is a perpetual headache. In almost all strong point defensive systems the development of Black's KB is the major problem.

So we come to the main reply: 2 .... Kt—QB3. While this move has the essential strong point characteristic in that it defends the KP directly, it leaves the way open for a more definite decision at some later stage.

Once more White has a wide choice after 1 P—K4, P—K4; 2 Kt—KB3, Kt—QB3.

Again he may try the basic idea: 3 P—Q4 (Scotch Game). And again he fails to secure any significant results. Why? Because the loose position of his pieces in the center endows Black's counter-attack with such force that an early .... P—Q4 is inevitable.

The fight goes on, again with indirect methods.

If the Pawn structure in *Diagram No. 1* is strong, that with White's Pawn at Q4 instead of at QB2 in addition must be much stronger. That is, if White prepares P—Q4 with P—QB3, in order to be able to recapture at Q4 with a Pawn, he will secure an overwhelming positional advantage with two powerful Pawns in the center against Black's none. This more subtle motif of preparing P—Q4 by P—QB3 is deadly against an inaccurate reply. Sometimes P—Q4 at once is impossible; then P—QB3 is indispensable.

Ponziani's Opening, 3 P—QB3, is the most obvious and immediate application of the idea. Yet it too fails, this time again because of the basic reply 3 .... P—Q4, though 3 .... Kt—KB3 is playable too.

It follows that White must adopt a line where he can prepare P—Q4 for the right moment *and* prevent the same liberating move by his opponent. By a process of elimination we have discovered that the only two openings which do that are the Giuoco Piano and the Ruy Lopez.

From a strictly theoretical point of view, i.e., one which insists that the only moves to be analyzed are those which promise White an advantage, the Four Knights' and the allied Three Knights' are of minor importance because White does not try to play P—Q4 early (if he does, he transposes into another opening). Yet the symmetry with its surface placidity may cover a barrel of dynamite. Sooner or later White will advance his QP, though in the more usual lines it is done at the expense of a weakened Pawn position. This leads to complicated jockeying, alternative Black defenses to wrest the initiative, etc. Thus these lines too are best understood in the light of our basic principles.

The Giuoco Piano and the Ruy Lopez have maintained their position as the strongest openings for White in this section longest because they adhere most faithfully to the pattern of waiting for the right time to advance the QP and simultaneously preventing the liberating enemy push.

In the Giuoco Piano White's major offensive thought is P—QB3 followed by P—Q4. Black has the usual two defenses at his disposal. The counter-attack is more exciting and theoretically a bit more adequate; the strong point is more subtle, but more likely to lead to a seriously cramped game.

Though modern masters have devoted relatively little attention to the Giuoco, its variations continue to pose many intriguing problems.

While the Giuoco yields the coveted advantage in many cases, it can do little against the best defenses. Why? Because it lacks the stimulating effect of a direct threat with a permanent effect. B—B4 does not continue the drive against the enemy KP.

Because the Giuoco Piano lacks punch, Black may resort to the speculative Two Knights' Defense, 3 .... Kt—KB3, instead of the more routine 3 .... B—B4. If White accepts the Pawn profferred—his only hope of getting the better of it—he is subjected to a difficult attack. It is no accident that Black's counter-action is initiated by the natural .... P—Q4. Yet analysis and practise indicate that White can come out with a considerable superiority by adopting the type of defense which is always effective against gambits—returning the extra Pawn for the sake of superior development. All the same, some unusual lines in the Two Knights' furnish a welcome opportunity for the exercise of the imagination.

Finally, we come to the opening which stands head and shoulders above all others in this section—the Ruy Lopez. What is the source of its persistent strength and popularity? It combines the soundness of the Giuoco with the punch of the Gambits by creating a direct threat. That is, for the first time Black must defend his KP against a menace by a piece before the Pawns come up. Since .... P—Q4 is prevented by the potential pin (after 3 B—Kt5) Black must take a radically different course.

It is fortunate for the defender that he can afford to neglect the threat for a while. The defenses with 3 .... P—QR3 lighten his problem considerably. After getting a piece out, he is then again faced with the choice of a strong point or a counter-attack defense. As so often, both are serviceable.

Despite all the efforts of players and theoreticians, White's claws in the Ruy Lopez are still as sharp as ever. That is not to say that he must necessarily get the better of it. But, other things being equal, he is more likely to get an advantage with the Ruy than with any other opening in this category and his chances are about as good with it as with one of the QP Openings.

THE GAMBITS

All gambits, of course, involve the sacrifice of one or more Pawns (on rare occasions a piece) for the sake of an attack. It has further become clear that all the gambits which occur after 1 P—K4, P—K4 have three important features in common:

1. The attack is directed against the most vulnerable point in Black's camp, his KB2.

2. If he wishes to hold on to the material Black must submit to a backward development.

3. The best way to meet the gambit is to accept the sacrifice (declining the gambit brings only equality at best though it is frequently psychologically powerful) and then concentrating on speedy development, if necessary returning the extra material. In particular, Black should try to play .... P—Q4 as early as possible.

One of the reasons for the third point is that experience has made most masters chary of defending a terribly cramped position because even though it may be theoretically adequate, it will be terribly difficult to find the correct replies in over-the-board play.

In many cases White's compensation for the Pawn is a strong center; in others it is only speedier or more effective development. Frequently (notably in the Evans Gambit) B—QR3 prevents Black from castling.

Apart from these basic ideas, there is little more that pure strategic considerations can teach us about these gambits. The remainder is the tactical elaboration, although in each gambit there are specific ideas which are helpful for both attack and defense.

In practical play, it will be found helpful to ask the question whether the attack which White has is strong enough to overcome the material disadvantage. The answer is usually indicated by the state of development: if Black's pieces are cramped, all on the back lines, his chances are poor, especially if his King is exposed, but if he has a free open game he should win or at least draw.

It may be noted that the gambits have not disappeared from tournament chess because they have been refuted. On the contrary, modern research has strengthened them in many important respects. The real reason why they are practically never seen is that defensive technique has become far stronger than in the days of Anderssen and Morphy.

KING'S GAMBIT: 1 P—K4, P—K4; 2 P—KB4

A. King's Gambit Accepted: 2 .... P×P.

The opening of the KB file makes it only too obvious that White's assault will be directed against the Black KB2. Again, the fact that the Black KP is out of the way indicates that White will play P—Q4 as soon as possible. First, however, a defense against the threatened .... Q—R5ch must be found.

In addition to the strong Pawn center, another idea which is often useful for White is the sacrifice of a piece to open the KB file. An instance is the Muzio Gambit: 3 Kt—KB3, P—KKt4; 4 B—B4, P—Kt5; 5 O—O!, P×Kt; 6 Q×P, etc. with about even chances.

On 3 Kt—KB3, the theoretically most adequate defense is 3 .... P—KR3, to be followed by .... P—KKt4. This is a very difficult line to handle. In practise the simplest is 3 .... P—Q4, and if 4 P×P, Kt—KB3; 5 Kt—QB3, Kt×P; 6

Kt×Kt, Q×Kt; 7 P—Q4, B—K2!; 8 B—Q3, P—KKt4 (8
.... B—KB4 is good enough to equalize, but the text is more
energetic); 9 Q—K2 (to prevent castling, regain the Pawn),
B—KB4! and Black is adequately developed and has much the
better of it.

The reply 3 .... P—KKt4 (to 3 Kt—KB3) leads to enormous complications, the discussion of which is beyond the
province of this book. No positional considerations other than
those mentioned above occur; the interested reader should consult the appropriate columns in PRACTICAL CHESS OPENINGS.

In the Bishop's Gambit (3 B—B4 instead of 3 Kt—KB3)
White is prepared to move his King to KB1, confident that his
strong center and excellent development will soon coordinate
all his pieces satisfactorily. The usual type of counter with
3 .... P—Q4! ; 4 B×P, Kt—KB3 is the simplest way for
Black to equalize: 5 Kt—QB3, B—QKt5; 6 Kt—B3, B×Kt; 7
QP×B, P—B3; 8 B—B4, Q×Qch; 9 K×Q, O—O; 10 B×P,
Kt×P etc. However, the counter-attack 3 .... P—Q4; 4
B×P, Q—R5ch; 5 K—B1, P—KKt4 (the older line) is not
good because Black has inadequate compensation for the dis-
location of his pieces.

Of the many alternate lines for both White and Black, the
decision as to their value rests as a rule with tactics, not with
strategy.

B. King's Gambit Declined.

The most important branch here is the Falkbeer Counter-
Gambit, 2 .... P—Q4, which is designed to turn the tables
and secure an attack for Black at the expense of a Pawn.

Opinions of the Falkbeer have varied widely. At one time it
was claimed that it was a complete refutation of the entire
gambit. Spielmann, who had secured renown as the greatest
living expert on gambits, was so impressed by it that he wrote
an article "From the Sickbed of the King's Gambit." While
the first extravagant claims had to be abandoned, it retained
its force. It remained for some profound masters of the present

generation—Stoltz, Milner-Barry, above all Keres—to confirm the old adage that Black can ill afford to undertake a counter-attack involving a sacrifice at an early stage. And once more White's play is based on a familiar principle—concentrate on speedy development rather than retention of the extra material.

After the normal 3 KP×P (3 BP×P??, Q—R5ch; 4 P—Kt3, Q×KPch is a typical trap), P—K5! the strength of Black's game rests entirely on his Pawn at K5. Consequently 4 P—Q3 (after 3 KP×P, P—K5) is natural. Now we find much the same situation as in the regular gambits, except that the colors are reversed. If Black recaptures his material, he drifts into a positionally inferior game. E.g., 4 .... Q×P; 5 Q—K2, Kt—KB3; 6 Kt—QB3, B—QKt5; 7 B—Q2, B×Kt; 8 B×B, B—KKt5; 9 P×P, Q×KP; 10 Q×Q, Kt×Q; 11 B×KKtP, etc. So Black must play a true gambit with 4 .... Kt—KB3. Again the analogy holds: if White tries to hang on to his material, he will only have equality at best, but if he disregards material and concentrates on getting his pieces out quickly, he will get the better of it. The ideal realization of this plan is 5 Q—K2!, Q×P; 6 Kt—QB3, B—QKt5; 7 B—Q2, B×Kt; 8 B×B, B—Kt5; 9 P×P, Q×KP; 10 Q×Qch, Kt×Q; 11 B×P with a clearly superior position. The strength of 5 Q—K2 lies in the fact that it forces a series of exchanges which deprive Black of his most effectively placed pieces. Black is left with Bishop and Knight against two Bishops and has bad Pawns besides, which is too much.

The other main line of the Gambit Declined is 2 .... B—B4, made possible by the fact that the tempting 3 P×P! allows the devastating check 3 .... Q—R5ch.

It should be remembered that the common 2 .... P—Q3? gives Black a cramped position and an inferior center for no good reason.

After 2 .... B—B4 the normal development sequence is 3 Kt—KB3, P—Q3; 4 Kt—B3, Kt—KB3; 5 B—B4, Kt—B3; 6 P—Q3.

Then on 6 .... B—KKt5 (to break up the White King position); 7 P—KR3!, B×Kt; 8 Q×B, Kt—Q5; 9 Q—Kt3!, Kt× Pch?; 10 K—Q1, Kt×R; 11 Q×P gives White a winning attack. Instead, however, Black can take the sting out of the White set-up with 6 .... B—K3!, which neutralizes the critical diagonal. True, after 7 B—Kt5, P—QR3; 8 B×Ktch, P×B; 9 Q—K2, P×P is advisable, when White gets a strong Pawn center, but that consideration is of minor importance because Black's pieces are all well placed.

As in the Vienna Game, on P—KB5 at any stage, Black should react by preparing a break in the center with .... P— Q4.

Instead of simple development, White may elect to try to force a strong Pawn center at an early stage with P—QB3. Thus: 2 .... B—B4; 3 Kt—KB3, P—Q3; 4 P—B3. Black, however, may take advantage of the opportunity and initiate a counter-attack 4 .... P—B4! with good effect. On other moves White is apt to secure too strong a Pawn center.

DANISH GAMBIT: 1 P—K4, P—K4; 2 P—Q4, P×P; 3 P—QB3

A. Accepted: 3 .... P×P.

With the usual 4 B—QB4 White gives up two Pawns to get excellent diagonals for his Bishops. Black can, if he wishes, accept everything and hold on to it, but even though his position may be theoretically adequate, the attack is extremely hard to meet.

Instead, he can force a favorable simplification by 4 .... P×P; 5 B×P, P—Q4!; 6 B×QP (after 6 P×P the critical diagonal QR2—KKt8 is blocked for White and Black can get his pieces out without any trouble), Kt—KB3; 7 B×Pch, K×B; 8 Q×Q, B—Kt5ch; 9 Q—Q2, B×Qch; 10 Kt×B, P— B4 and Black has much the better of the ending because his Q-side Pawn majority can advance rapidly.

If White sacrifices only one Pawn (4 Kt×P instead of 4 B—QB4) or if Black does not take the second Pawn, Black must make sure that his Pawn position on the K-side will not be ruined. This can usually be done by .... B—K3 early. E.g., 4 .... P—Q3; 5 Kt×P, Kt—QB3; 6 Kt—B3, B—K3! (this takes the sting out of Q—Kt3) or 4 Kt×P (instead of 4 B—QB4), Kt—QB3; 5 B—QB4, P—Q3; 6 Q—Kt3, Q—Q2; 7 Kt—B3, Kt—QR4! etc. Exchanges are the best way to reduce the force of an attack.

B. Danish Gambit Declined.

There is no good way to decline the first Pawn, since the center would then be imperiled. But after 2 .... P×P; 3 P—QB3, P—Q4! is, as expected, quite sufficient. Then 4 KP×P is virtually forced, when either 4 .... Q×P; 5 P×P, Kt—QB3; 6 Kt—KB3, B—KKt5 (developing and bringing pressure to bear on the QP); 7 Kt—B3, B—Kt5; or 4 .... Kt—KB3; 5 P×P, B—Kt5ch; 6 B—Q2, B×Bch; 7 Q×B, O—O is good enough for equality. Note how here too Black's main concern is speedy development.

VIENNA GAMBIT: 1 P—K4, P—K4; 2 Kt—QB3, Kt—QB3; 3 P—KB4, P ×P

This is one of the few cases where Black can afford to hold on to his material. The reason is that the development of the QKt at QB3 is not particularly favorable in the King's Gambit or allied lines. The line with 4 Kt—B3, P—KKt4; 5 P—Q4, P—Kt5; 6 B—B4, P×Kt (Pierce Gambit) has been refuted; likewise 5 P—KR4, P—Kt5; 6 Kt—KKt5, P—KR3; 7 Kt×P, K×Kt; 8 P—Q4, P—Q4! is not adequate because of the loss of time.

SCOTCH GAMBIT: 1 P—K4, P—K4; 2 Kt—KB3, Kt—QB3; 3 P—Q4, P ×P

This is somewhat more promising for the attacker, though it need not be feared by Black. On 4 B—QB4, B—B4; 5 P—B3, P×P (5 .... P—Q6 and straight development equalizes); 6 Kt×P, P—Q3; 7 Q—Kt3!, Q—Q2; 8 Kt—Q5!, KKt—K2; 9 Q—B3, O—O leaves the chances about even. Note that

White's trumps are his superior development and the pressure on Black's KBP.

The Scotch may also transpose into a variety of other openings.

EVANS GAMBIT: 1 P—K4, P—K4; 2 Kt—KB3, Kt—QB3; 3 B—B4,
B—B4; 4 P—QKt4

A. *Evans Gambit Accepted: 4 . . . . B×P; 5 P—B3, B—R4;*
6 P—Q4.

One theoretical reason why this gambit has retained its virulence is that the freeing . . . . P—Q4 is not feasible.

In addition to the usual ideas of pressure against the KBP and cramping the Black game generally, there are two valuable subsidiary ideas here: setting up a strong Pawn center and preventing castling by B—QR3.

The older defenses run 6 . . . . P×P; 7 O—O, P—Q3; 8 P×P. Black's position is then constricted, but playable, although as so often there would perhaps be immense difficulties in practise. The great trouble for the defender is that the White Pawn center cannot be budged, so that Black must resort to many a peculiar maneuver to get his pieces out decently.

The Lasker Defense, which put the Evans out of business, envisages giving the Pawn back in order to secure the better ending. It is: 6 . . . . P—Q3 and if then 7 O—O, B—Kt3! Black hits at the White center immediately, for it is these Pawns which constrict his pieces. Then 8 P×P, P×P; 9 Q×Qch, Kt×Q; 10 Kt×P, B—K3 leads to an ending where Black's Pawn structure is superior. Moreover, the mere fact that an ending has been reached is psychologically depressing for the gambit player. Again, if White does not recapture the Pawn, he will find that the constant threat to his center puts a crimp in his attacking plans.

The most promising for White after 6 . . . . P—Q3 is 7 Q—Kt3, to hit at the enemy's weakness before the center is cleared. Then 7 . . . . Q—Q2; 8 P×P!, B—Kt3!; 9 QKt—Q2! regains the Pawn and retains some attacking prospects. Black cannot afford to recapture because of B—QR3 later, preventing castling.

B. *Evans Gambit Declined: 4 .... B—Kt3.*

The ideas in the resulting positions do not differ much from the similar lines in the Giuoco Piano, into which White may transpose. It should be noted that White cannot afford to take the KP after 5 P—Kt5, Kt—R4; because of 6 Kt×P, Kt—R3! White may try to get the upper hand in the center by 5 B—Kt2, P—Q3; 6 P—QR4, P—QR3; 7 P—Kt5, P×P; 8 P×P, R×R; 9 B×R for if 9 .... Kt—Kt1; 10 P—Q4 is strong. But both 9 .... Kt—QR4 and 9 .... Kt—Q5 are playable although on the latter White may secure a target by 10 B×Kt, P×B; 11 O—O, Kt—B3; 12 P—Q3 and eventually hitting at the QP and penetrating on the QR file.

Chapter III

KING PAWN OPENINGS
PART II

ALL REPLIES TO 1 P—K4 OTHER THAN 1 .... P—K4

While the defenses here differ radically in some respects, they are very much alike in others.

In the first place, in all, the attack on Black's vulnerable KB2, which played so predominant a role in the 1 P—K4, P—K4 lines, is virtually non-existent here. For this reason the game is much more positional in character.

In the second place, Black's Pawn structure is as a rule inferior in the opening. This should not be surprising, since he omits the natural .... P—K4. It does not follow, however, that all these openings are therefore poor: the only justifiable conclusion is that the struggle for equality (or counter-attack) becomes far more complex and depends to a far larger extent on the Pawn skeleton.

The role of .... P—Q4 by Black points to a further essential similarity and dissimilarity. We saw in the 1 P—K4, P—K4 group that if Black can succeed in playing .... P—Q4 without immediate ill effects, his opening problem is solved. We also saw how difficult it is for him to force the advance against good play, especially against the Ruy Lopez or Giuoco Piano.

In these openings, however, ... P—Q4 is relatively easy (except for the Sicilian Defense) but does not yield immediate equality. For Black's objective is to liquidate or neutralize the entire center and when he does play .... P—Q4 he has only taken care of the White KP. He must then also hit at the White QP, assuming, as is almost always the case, that that has been played to Q4. Consequently, to secure complete freedom, ... P—Q4 must be followed by .... P—QB4, or .... P—K4 (just as .... P—K4 had to be followed by .... P—Q4 or .... P—KB4). Unlike the analogous case in 1 P—K4, P—K4, where .... P—KB4 has to be prepared carefully because it weakens the K-position, here .... P—QB4 can and should be played whenever it is physically possible. Sometimes (as in the Sicilian), ... P—QB4 comes first: in that event .... P—Q4 must be the goal. In other words, Black must hit at the center with his Pawns to secure equality, and he can do it in these openings by .... P—Q4 and .... P—QB4 (usually) or .... P—Q4 and .... P—K4 (less often) or .... P—QB4 and .... P—Q4 (exceptional).

FRENCH DEFENSE: 1 P—K4, P—K3

The French Defense is ideal for a good defensive player. Because there are so many variations where Black must assume a temporarily cramped position, some masters have felt—and tried to demonstrate—that it is unsound, but ever and again the attacks have been made to recoil. Most of Black's problems arise from the lack of development of his QB (which explains why the opening has so much in common with the Queen's Gambit) and of his K-side. White usually tries to take advantage of his opponent's lack of room by a K-side attack coupled with a cramping bind in the center; Black's defense consists of a center break and judicious development. From time to time it would appear that one side has the upper hand, but the balance is always restored.

One great merit of the opening is that it affords plenty of scope for the imagination.

After the natural 2 P—Q4, P—Q4 an examination of the Pawn structure will reveal the objectives for both sides.

White's center Pawns are better, so he is out to keep the status quo or to improve it by P—K5, P—KB4, etc., eventually P—KB5. Black has a cramped position and can free himself only by hitting at the White Pawns. For this reason .... *P—*

QB4 is vital for Black in the French Defense. He can usually, though not always, equalize by playing .... P—QB4, but he can never get an even game if he does not advance his QBP. A subsidiary freeing maneuver is .... P—KB3, when White has moved his KP up. Further, Black's QB is a special problem because it is bound to be blocked behind a mass of Pawns for quite a while. Unless .... P—K4 can be forced, which is rarely the case, the B must be kept inactive in the opening or at best fianchettoed at QKt2.

White can prevent the liberation of the Black QB once and for all by playing P—K5. As long as White Pawns remain at Q4 and K5, Black's QB is hemmed in and his Kt is deprived of its best square. We shall refer to such a set-up with White Pawns at Q4 and K5, Black Pawns at Q4 and K3, as *the cramping Pawn chain.*

For the next few moves there are three principal motifs for White: 1) simplification; 2) keeping the tension in the center; 3) creation of the cramping Pawn chain with P—K5. In general, simplification is too simple and poses no real problems, while the trouble with the cramping Pawn chain is that it exposes White to an immediate counter-attack against his center Pawns, which usually results in disrupting them. However, the question as to whether the Pawns can be maintained or not at Q4 and K5 at any given time can only be answered tactically. Finally, the longer White can maintain the tension the better it is for him.

There are four principal continuations for White on his third move: 3 P×P (simplification), 3 Kt—QB3, 3 Kt—Q2 (keeping the tension) and 3 P—K5 (setting up the cramping Pawn chain).

I. 3 P×P (The Exchange Variation) is rarely adopted if White hopes to secure an advantage. The reason is clear enough: after 3 P×P, P×P the positions are perfectly symmetrical when all that White can rely on is his extra move. Note too that Black's QB is no longer a problem and that since there is no superior White Pawn in the center, the necessity for

.... P—QB4 by Black has been removed. Straight development equalizes.

Frequently the Exchange Variation is played by White in order to force a draw. In that event, Black, if he so chooses, can well afford to play for a win by breaking the symmetry. E.g., 4 Kt—KB3, B—Q3; 5 B—Q3, Kt—QB3!; 6 P—B3, KKt—K2!; 7 O—O, B—KKt5; 8 R—K1, Q—Q2; 9 B—KKt5, P—B3 etc. with attacking prospects (10 B—R4, P—KR4!; 11 QKt—Q2, P—KKt4; 13 B—Kt3, B×B; 14 RP×B, O—O—O).

II. 3 Kt—QB3 is the most obvious way to maintain the tension. Now it is up to Black to choose the mold into which the game is to be poured. He can either simplify, or counter-attack, or maintain the tension as well.

A. Simplification: 3 .... P×P. While this avoids many pitfalls and difficulties, its weakness is that it abandons the center, so that Black can at best equalize after a long and hard fight. The question then to be determined is whether Black will be able to play .... P—QB4 or not. It appears that he can, after 4 Kt×P, Kt—Q2; 5 Kt—KB3, KKt—B3; 6 Kt×Ktch, Kt× Kt; 7 B—Q3, P—B4!; 8 P×P, B×P; 9 O—O, O—O; 10 B— KKt5, P—QKt3; 11 Q—K2, B—Kt2; 12 QR—Q1 (*Diagram No. 14A*). While Black's game is playable it is not wholly satisfactory. White has the majority of Pawns on the Q-side (a great endgame advantage), a possible K-side attack.

B. Counter-attack: 3 .... B—Kt5. This threatens to win a Pawn and thus compels White to take some action about the center. (It should be noted that the alternative counter-attack 3 .... P—QB4? is refuted by 4 KP×P, KP×P; 5 Kt— KB3, Kt—KB3; 6 B—KKt5 and Black's center is too weak.)

Again White has a large gamut of possibilities. These fall into the usual three classes of simplification, keeping the tension and cramping Pawn chain, but there are two more now because Black has weakened his K-side by playing out his B: attack against the Black King's wing and sacrifice of the center Pawn to secure quick development.

Simplification with 4 P×P, as usual, leads to nothing better than equality.

Keeping the tension is possible with either 4 B—Q2 or 4 B—Q3. 4 B—Q3 fails because it does not prevent .... P—QB4, while on 4 B—Q2, Kt—K2; the only important independent line is 5 P×P, when 5 .... P×P equalizes as always.

Setting up the cramping Pawn chain with 4 P—K5 is most popular. Then the natural 4 .... P—QB4 follows. Now the struggle revolves around whether White will be able to maintain his Pawns in the center or not. The thought which comes to mind first is 5 B—Q2, to unpin the Kt and exchange the enemy KB, thus gaining the upper hand on the Black squares. But this can be met adequately by the immediate 5 .... Kt—QB3, hitting at the White center. Then on 6 Kt—Kt5, B×Bch; 7 Q×B, Kt×QP!; 8 Kt×Kt (8 Kt—Q6ch is meaningless), P×Kt; 9 Q×P, Kt—K2 and Black will soon be able to exchange the White KP or gain adequate counterplay by strengthening his center.

More enterprising for White is 5 P—QR3, when the game may again branch off. On 5 .... B×Ktch; 6 P×B White has the two Bishops and superiority on the Black squares, but the inferior Pawn position on the Q-side. His policy should be an attack against the enemy K-side Pawn position (P—KB4, P—KKt4, eventually P—B5), which will give him a good attack regardless of which side Black castles on. Black can, however, take the sting out of such an advance by suitable exchanges. 5 .... P×P (instead of 5 .... B×Ktch); 6 P×B, P×Kt involves a Pawn sacrifice by White, since 7 P×P?, Q—B2! is bad. But 7 Kt—B3, followed by Q—Q4, B—Q3, etc gives White enough for the Pawn.

The attack against the Black King's wing is initiated by 4 Q—Kt4. This looks plausible, but is refuted by vigorous counter-action in the center: 4 .... Kt—KB3; 5 Q×KtP, R—Kt1; 6 Q—R6, R—Kt3; 7 Q—K3, P—QB4! etc.

The sacrifice to secure quick development with 4 Kt—K2 is good if Black tries to hold on to the Pawn, but is refuted by the usual strong reply to a gambit—concentration on getting the pieces out: 4 .... P×P; 5 P—QR3, B—K2!; 6 Kt×P, Kt—QB3 (violation of the rule that .... P—QB4 is vital for Black but nevertheless not to be censured because White is thereby forced on the defensive); 7 B—K3, Kt—B3 and Black's game is satisfactory.

Finally, there is a move which unites a number of motifs: 4 P—QR3. White wishes to strengthen the center and then attack the Black K-side. After 4 .... B×Ktch; 5 P×B, P×P followed by counter-action on the Q-side leads to a game with chances for both sides.

It should be remembered that after 3 .... B—Kt5 the idea of weakening the defender on the Black squares plays an important part in the proceedings.

C. Keeping the Tension: 3 .... Kt—KB3. The most common and, in a sense, the most natural. The many variations and sub-variations are best understood in the light of the following *main line:* 4 B—KKt5, B—K2; 5 P—K5, KKt—Q2; 6 B×B, Q×B; 7 Q—Q2, O—O; 8 P—B4, P—QB4; 9 Kt—B3, Kt—QB3; 10 O—O—O, P—B3; 11 KP×P, Q×P; 12 P— KKt3, P×P; 13 KKt×P *(Diagram No. 13F)*. In the final position we must concede White a slight plus because of Black's weak and exposed KP. Black may try to build up an attack, but he is not likely to be successful. On the other hand, White's advantage is so minimal that he can readily be pardoned for attempting to secure more. Thus improvements for both sides must be examined.

First let us review the motifs for both sides in the light of what has been said.

1. White kept the tension as long as he was able to. On his 5th move he had to break and, rather than simplify, (which leads to nothing) he set up the cramping Pawn chain.

2. Once this Pawn chain is set up, Black is constrained to try to dissolve it by .... P—QB4 and .... P—KB3. He succeeds, but must avoid certain other weaknesses. One positive feature of this defense is that the square KB4 should be used

for the Kt, which should be safeguarded there by .... P—
KR4 (*Diagram No. 14B*). Sometimes White may be able to
chase the Kt away, but only by the sequence P—KKt3, P—
KR3 (the order is important—if first P—KR3, P—R5 blocks
the KtP) and P—KKt4, which always costs a good deal of
time and frequently weakens the K-position.

3. Since the Pawn structure is so crucial in this opening,
it is essential to examine the various possibilities in greater detail, as illustrated in *Diagrams No. 13A–E*.

First of all, we have the case which is best for Black, 13A.
Here his only weakness is the KP, but he need not fear any attack on the K-side (structure of the main line). It goes almost
without saying that the liberating .... P—K4 must always be
prevented by White.

Next, in 13B, Black plays only .... P—QB4. The difference
between this and the previous line is great. White exchanges,
and has a position which is superior in both endgame and middle game. In the ending, he will stand particularly well if he
has a Kt vs. a B, because so many Black Pawns are on White.
The key square for his pieces is Q4, the key move for the attack
is P—KB5 (after P—KKt4).

13C is again inferior for Black. Here he has tried only ....
P—KB3 and White has captured. The result is that his KP is
held in a vise and he has no compensatory play on the Q-side,
as in A. White has both the better ending and a strong attack
against Black's K-side.

13D is the result of bad timing: Black has played both
freeing moves, ... P—QB4 and .... P—KB3, but has allowed White to reinforce the Pawns so that the result is a
White center more solid than ever. In this type of Pawn position the White attack is usually overwhelming, but in the ending, White's plus is minimal.

Finally, in 13E we have the do-nothing position: Black
makes no attempt to free himself. Here White of course has
the better ending, but can secure a crushing attack with P—
KKt4, P—KB5.

POSITIONS IN THE FRENCH DEFENSE

(Black makes no Pawn moves other than those shown)

No. 13A

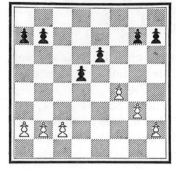

White's advantage is minimal.

No. 13B

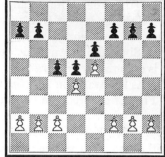

White is a little better off.

No. 13C

White is a little better off.

No. 13D

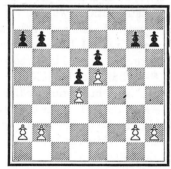

White has much the better of it.

Now we can return to the variations, which will be treated as deviations from the main line.

On White's 10th move, White may wish to exchange Pawns and castle on the K-side, thus eliminating any Black counterchances based on attack. The trouble with this is that he cannot then prevent the freeing .... P—K4. On 10 P—KKt3, P—B3; 11 P×KBP, Kt×BP!; 12 B—Kt2, P×P; 13 KKt×P, P—K4! gives more than adequate counterplay. Or 10 P×P,

POSITIONS IN THE FRENCH DEFENSE

No. 13E

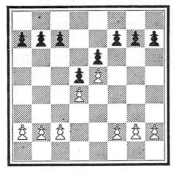

White's game is crushing.

No. 13F

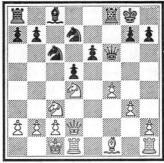

Position reached in the main line; White has a slight plus.

No. 14A

French Defense Position after 12 QR —Q1. White has both a middle game and an endgame advantage.

No. 14B

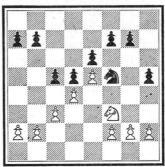

Typical French Defense Structure; KB4 is a Powerful Post for the Black Kt.

Kt)(BP; 11 B Q3, P B3; 12 P)(P, Q)(P, when the KBP is attacked, and after 13 P—KKt3, Kt×Bch; 14 P×B, P—K4! is adequate.

On White's 8th move he may try to make room for his QBP and thus hold the center Pawns to secure 13D. The monkey wrench which disrupts the machinery here is *the sacrifice of the exchange at KB6 to disrupt White's Pawns* (a motif of frequent occurrence): 8 Kt—Q1, P—QB4; 9 P—QB3, Kt—QB3; 10 P—

KB4, P—B3; 11 Kt—B3, P×QP; 12 BP×P, P×P; 13 BP×P, R×Kt!; 14 P×R, Q—R5ch and Black will get at least two Pawns for the exchange, in addition to a strong center.

The importance of correct timing for Black may be seen from the sad results of 7 .... P—QR3, instead of 7 .... O—O. Then 8 P—B4, P—QB4; 9 Kt—B3, Kt—QB3; 10 P×P, Kt× BP; 11 B—Q3, B—Q2 (11 .... O—O would be even worse); 12 O—O, P—KR3 (to castle without allowing B×Pch); 13 QR—K1 and White has all the play (structure 13B).

The attempt *on White's 7th move* to solidify the center Pawn position introduces a new motif for Black. 7 Kt—Q1, P—QB4; is refuted by the exchange sacrifice as above. But 7 Kt—Kt5 is harder to meet. Then 7 .... Kt—Kt3; 8 P—QB3, P—QR3 (necessary to prevent Kt—Q6); 9 Kt—QR3, P—QB4!; 10 Kt—B2, Kt—R5; 11 R—Kt1, P—QKt4; 12 P—KB4, Kt— B3; 13 Kt—B3, B—Q2. White has succeeded in keeping his Pawns straight, but at the cost of weakening his Q-side, where Black's counter is sufficient.

On White's 6th move, we get the most important strengthening of the attack: 6 P—KR4! Theoretically, the reason why this sacrifice is good is that it prevents normal development by Black and creates tension all over again. It is essential to recognize that accepting the sacrifice is not advisable because of White's subsequent command of the KR file: 6 .... B×B; 7 P×B, Q×P; 8 Kt—R3, Q—K2; 9 Kt—B4, P—QR3; 10 Q— Kt4!, P—KKt3; 11 O—O—O and Black's extra Pawn is useless. Likewise the normal 6 .... O—O is refuted by 7 B—Q3, P—QB4; 8 Kt—R3! etc. with a powerful attack.

There are no new positional motifs introduced by Black's replies. The chief point worth noting is that after 6 .... P— QB4; 7 B×B, K×B! (better than 7 .... Q×B; 8 Kt—Kt5); 8 P—B4, Kt—QB3; 9 P×P, Kt×BP; 10 Q—Kt4!, K—B1; 11 O—O—O the attack can be effectively continued with R— R3! —Kt3 etc.

It has been established that the most adequate defense for Black is 6 .... P—KB3! Then 7 P×P, Kt×P leads to Pawn structure 13A after .... P—QB4, which is enough to equalize for Black. The most promising appears to be 7 B—Q3!, P—QB4!; 8 Q—R5ch, K—B1; 9 KP×P, Kt×P; 10 B×Kt when White has some hopes of getting the better of it because of Black's exposed King position.

All told, Alekhine's attack (6 P—KR4) remains a powerful weapon.

The attempt by Black to avoid a constricted position with 5 .... Kt—K5 (instead of 5 .... KKt—Q2 in the main line) is refuted by 6 B×B, Q×B; 7 Kt×Kt, P×Kt; 8 Q—K2!, when the KP is too weak.

On White's 5th move he may try to build up a vigorous attack with 5 B×Kt! (in the main line), B×B; 6 P—K5, B—K2; 7 Q—Kt4. Here White intends to castle long and hammer at the Black King. The plan is not easy to meet: the best is to get rid of the cramping KP: 7 .... O—O; 8 B—Q3, P—QB4; 9 P×P, P—KKt3!; 10 Q—R3, Kt—B3; 11 P—B4, B×P; 12 Kt—B3, P—B3!. Should Black defend with 9 .... P—B4 (instead of 9 .... P—KKt3); 10 Q—R3!, B×P; 11 O—O—O and eventually P—KKt4 the assault is not easy to ward off. This variation has speculative possibilities for both sides: White is active on the K-side, Black on the other wing.

On Black's 4th move there are two promising deviations: the counter-attack 4 .... B—Kt5 (the McCutcheon Variation) and simplification with 4 .... P×P.

In the McCutcheon, 4 .... B—Kt5, improvements have lately appeared for both sides.

Simplification with 5 P×P is much better than in other lines because 5 .... Q×P allows the weakening of the Black K-side with 6 B×Kt, P×B. However, Black's two Bishops and otherwise sound position make this slight advantage too slight to be of value.

It had always been believed that the refutation of the McCutcheon was 5 P—K5, P—KR3; 6 B—Q2, B×Kt; 7 P×B, Kt—K5 (Black's moves are all forced); 8 Q—Kt4, with a vigorous attack. But since Black's only weakness consists of his cramped position, if he can develop in time and castle long, he will be out of danger: 8 .... P—KKt3; 9 B—Q3, Kt×B; 10 K×Kt, P—QB4. Here on the older 11 P—KR4, Kt—B3!; 12 R—R3, P×P; 13 P×P, Q—Kt3! foils the sacrifice B×P and initiates a strong assault for the second player. But the newer 11 Kt—B3! gives White excellent attacking chances, e.g. 11 .... Kt—B3?; 12 P×P!, Q—K2; 13 Q—KB4, Q×P; 14 Kt—Q4, or 11 .... P×P; 12 P×P, Kt—B3; 13 QR—Kt1, and Black's game remains uncomfortably cramped.

The simplification 4 .... P×P (in the main line) is much stronger than on the previous move because the pin 4 B—KKt5 is then deprived of most of its value. There are several unusual possibilities: if Black avoids the weakening of his K-side Pawns, White can secure better endgame prospects by exchanging P×P on an eventual .... P—QB4 and capitalizing on his Q-side majority of Pawns: 5 Kt×P, B—K2; 6 B×Kt, B×B (better 6 .... P×B); 7 Kt—KB3, Kt—Q2; 8 P—B3, Q—K2; 9 Q—B2, P—B4; 10 P×P, Kt×P; 11 B—Kt5ch, B—Q2; 12 B×Bch, Kt×B; 13 O—O—O. Since this normal line is not quite good enough Black is better off if he recaptures with the Pawn on his 6th move above. Then he has a cramped position, it is true, but without any tangible objects for attack. He develops by .... Kt—Q2, ... P—QKt3, ... P—QB3, ... Q—B2, ... O—O—O and can then count on the open KKt file to get some counterplay. An early .... P—KB4 is also feasible.

Finally, we come to alternatives on White's fourth move (instead of 4 B—KKt5). 4 B—Q3 is, as always, refuted by .... P—QB4. 4 P—K5 is, however, harder to meet. Then 4 .... KKt—Q2 must be followed by an immediate assault on the White center: 5 QKt—K2 (5 P—B4, P—QB4; 6 P×P, Kt—QB3 is similar to the 5 B×Kt line above), P—QB4; 6 P—QB3 and now 6 .... P×P; 7 P×P, P—B3!, for if 8 P—B4, P×P; and now 9 BP×P? is refuted by 9 .... Q—R5ch; 10 Kt—Kt3, B—Kt5ch etc. On the other hand, if Black takes no immediate measures against the center Pawns, White secures a

strong attack: 5 .... P—QB4; 6 P—QB3, Kt—QB3; 7 P—
KB4, Q—Kt3; 8 Kt—B3, P—B3; 9 P—QR3 (to clarify the
Pawn situation), P×KP (better 9 .... P—QR4); 10 BP×P,
P×P; 11 P×P, B—K2; 12 Kt—B4 and Black has insufficient
compensation for his weakened King position.

III. 3 Kt—Q2 also holds the tension, but avoids the pin,
which was so strong in many 3 Kt—QB3 variations, and leaves
the QBP free to support the QP. Thus it has much theoretical
support, but its great drawback is that it offers no adequate
refutation of 3 .... P—QB4. On 4 P×KP, KP×P (4 ....
Q×P is also possible); 5 B—Kt5ch (or 5 KKt—B3, KKt—B3),
B—Q2; 6 Q—K2ch, Q—K2; 7 Q×Qch, B×Q; 8 B×Bch,
Kt×B; 9 P×P, Kt×P; 10 Kt—Kt3, Kt—R5! the isolated
QP is too slight a weakness for practical purposes. In all varia-
tions with the isolated QP White posts a piece (preferably a
Kt) at Q4, while Black counters by placing his Kt at K5 and, if
possible, at QB5. It is worth noting that the normal 3 ....
Kt—KB3 though risky may be played with the finesse 4 P—
K5, KKt—Q2; 5 B—Q3, P—QB4; 6 P—QB3, P—QKt3!; 7 Kt
—K2, B—R3; 8 B×B, Kt×B; 9 O—O, P—Kt3; 10 Kt—
B3, B—Kt2 and White, shorn of his Bishop, cannot do much.

IV. 3 P—K5 sets up the cramping Pawn chain and judgment
of the variation depends on the tactical problem of how well
the Pawns can be maintained. After 3 .... P—QB4, there are
two possibilities for White: hold the Pawns in the center at any
cost, or give up one Pawn in order to retain the other.

The first fails after 4 P—QB3, Kt—QB3; 5 P—KB4?, P×P;
6 P×P, Q—Kt3; 7 Kt—KB3, Kt—R3; 8 B—Q3, B—Q2 and
White is in trouble.

To hold the QP White must resort to unnatural develop-
ment: 4 P—QB3, Kt—QB3; 5 Kt—KB3, Q—Kt3; 6 B—Q3,
P×P; 7 P×P, B—Q2; 8 B—K2, KKt—K2; 9 P—QKt3,
Kt—B4; 10 B—Kt2, B—Kt5ch; 11 K—B1, P—KR4; 12 P—
Kt3, R—QB1; 13 K—Kt2, P—Kt3 and eventually .... P—
KB3 or play on the QB file is sufficient.

One good idea for White which can, however, rarely be realized, is to play P×BP at an appropriate moment, since it is chiefly the KP which cramps the opponent's game.

4 Q—Kt4 is played with a view to sacrificing the QP (often only temporarily) in order to hold the Pawn at K5 and keep Black's K-side cramped. But it too fails against a determined assault on the White center: 4 .... Kt—QB3 (or 4 .... P×P followed by hitting at the KP and .... P—KB3 early); 5 Kt—KB3, KKt—K2; 6 P—B3, Kt—B4; 7 B—Q3, P×P! and White must resort to an inadequate sacrifice or a levelling exchange.

Least pretentious is 4 Kt—KB3, to which, however, there is the usual variety of good replies based on hitting the White center Pawns. One interesting idea for Black is to play the KKt to QB3 and the QKt to Q2. An idea worth remembering for White is to allow the exchange of his KP in order to substitute a piece for the Pawn: e.g., 4 Kt—KB3, Kt—QB3; 5 B—Q3, P×P; 6 O—O, P—B3; 7 B—QKt5!, B—Q2; 8 B×Kt, P×B; 9 Q×P, P×P; 10 Q×KP, Kt—B3; 11 B—B4, but Black's two Bishops and otherwise strong center are adequate.

On White's third move, inferior lines (any alternative to the four given) are refuted by advance of the QBP.

An excellent rule in all variations for Black is never to block his QBP with his QKt.

Alternatives on White's second move have little more than academic interest, since by advancing in the center Black secures theoretical equality at once. The most interesting is 2 Q—K2 (Tchigorin's Attack), which is played with a view to leaving the Q4 square in Black's control and instead concentrating on the K-side: 2 .... P—QB4; 3 P—KB4, Kt—QB3; 4 Kt—KB3, KKt—K2; 5 P—KKt3, when 5 .... P—Q4; 6 P—Q3 does leave Black's game somewhat cramped, but 5 .... P—KKt3, to strengthen control of Q5, is enough to equalize.

CARO-KANN DEFENSE: 1 P—K4, P—QB3

This defense is motivated by a desire to secure the good features of the French (prevention of any attack on KB2) and to avoid the bad ones (cramped game, especially due to the fact that the QB is shut in). However, it is subject to the theoretical disadvantage of supporting a center Pawn (Q4) not with another center Pawn (as in the French) but with a side Pawn. It thus becomes easier for White to get the upper hand in the center. On the whole, it is safer than the French, but offers fewer opportunities for counterplay.

After the normal 2 P—Q4, P—Q4 White has four distinct motifs, the elaboration of which vary a good deal from their analogues in the French. They are: maintaining the tension, attack, simplification, and setting up the cramping Pawn chain.

I. 3 Kt—QB3, maintaining the tension, is much less complicated than its analogue in the French because the reply 3 .... P×P is virtually forced. (Both 3 .... P—K3 and 3 .... Kt—KB3; 4 P—K5 lead to unfavorable lines of the French since Black must eventually play .... P—QB4 and has thus lost a move.) After 3 .... P×P; 4 Kt×P Black's replies are again more limited. He can develop in one of three ways:

A. 4 .... Kt—KB3 challenges the domineering enemy horseman. To secure an advantage there are now two motifs for White: to try to disrupt the Black Pawn position, or to avoid exchanges, relying on his lead in development. 5 Kt× Ktch breaks up the Black Pawns, and yields a minimal endgame advantage. After 5 .... KP×Kt (*Diagram No. 15A*); Black has no compensation for his minority of Pawns on the Q-side; the sole reason why he can so often draw in practise is that the White majority is so hard to exploit. Nevertheless, regardless of how White continues, Black's game remains too passive. The Pawn position on 5 .... KtP×Kt is much less favorable for White.

One point is noteworthy in both the above lines. It is that White must handle his Pawn majority more skillfully than might be supposed because an unsupported Pawn at Q4 may well be a handicap in the ending. Its value is *restrictive;* once there is nothing to restrict its value is virtually gone. Hence he should play for an attack by avoiding exchanges. In the

first line, after 5 .... KP×Kt, an early Q—R5! surprisingly
is hard to meet. E.g., 6 B—QB4, B—Q3; 7 Q—R5!, O—O;
8 Kt—K2, P—KKt3; 9 Q—B3, R—K1; 10 B—KR6, B—
KB4; 11 O—O—O, B—K5; 12 Q—QKt3 yields a strong attack.
In the above 7 Q—K2ch, B—K2 and then 8 Q—R5 may be
even stronger. In the second line, after 5 .... KtP×Kt; 6
Kt—K2! preserves the pressure, e.g., 6 .... B—B4; 7 Kt—
Kt3, B—Kt3; 8 P—KR4, P—KR3; 9 P—R5, B—R2; 10
P—QB3, Q—Kt3; 11 B—QB4 and Black remains cramped.
The point here is that Black's pieces are thoroughly disorganized, while White's work together as a perfect team. White
need not hurry matters; all that he has to do is develop nor-
mally, and then when Black has castled build up an attack
there.

5 Kt—Kt3, P—K3; 6 Kt—B3, P—B4!; 7 B—Q3, Kt—B3
(*Diagram No. 15B, also 14A*) leads to a type of Pawn position
which frequently occurs. Here there are two motifs for White:
he may rely on his Q-side majority and play P×P, P—QR3,
P—QKt4, P—QB4, when his advantage will tell most in the
endgame, as a rule, though he may also quite justifiably play
for an attack against the cramped Black King position (B—
Kt2, B—Q3, O—O, Q—K2, Kt—K5, P—B4, Kt—R5—often
effective sacrifices are feasible). Black's counterplay in such
cases consists of judicious exchanges and securing control of the
Queen's file. Or White may submit to the isolated Pawn in
order to secure a powerful outpost for his Kt at K5. Here he
speculates solely on attack. He expects to continue with B—
Q3, Kt—K5, O—O, B—KKt5 (or B—K3), P—B4, eventually
either P—B5 or Kt—R5, or both, depending on circumstances.
Black's counterplay then will be based on the unassailable
anchor at Q4, while exchanges will lead to an ending which is
favorable for him, rather than merely equal.

B. 4 .... B—B4 avoids the Pawn structure pitfalls of the
alternative, but loses an extra move in development, so that
after 5 Kt—Kt3, B—Kt3 Black's role is more passive than
ever. The Black QB may be able to assist Black in building up

pressure against the White Q-side, so that it is a good idea to offer to exchange it. Eventually White will then have the superior Pawn structure and Black will have no compensation.

PAWN POSITIONS IN THE CARO-KANN DEFENSE

No. 15A

White has the better endgame.

No. 15B

White has an advantage in both middle game and endgame.

No. 15C

White has the better endgame.

No. 15D

The chances are even.

Black's Pawn structure is superior.

To pursue this motif effectively, there are three points for White to remember: the position of the Black QB must be undermined to force the exchange; White will get Pawn position 15B under favorable circumstances; he can exploit this

Pawn structure best by avoiding unnecessary changes. As mentioned above, Black's role is passive and he cannot put any meaningful obstacles in White's way, but must await events as they come.

White can execute his plan (after 5 Kt—Kt3, B—Kt3) by 6 P—KR4!, P—KR3 (forced); 7 Kt—B3, Kt—B3; 8 B—Q3, B×B (as a result of the move of the RP there is no choice); 9 Q×B, QKt—Q2; 10 B—Q2, P—K3; 11 O—O—O (White castles long because his K-side has been weakened), Q—B2 and now 12 K—Kt1! (rather than 12 KR—K1, B—Q3; 13 Kt—K4, Kt×Kt; 14 Q×Kt, Kt—B3; 15 Q—K2, B—B5 when the excessive blood-letting has relieved Black), B—Q3 (though Black is better off if he defers this for a while); 13 Kt—K4, Kt×Kt; 14 Q×Kt, Kt—B3; 15 Q—K2. White has reached his goal: there are still two minor pieces on each side, he has the upper hand in the center. It should be noted that improvements in Black's play are based on the thought that the more pieces he exchanges the less cramped and more playable his position becomes.

C. 4 .... Kt—Q2 (or 4 .... P—K3, which amounts to the same thing) is a less forceful version of line A. White does not exchange. Pawn position 15B is reached, when White may continue as he pleases.

II. 3 P×P, P×P; 4 P—QB4 is the *attacking line* which almost put the Caro-Kann out of business some years ago.

The strength of the attack is due to the fact that it hits at the Black center immediately, and hits hard. Instead of coasting along as in other lines, Black has to solve a troublesome problem immediately: how to maintain the center and find a suitable place for his QB. If he shuts in his B with .... P—K3, he is deprived of the chief advantage of the Caro-Kann. But if he plays his B out to B4 or Kt5 (eventually) he may be unable to hold the center or his Q-side may be badly weakened. These possibilities form the background for Black's play.

Black is, of course, at liberty to develop his Kt's first without committing himself about his B. Thus 4 .... Kt—KB3;

5 Kt—QB3 (more energetic than the alternative Kt move because it brings another piece to bear on Q5), Kt—B3. Now White is at the parting of the ways. He may continue the pressure on the center with 6 B—Kt5, in which event 6 .... P—K3 is virtually forced (6 .... P×P; 7 P—Q5 is practically a lost game). Now Black's center is solidified (especially after .... B—K2) so that White can attempt to retain the advantage in one of two ways: by building up an attack, or by setting up a majority of Pawns on the Q-side. The first can be done with 7 Kt—B3, P×P; 8 B×P, B—K2, when we have Pawn position 15C. This is somewhat stronger here than is otherwise the case because Black's control of his Q4 is not absolute, i.e., he has trouble maintaining a piece there favorably. The Q-side majority can be set up with 7 P—B5, when Black must break up or weaken the White Pawn formation with .... P—QKt3. If White can hold his Pawns in such cases without allowing the crippling break .... P—K4 or cramping himself so much that Black gets adequate counterplay, he gets the better of it. The question can only be resolved tactically in this and all similar positions.

The ideas remain essentially the same if White develops his Kt on his 6th move, 6 Kt—B3, instead of 6 B—Kt5. Only the reply 6 .... B—Kt5, now not wholly bad, creates any different variations. This time the pin prevents White from building up an attack, so that he may either set up the Q-side majority as above or try to exploit the weakened state of the Black Q-side. This latter line yields him a light plus: 7 P×P, KKt×P; 8 Q—Kt3, B×Kt; 9 P×B, P—K3; 10 Q×P, Kt×P; 11 B—Kt5ch, etc.

III. 3 P×P, P×P; 4 B—Q3 is the more quiet *simplification* line, much less promising than II. After the normal 4 .... Kt—QB3; 5 P—QB3 the Pawn structure is that shown in *Diagram No. 15D*. Here White's source of strength is his control of K5, which should be occupied with a Kt at an early stage. If P—KB4, followed by pouring his pieces into the K-side, is then possible, White will secure a strong attack. But he has no long-run prospects; in the ending he is inferior. Black has the famous Pawn minority on the Q-side, which may be exploited by advancing the KtP to Kt5, thus creating weaknesses in the White camp (see page 105). He may defend himself against the White attack either by a fianchetto or by maneuvering to exchange the White KB, though the K fianchetto is more lasting.

Thus on 5 .... Kt—B3; 6 B—KB4, P—KKt3 is best, when the QB may be developed at KB4. But on 6 .... B—Kt5; 7 Kt—B3, P—K3; 8 Q—Kt3!, Q—B1; 9 QKt—Q2, B—K2; 10 O—O, O—O; 11 P—KR3, B—R4; 12 QR—K1, B—Kt3; 13 B×B, RP×B; 14 Kt—K5 White has the better of it. This variation is even stronger if Black plays .... P—K3 without developing his B first.

IV. 3 P—K5 sets up the *cramping Pawn chain*, but there is nothing cramped, which makes the move entirely useless, un' like its analogue in the French. After 3 .... B—B4; 4 B—Q3, B×B; 5 Q×B, P—K3 Black really has all the advantages of the French without any of the disadvantages. After .... P—QB4 he will have at least equality. The point KB4 will again be a strong post for his Kt, as in many lines of the French. (*Diagram No. 14B.*)

V. 3 P—KB3 is the only other move beside 3 Kt—QB3 which *keeps the tension* and retains possibilities of an advantage. The counter-attacking reply 3 .... P×P!; 4 P×P, P—K4; 5 Kt—KB3, P×P; 6 B—QB4! fails because of Black's exposed KB2, but 3 .... P—K3 transposes into French Defense lines eventually because White cannot maintain the tension indefinitely.

Irregular continuations on White's second move lead to few new ideas. The most interesting is 2 P—QB4, when Black frequently offers the QP for several moves. E.g., 2 .... P—Q4; 3 KP×P, P×P; 4 P×P, Kt—KB3 (4 .... Q×P goes into regular lines). This creates tactical possibilities for the utilization of the extra Pawn. He may either try to hold on to it (which usually does not work out well) or give it up to create a Black weakness. E.g., 5 B—Kt5ch, QKt—Q2; 6 QKt—B3, P—KKt3; 7 Kt—B3, B—Kt2; 8 P—Q6!, P×P and the Black QP is a target.

Unfavorable transpositions must also be guarded against. Thus on 2 Kt—QB3, P—Q4; 3 Kt—B3, P—K3?; 4 P—Q4 gives a variation of the French which is bad for Black. Instead straight development equalizes.

It should be noted that the Caro-Kann has a number of points of similarity with the Queen's Gambit. Pawn position 15C can come out of the Q.G.A., while 15D may occur in the Colle System.

SICILIAN DEFENSE: 1 P—K4, P—QB4

Like the Caro-Kann, the Sicilian begins by breaking the symmetry. But unlike that defense, it does not do so merely to hold the center, but to institute a counter-attack on the Queen's wing. For that reason *the outstanding characteristic of the Sicilian Defense is that it is a fighting game.* Both players must necessarily seek their objectives on different sides, which can lead to deliciously complicated and exciting variations.

Because the Sicilian is more of a unit than most other defenses it is possible and worth while to lay down a number of general principles which will be found to be valid in a large majority of cases.

White almost invariably comes out of the opening with more terrain. Theory tells us that in such cases he must attack. He does so, normally, by P—KKt4, followed by a general advance P—Kt5, P—B5, eventually P—B6. In some cases he may castle long (in that event he must weigh the counterplay which Black can undertake). One of White's major positional objectives is the prevention of .... P—Q4.

Normal play for Black consists of pressure on the QB file, especially his QB5. Coupled with this is keeping White's KP under observation. The counter-attack against the KP may also be quite strong independently of the play on the QB file. Sometimes he can secure the two Bishops by moving his Kt to

QB5 in a position where the reply B✕Kt is virtually compulsory. Whenever .... P—Q4 is feasible without allowing the reply P—K5 it should be played; it is almost certain to at least equalize.

In the Sicilian the middle game is all-important. Markedly favorable or unfavorable endgame Pawn structures have no immediate relationship to the opening as such.

There are, further, three important considerations in all variations:

1. Black must never allow White to play P—QB4 in the opening because he then has no counterplay on the QB file and is thereby doomed to passivity.

2. After White has played P—Q4, Black must not move .... P—K4, leaving his QP backward on an open file.

3. White must not be passive: he must attack because time is on Black's side (it usually is in cramped positions). That is why the Sicilian is so effective against a pussyfooter.

It may also be noted that White should try to get his B to the diagonal KR1—QR8 as a rule, while it is always bad for him to place it at QB4. The B at QB4 will rarely help to prevent .... P—Q4 permanently. Even if it does, it will do so only in a purely passive way. Further, if .... P—Q4 does become possible, Black will gain an extra tempo against a White B at QB4.

There are two main lines, depending on whether Black plays his KB to K2 (usually leading to the Scheveningen Variation— the name comes from a small Dutch seaside resort, where a tournament was held in 1923 at which the variation first became popular) or to KKt2 (the Dragon Variation). The Scheveningen is the less energetic of the two, though it is somewhat more involved.

The normal line in the Scheveningen runs 2 Kt—KB3, P—K3; 3 P—Q4, P✕P; 4 Kt✕P, Kt—KB3; 5 Kt—QB3. The order of moves is by no means essential, except that Black must forestall P—QB4 by forcing the White Kt out to QB3 early. That these moves are so frequently interchangeable is often disconcerting, even confusing, but once the ideas become familiar the air is clear.

Black's objectives are, as we know, to finish his development and get his Kt to QB5 effectively. He therefore proceeds according to the following scheme (the order is not essential): .... P—Q3, ... B—K2, ... O—O, ... P—QR3, ... P—QKt4 (if possible), ... B—Q2 (or preferably .... B—QKt2), ... Q—B2, ... QR—B1, ... Kt—QR4, ... Kt—QB5. It

No. 16   No. 17

   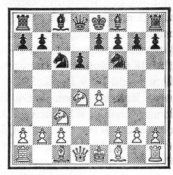

Position after 5 Kt—QB3 in the Sicilian Defense (leading to the Scheveningen Variation).

Position after 5 .... P—Q3 in the Sicilian Defense (leading to the Dragon Variation).

is assumed all along that .... P—Q4 is not feasible, which is the case if White makes no mistake. If he does go astray, the thrust in the center will at least equalize for the defender.

White's plan of campaign against the above scheme is based on the twin ideas of warding off danger on the Q-side and building up an attack on the K-side. We already know that he can and should start the attack with P—KB4, P—KKt4, but the timing is not so clear. Experience has shown that it is not essential for him to safeguard his Q-side first, but that he can do so without harm. Thus his developmental schedule runs as follows (this time the order is significant and should be adhered to): O—O, B—K3, Kt—Kt3 (not always essential), P—KB4,

B—KB3, Q—K2 (or Q—K1), QR—Q1, B—QB1 (if needed) and then P—KKt4, which has been adequately prepared.

By following the ideas sketched above for both sides we get the main line. From *Diagram No. 16*: 5 .... P—Q3; 6 B—K2, Kt—B3; 7 O—O, B—K2; 8 K—R1, P—QR3; 9 P—B4, Q—B2; 10 B—K3, O—O; 11 Q—K1, B—Q2; 12 R—Q1, P—QKt4; 13 P—QR3, Kt—QR4; 14 Q—Kt3, Kt—B5; 15 B—B1 and White's game is most promising.

To understand this line better a little explanation is in order: White's 8th move is designed to avoid any compromising checks or pin of the Kt at Q4 which might arise if the K remains on the diagonal. Black's 8th move serves the twofold purpose of preparing .... P—QKt4 and preventing the pin of the QKt. Note that the answer to 8 .... P—Q4 by White here would be 9 B—Kt5, B—Q2; 10 P×P and Black has a weak isolated Pawn. At a later stage, when the pin is no longer feasible, White may either move the Kt away from Q4, or prepare to meet .... P—Q4 with P—K5. On White's 10th move the B is played out to complete the development of the Q-side. P—QR4, to prevent .... P—QKt4, is not vital.

Since this variation is in White's favor it is up to Black to find improvements. One try is the postponement of castling, e.g., 7 .... P—QR3 (instead of 7 .... B—K2) but then White's assault is just as strong with B—K3, P—B4, etc. More popular is the Paulsen line, which involves moving the Black Kt to Q2 instead of to QB3. The idea is to hit at the KP, either directly or indirectly, while reserving the route to QB5 via K4. Here too, however, Black emerges with a terribly cramped position. E.g., 5 .... P—Q3; 6 B—K2, P—QR3 (instead of 6 .... Kt—QB3 in the main line); 7 O—O, Q—B2; 8 B—K3, B—K2; 9 P—B4, O—O; 10 B—B3, QKt—Q2; 11 Kt—Kt3, R—QKt1; 12 P—QR4, etc. An interesting try for Black is 12 .... P—K4, to prevent the explosive P—K5 once and for all. Black has then averted the most immediate danger, but is saddled with a permanently weak QP.

Some of the alternatives in the first six moves are promising.

White can reason that since he plays his KB to the long diagonal via K2 (B—K2—B3) it might be simpler to get it there directly by fianchettoing. There would then also be a further obstacle to Black's .... P—Q4. Such a set-up is quite strong, especially in conjunction with the fianchetto of the QB, which deprives Black of any counterplay against QB5. Tactically, the chief danger to guard against in such a system is an early .... P—Q4 before the KB is out. An example of the strength of White's position with the double fianchetto is 6 P—KKt3 (instead of 6 B—K2 in the main line), Kt—B3; 7 B—Kt2, B—K2; 8 O—O, O—O; 9 P—QKt3, B—Q2; 10 B—Kt2, etc.

It is not surprising that there are no other good alternatives for White in this line, since the main variation is favorable. The placement of the KB at Q3 is sometimes seen, with a view to preparing P—QB4, but the trouble is that the KKt is then left undefended, so that on .... Kt—QB3 time must be lost. Thus 5 B—Q3 in the main line (instead of 5 Kt—QB3) is more than adequately met by 5 .... Kt—B3, for if 6 Kt—K2, P—Q4, while if 6 Kt×Kt, QP×Kt; 7 O—O, P—K4 with complete equality. The B should go to Q3 only when Kt×Kt followed by P—K5 is advantageously possible in reply to the natural .... Kt—QB3. Black may on occasion even try to get the better of it.

The only really worthwhile alternative for Black is the counter with .... B—Kt5. We return to *Diagram No. 16*. Black may reason that a further attack on the KP would necessitate either B—Q3 or P—B3, both unfavorable because they do not fit into White's plans at such an early stage. 5 .... B—Kt5 does indeed present some knotty problems and is most powerful against defenses such as 6 B—Q3, P—K4! or 6 B—K2, Kt×P! or 6 P—B3, O—O, threatening .... P—K4 followed by .... P—Q4. But the Pawn advance 6 P—K5! leaves Black too cramped: 6 .... Kt—Q4; 7 B—Q2, Kt×Kt; 8 P×Kt, B—B1; 9 B—Q3, Kt—B3; 10 Kt×Kt, QP×Kt; 11 Q—Kt4 etc., when White's mobility is much too great.

Much stronger for Black is the Sicilian Four Knights': 5 ....
Kt—QB3 (*Diagram No. 16*). The difference is that now on 6
B—K2, B—Kt5 cannot be met by P—K5, while we already
know that other rejoinders are inferior. However, even here
6 KKt—Kt5 or 6 P—KKt3 gives White a slight advantage,
e.g., 6 P—KKt3, B—Kt5; 7 B—Kt2, P—Q4; 8 P×P, Kt×P;
9 O—O!, O—O; 10 QKt×Kt, P×Kt; 11 P—QB3, B—K2;
12 Kt—K2 and the isolated Pawn remains a burden. This
idea of the fianchetto of the White KB is one which can be applied in a number of variations of the Sicilian.

Two rather common mistakes on Black's part are worth
mentioning. First, if P—QB4 is allowed, the defender gets a
terribly cramped game. One example will do: 2 Kt—KB3,
P—K3; 3 P—Q4, P×P; 4 Kt×P, P—QR3; 5 P—QB4, Kt—
KB3; 6 Kt—QB3, P—Q3; 7 B—K2, Kt—B3; 8 O—O, Q—B2;
9 P—QKt3, B—K2; 10 B—Kt2, O—O; 11 Kt—B2, R—Q1;
12 Kt—K3 and Black is in a bad way. Second, a premature
.... P—Q4 gives the second player a permanently weak QP.
E.g., 2 Kt—KB3, P—K3; 3 P—Q4, P—Q4?; 4 KP×P, KP×
P; 5 B—K2, Kt—KB3; 6 O—O, B—K2; 7 P×P, O—O; 8
QKt—Q2, B×P; 9 Kt—Kt3, B—K2; 10 B—KKt5 and Black's
headaches are only beginning. This variation may also arise
from the French Defense.

In view of the theoretical inadequacy of the Scheveningen,
its competitor, the Dragon, has come to the fore more and
more in recent years. While the exact order may vary, a
normal sequence of moves is 2 Kt—KB3, Kt—QB3; 3 P—Q4,
P×P; 4 Kt×P, Kt—KB3; 5 Kt—QB3, P—Q3 (*Diagram No.
17*); 6 B—K2, P—KKt3.

Now we can note several similarities with and differences
from the Scheveningen. As before, Black's counterplay lies on
the QB file, with the square QB5 most important. The B on
the long diagonal means that this counter will be even more
effective than in the previous case, so that White must be more
careful. Time again works for him, which means that White is
well advised to attack. The advance of the K-side Pawns is

not quite so strong as in the Scheveningen, but nonetheless quite cramping for Black. Another possibility arises from the weakness of Black's Q4: since . . . . P—K3 would leave the QP hopelessly weak, if White were able to post a Kt at Q5, he would have a strong bind. Other factors remain unchanged; thus again . . . . P—Q4 by Black equalizes.

The development set-up follows the old pattern (variants will be considered later): Black hastens to post a Kt at QB5, White to push his K-side Pawns up. Seen in this light, the main line is easily understood: 7 B—K3, B—Kt2; 8 O—O, O—O; 9 Kt—Kt3, B—K3; 10 P—B4, Kt—QR4; 11 P—B5!, B—B5!; 12 P—Kt4! (the latest find), Kt—Q2; 13 Kt×Kt, B×B; 14 Q×B, Q×Kt; 15 Kt—Q5, KR—K1; 16 Q—B2, Kt—K4; 17 P×P, RP×P; 18 B—Q4 with a good attack.

This last variation is not too palatable for Black, and he should try for improvements earlier. On his 9th and 10th moves he has two good alternatives, both of which avoid an immediate occupation of QB5. One is 9 . . . . P—QR3, followed by placing the B at Q2, and building up to . . . . Kt—QB5 gradually. The other is to play 10 . . . . Q—B1, later . . . . Kt—Q2, and get the other Kt to QB5. With either of these he can manage to achieve equality. White will therefore search for some improvements.

On White's 9th move he may prefer not to play his Kt away from its strong central post. But 9 P—KR3 or 9 Q—Q2 can be met by the natural . . . . P—Q4. E.g., 9 P—KR3, P—Q4; 10 P×P, Kt×P; 11 QKt×Kt, Q×Kt; 12 B—B3, Q—B5 and White has nothing. More interesting is 9 P—B4, to reply to 9 . . . . P—Q4? with P—K5. Delectable complications ensue on 9 . . . . Q—Kt3!; 10 Q—Q3!, Kt—KKt5!; 11 Kt—Q5!, B×Kt!; 12 Kt×Q, B×Bch; 13 K—R1, B×Kt, when the three pieces just about counterbalance the Queen. This is an instance of a common motif when White leaves his Kt at Q4: simplification by . . . . Kt—KKt5.

The chief reason why White's attack is less vigorous here is that to exploit a K position of the type which Black has (with

B fianchetto) White should be castled on the other side in order to be able to storm on freely with his Pawns. Consequently many attempts have been made in that direction, but none has held its ground against a vigorous counter-thrust. Black's offensive chances against the Q-side when White castles long are considerable. On 8 Kt—Kt3 (instead of 8 O—O in the main line), B—K3; 9 P—B4, O—O; 10 P—KKt4, P—Q4! is adequate, for if 11 P—B5, B—B1! while if 11 P—K5, P—Q5! with equality. The rule that any attack begun before development is completed is best met by a break in the center is again justified. On 8 Q—Q2, O—O; 9 Kt—Kt3, B—K3, threatening .... P—Q4 is good enough. More complicated is 8 Q—Q2, O—O; 9 O—O—O, when both sides attack with all vigor. While the results are not quite clear, because the line has almost never been tested, experience with similar assaults leads one to the conclusion that Black will be able to weather the storm.

A refutation which tries to capitalize on the vulnerability of Black's Q4 is a move which Euwe has tried: 8 Kt—Kt3 (in the main line), O—O; 9 P—B3! If now 9 .... B—K3; 10 Kt—Q5!, Kt—QR4; 11 P—QB4 with an overwhelming position in the center and on the Q-side. 9 .... B—Q2, to be able to capture at Q5, is undoubtedly better: if then 10 Kt—Q5, Kt× Kt, P×Kt, Kt—QR4 and White cannot avoid levelling exchanges.

By far the most tricky method of strengthening White's prospects is the Richter Attack, 6 B—KKt5 in *Diagram No. 17*. The purpose of this at first sight rather pointless move (White's QB is rarely of any use at KKt5 in the Sicilian) is twofold: to prevent normal development by Black with .... P—KKt3, and to prepare castling long, which would be accompanied by immediate threats. 6 .... P—KKt3? would of course be a mistake, since 7 B×Kt leaves the Pawns hopelessly shattered. Likewise after 6 .... Q—R4?; 7 B×Kt the Pawns are too weak. 6 .... P—K3 is essential, even though the Black QP is a distinct weakness. White concentrates his forces on this feeble link in the chain: 7 Q—Q2, B—K2; 8 O—O—O. Here we have one of those cases where the threat is stronger than its fulfillment. If, e.g., 8 .... O—O; 9 B×Kt?, B×B!; 9 Kt×Kt, P×Kt; 10 Q×P, Q—R4! Black has quite enough for the Pawn. Still, Black can reply with 8 .... O—O!; 9 P—B4 (if 9 KKt—Kt5, Q—R4! with an attack), P—QR3; 10 B—K2, B—Q2; 11 Kt—Kt3, R—B1; 12 B—B3, R—B2 and the counter-attack is quite powerful. 8 .... P—QR3 (instead of 8 .... O—O) is also playable. Note that the main defensive idea is to concentrate on the attack.

Players fearful of the Richter Attack have tried to sidestep it by postponing the development of both Kt's. The remedy is much worse than the disease. On 2 Kt—KB3, Black then plays 2 .... P—Q3; 3 P—Q4, P×P; 4 Kt×P, Kt—KB3; 5 Kt—QB3, P—KKt3. White now has a large number of continuations any one of which yield an advantage. The most energetic is 6 P—B4!, so that if 6 .... B—Kt2; 7 P—K5!, Kt—Kt5; 8 B—Kt5ch and Black's monarch must bestir himself with disastrous results, e.g., 8 .... K—B1; 9 P—KR3, Kt—KR3; 10 B—K3, Kt—B3; 11 P×P, Kt×Kt; 12 B×Kt, Q×P; 13 B×Bch, K×B; 14 Q×Q, P×Q; 15 O—O—O with a won ending. After 6 P—B4!, Kt—B3 is best, when 7 Kt×Kt, P×Kt; 8 P—K5, P×P; 9 Q×Qch, K×Q; 10 P×P, Kt—Q2; 11 B—KB4, KB—Kt2; 12 O—O—O, K—K1; 13 R—K1 leads to an ending in White's favor because of Black's weak Pawns and cramped pieces. Another good line for White is 6 P—KKt3, to hold back the QP. E.g., 6 .... B—Kt2; 7 B—Kt2, O—O; 8 P—KR3, Kt—B3; 9 KKt—K2, P—QR3; 10 O—O, Kt—K4; 11 K—R2, B—Q2; 12 P—B4, Kt—B5; 13 P—Kt3 and White has all the play on all three sides of the board. Even 6 P—KR3 works out well, e.g., 6 .... B—Kt2; 7 B—K3, Kt—B3; 8 Q—Q2, O—O; 9 O—O—O, Kt×Kt; 10 B×Kt, B—K3; 11 K—Kt1, Q—B2; 12 P—KKt4, QR—B1; 13 B—Kt2 and White's attack is stronger than Black's. This King-side attack by White is one of his most powerful weapons in the Sicilian.

On the older try 5 P—KB3 (instead of 5 Kt—QB3 in the

above line) the anti-theoretical 5 .... P—K4! is satisfactory, because Black can sooner or later manage to squeeze in .... P—Q4. E.g., 6 B—Kt5ch, B—Q2; 7 B×Bch, QKt×B; 8 Kt—B5, P—Q4!; 9 P×P, Kt—Kt3; 10 O—O, B—B4ch; 11 K—R1, O—O; 12 Kt—B3, KKt×P with equality. If Black refrains from .... P—K4, an early P—QB4 by White will keep his position too cramped.

Of the remaining variations, three are worth brief mention.

Nimzovitch's Line, 2 Kt—KB3, Kt—KB3, is motivated by the same idea as Alekhine's Defense: to tempt the White Pawns on in the hope or expectation that they will then become weak. E.g., 3 P—K5, Kt—Q4; 4 P—Q4, P×P; 5 Q×P, P—K3; 6 P—B4, Kt—QB3; 7 Q—Q1, KKt—K2! and White cannot develop normally because of his exposed KP. After 3 P—K5, Kt—Q4; 4 Kt—QB3, however, 4 .... Kt×Kt leads to equality. On 3 Kt—QB3 (instead of 3 P—K5) transposition into more regular lines with 3 .... P—Q3 is advisable. All told, Nimzovitch's Defense is a sound and welcome alternative.

When White omits P—Q4, of the ways in which he may develop the two most important are the K-fianchetto and the Wing Gambit.

To fianchetto he must first prevent .... P—Q4, so 2 Kt—QB3. Then 2 .... Kt—QB3; 3 P—KKt3. Now that White has discarded the most powerful, P—Q4, for the time being, it behooves Black to prevent it once and for all by tightening his grip on Q5. Thus: 3 .... P—KKt3; 4 B—Kt2, B—Kt2; 5 KKt—K2, P—K3!; 6 O—O, KKt—K2, eventually, ... Kt—Q5 and .... KKt—B3, followed by an advance on the Q-side. Here White's chances lie in an eventual P—KB4—KB5, while Black will try .... P—QKt4—Kt5. The line is too passive to afford any real chance of an advantage for the first player.

In the Wing Gambit, 2 P—QKt4, White is guided by the motif of sacrificing a Pawn to secure a strong center and cramp the enemy position. It had always been thought that the natural 2 .... P×P; 3 P—QR3, P—Q4! takes all the sting out of White's offer. But Marshall has shown that White can continue with 4 KP×P, Q×P; 5 Kt—KB3!, P—K4; 6 P×P, B×P; 7 Kt—R3!, P—K5; 8 Kt—QKt5!, K—Q1; 9 KKt—Q4 with a complicated attack. This line is a good speculative bet for first players so inclined. 7 B—R3, instead of 7 Kt—R3 above, is another Marshall suggestion worth a try.

ALEKHINE'S DEFENSE: 1 P—K4, Kt—KB3

It is only too obvious that this defense represents a radical break from the classical tradition, which insisted that nothing could be done without a firm Pawn basis in the center. Historically, it was the first of the hypermodern lines to be taken seriously. As such, it helped to clarify the notions of what a good and bad center are.

The basic idea—a great contribution to chess thought—is to tempt the White Pawns on in the hope that they will become weak. Many instances may be found: only too often have over-optimistic attackers gone to pieces on its reefs. It may be asked whether such a defense does not refute our general principles that a Pawn in the center is stronger than one on the side. The answer is, of course, no. All rules in chess have a proviso either expressed or implied: other things being equal. That leads immediately to the corollary that a Pawn in the center is effective if and only if it can be kept there for a reasonable length of time. We also know that the value of center Pawns is that they safeguard bases for one side's pieces and prevent the enemy from developing properly, with the emphasis on the latter. Consequently, the question at issue is *whether White can maintain his center Pawns after they have gone forward.* The entire defense stands or falls by the answer to this question.

Perhaps it is needless to add that the answer is no: all efforts at refutation have consistently failed.

White's most natural plan is to gain time by getting in as many kicks at the enemy Kt as he can: 2 P—K5, Kt—Q4; 3 P—QB4, Kt—Kt3; 4 P—Q4, P—Q3. Note that Black must

hit at the enemy center in some way. 4 .... P—QB4? would
be bad because of 5 P—Q5, 4 .... P—Q4? because of 5 P—B5.
Then after 4 .... P—Q3 the main line continues: 5 P—B4 (to
exchange would be equivalent to dissipating any potential
advantage, which must necessarily derive from the superior
Pawn center), P×P; 6 BP×P, Kt—B3 (still hitting at the
center!); 7 B—K3, B—B4; 8 Kt—QB3, P—K3; 9 Kt—B3
(*Diagram No. 18*).

Normal development has brought Black to the parting of the
ways. He must now decide how and where he is going to smash
at the White center. There are obviously two possibilities:
.... P—QB4, or .... P—KB3.

.... P—QB4 must be prepared with 9 .... Kt—QKt5; 10
R—B1, P—B4. Strategically, Black's main opening problem
(to take the sting out of White's Pawn center) is now solved.
There remain only the tactical skirmishes which, it so happens,
turn out all right for him: 11 B—K2, P×P; 12 Kt×P, B—
Kt3; 13 P—QR3, Kt—B3; 14 Kt×Kt, P×Kt and the weakness of the Black Q-side Pawns is offset by White's exposed KP.

The other type of freeing maneuver from *Diagram No. 18*
can be carried out either as pure defense (Black castles short)
or as the introduction to an attack (Black castles long, specu-
lates on the KKt file, which will eventually be opened.)
Neither of these is entirely satisfactory. On 9 .... B—K2;
10 B—K2, O—O; 11 O—O, P—B3; 12 P×P, B×P; 13
Q—Q2 Black's pieces get in one another's way, e.g., 13 ....
Q—K2; 14 QR—Q1, QR—Q1; 15 Q—B1! etc. And in the
second variant, which begins with 9 .... Q—Q2 (*Diagram
No. 18*), Black again does poorly: 10 B—K2, O—O—O; 11
O—O, P—B3; 12 P×P, P×P; 13 P—Q5, Kt—K4; 14 B×Kt,
Kt×Ktch and now 15 B×Kt! with an overwhelming position.
E.g., 15 .... RP×Kt?; 16 Kt—Kt5!, B—B4ch; 17 K—R1,
K—Kt1; 18 Q—R4 and wins.

Still, there is one equalizing line in the 4-Pawn attack, which
compels White to search for an alternative that will be better. It may be noted for the benefit of speculative players

that the sacrifice P—K6, when Black is compelled to take with the BP (which happens when his Kt is at QB3), in some cases offers considerable attacking possibilities.

We have already seen that the exchange 5 P×P (all numbers refer to the main line above) is too levelling: after 5 .... KP×

No. 18

Position after 9 Kt—B3 in Alekhine's Defense.

P White's only conceivable advantage lies in Black's somewhat misplaced Kt at QKt3. Practise shows, however, that this is too little: straight development nullifies White's plus. Black has some choice on 5 P×P: he may try either 5 .... BP×P, or 5 .... Q×P, to break the symmetry. Such lines, particularly the first, are good only against inferior players because the stronger Pawn center gives White a theoretical superiority.

With hopes based on the obvious swashbuckling forward march dashed, White must resort to something more subtle at an early stage. 5 P—B4—in contrast to 5 P×P—is an instance of the common motif of keeping the tension. Another way of carrying out this idea is 5 Kt—KB3, to maintain the Pawn at Q4 and to be able to recapture at K5 with the Kt. On 5 .... Kt—QB3; 6 P—K6! would bottle Black up badly.

After 5 Kt—KB3, B—Kt5, to continue the pressure against White's center, is customary (though perhaps 5 .... B—B4 would be just as good). Normally Black's B is more effective at KB4, so 6 P×P is a possibility. Then 6 .... KP×P; 7 B—K2 (or 7 P—KR3), B—K2; 8 Kt—B3, O—O; 9 P—QKt3, R—K1; 10 B—K3 gives White a most minimal plus, which does not mean much in practise. An attempt full of tactical surprises is 5 Kt—KB3, B—Kt5; 6 B—K2, P×P; 7 P—B5!, P—K5!; 8 P×Kt, P×Kt; 9 B×P, B×B; 10 Q×B, RP×P (or 10 .... Kt—B3) and Black's chances are adequate. The main consideration here is quick development.

Since 5 Kt—KB3 is unsatisfactory, we try again, this time on move 4: Lasker's 4 P—B5, which is designed to keep Black badly cramped. Yet, after 4 .... Kt—Q4; 5 Kt—QB3, Kt×Kt; 6 QP×Kt, the natural 6 .... P—Q3 (or even 6 .... P—K3) followed by straightforward development is good enough for equality.

Still on the search for the magic refutation, we can try Lajos Steiner's 4 P—QKt3 (in the main line, instead of 4 P—Q4). The idea here is that by postponing the advance of the QP Black will not have any target which he can use to free his game. Sometimes this works out well, but again the simplest reaction—quick development—will equalize. That is a recurrent difficulty with many esoteric ideas—they fail against the moves a well-instructed child would pick.

After 2 P—K5, Kt—Q4; 3 P—Q4 has led to some success, partly due to the fact that Black, after being pushed around for weeks is suddenly told to do as he pleases. On the normal 3 .... P—Q3; 4 Kt—KB3, B—Kt5; 5 B—K2 White hopes that Black will sooner or later capture his KP at a point where he will be able to recapture with his Kt. Of course, 5 .... B×Kt; 6 B×B, P×P; 7 P×P, P—K3? is bad because of 8 P—B4. Instead the move considered best after 5 B—K2 turns out to be 5 .... P—K3, to facilitate development, e.g., 6 P—B4, Kt—K2; 7 Kt—B3, Kt—B4; 8 P—KR3, B×Kt; 9 B×B, Kt—B3 with satisfactory counter-play. On the alternative 5 .... P—QB3 (instead of 5 .... P—K3), 6 Kt—Kt5!, B—B4; 7 P—K6!, P×P; 8 P—KKt4! gives White a dangerous attack.

All the efforts of both classicists and moderns have been in vain: Alekhine's Defense remains sound.

Attempts at refutation other than those mentioned above are mere stabs in the dark, though they may be successful on occasion. One instance is 2 Kt—QB3 (after 1 P—K4, Kt—KB3), when 2 .... P—Q4; 3 P×P, Kt×P; 4 B—B4, Kt—Kt3, while perfectly correct theoretically, may get Black into difficulties. 2 .... P—K4 is wholly satisfactory. Equally on 2 P—Q3, P—K4! is the simplest, though 2 .... P—Q4 is also playable.

CENTER COUNTER GAME: 1 P—K4, P—Q4

Black's basic idea here is unusual: he wishes to get freedom for his pieces at the cost of a theoretically inferior Pawn structure and (on occasion) loss of time, in the hope that good development will make it possible to get adequate compensation, either in the form of a counter-attack or of a neutralization of White's powerful center Pawn. There is, however, only one line where compensation is theoretically sufficient and even there Black's game is extremely cramped. The defense cannot be recommended.

White's only reply is the obvious 2 P×P. Then there are two main lines, depending on whether Black recaptures at once or waits a move.

After 2 .... Q×P; 3 Kt—QB3, Q—QR4; 4 P—Q4, Kt—KB3; 5 Kt—KB3 Black tries his hardest to build up some real attacking chances by castling long, but without success. One typical case is 5 .... B—Kt5; 6 P—KR3!, B—R4; 7 P—KKt4, B—Kt3; 8 Kt—K5, P—B3; 9 P—KR4! and Black's game is far from easy. Nor could he get anywhere with 3 .... Q—Q1 (instead of 3 .... Q—QR4); 4 P—Q4, Kt—KB3; 5 B—K3, P—B3; 6 B—Q3 (he is preparing to develop his Kt at K2) when White simply has the better Pawn center, with all that that entails.

More promising is 2 .... Kt—KB3. To try to hold the Pawn with 3 P—QB4, P—QB3; 4 P×P is playable, but yields

Black a good attack in view of the backward QP. Instead White can secure a minimal advantage in a variety of ways, all of which involve keeping his Pawn at Q4. Perhaps the best is 3 P—Q4, Kt×P; 4 P—QB4, Kt—KB3; 5 Kt—KB3, P—B3; 6 Kt—B3, B—Kt5; 7 B—K3, P—K3; 8 B—K2, B—K2; 9 O—O, O—O; 10 Kt—K5 with the freer game.

NIMZOVITCH'S DEFENSE: 1 P—K4, Kt—QB3

Black's objective in this unusual defense is threefold: first there is the usual hypermodern motif of tempting White's Pawns on in the hope that they will become weak; second (really a corollary of the first) Black wishes to lock the center; third, the entire Black set-up is to be used as a prelude to an attack by castling long and storming White's K-side.

With careful play, however, White's offensive is easier than Black's, which means that the defense is not wholly sound theoretically.

The main line runs: 2 P—Q4, P—Q4; 3 P—K5, B—B4; 4 P—QB3 (to be able to develop the B), P—B3 (to weaken White's K4); 5 P—KB4, Q—Q2; 6 B—Q3, Kt—R3! (to post the Kt at KB4, if opportunity offers—*Diagram No. 14B*); 7 Kt—B3, B—K5; 8 Q—K2, P—B4; 9 B—K3, P—K3; 10 QKt—Q2. Now the best is 10 .... O—O—O, when White should eventually castle and storm the other wing with P—QKt4, P—QR4, P—R5, P—Kt5, P—Kt6, eventually P—QB4. Practise indicates that White's chances are superior.

3 Kt—QB3 (instead of 3 P—K5 in the main line) is a worthwhile alternative. Black's best is 3 .... P—K3, when we have a French Defense with the inferior .... Kt—QB3.

Interesting is 2 .... P—K4 (instead of 2 .... P—Q4). Here Black reverses roles, aims to get his KB out. If this is stopped White is bound to get the better of it. Thus: 3 P×P, Kt×P; 4 P—KB4, Kt—Kt3; 5 B—K3, etc.

2 Kt—QB3 or 2 Kt—KB3 (instead of 2 P—Q4) are both all right if Black pursues his original idea. E.g., 2 Kt—KB3, P—K3; 3 P—Q4, P—Q4; 4 P—K5, P—QKt3; 5 P—B3, QKt—K2;

6 B—Q3, P—QR4; 7 Q—K2, Kt—B4; 8 P—KR4 with an overwhelming game. In reply to either of these moves, though, Black may choose the simple 2 .... P—K4, transposing to regular lines. However, it is a safe assumption that if Black does not play 1 .... P—K4 to begin with he will not do so later.

Other defenses will be handled under Irregular Openings.

Chapter IV

QUEEN PAWN OPENINGS

PART I

QUEEN'S GAMBIT AND MINOR OPENINGS
WITH 1 P—Q4, P—Q4

The basic ideas in the QP openings are, in a manner of speaking, a mirror of those in the KP section. Here after P—Q4, White's goal is to get his P to K4, just as it was P—Q4, after 1 P—K4. Essentially, the idea is the same in both: to set up Pawns at Q4 and K4. Again, on the one hand there are the older and regular lines from 1 P—Q4, P—Q4, with analogues to the strong point and counter-attack defenses, on the other newer (many based on hypermodern theories) which are more involved. On the whole, one great defensive question in the KP openings was the proper development of the KB; in the QP openings the QB is the eternal problem child for Black. Other similarities will be pointed out.

After 1 P—Q4, the advance of White's KP may be prevented by a Pawn (1 .... P—Q4, 1 .... P—KB4) or a piece (1 .... Kt—KB3) or a counter-attack (1 .... P—QB4). As indicated above, the traditional reply, in accordance with the classical theories of Steinitz and Tarrasch, is 1 .... P—Q4. It will be treated here; all others will be considered in the next chapter.

Just as White can only hope to derive an advantage from the KP openings by developing with a move which attacks the Black center (there 1 P—K4, P—K4; 2 Kt—KB3), here his best chance lies in a similar assault. But this time the Black QP is defended, so he must hit at it with a Pawn, rather than with a piece. Thus we get to 2 P—QB4, which is essential from a theoretical point of view. (Variants will be treated at the end of this chapter.)

(See *Diagram No. 19.*) The force of White's play is due to the fact that there is an immediate threat: 3 P×P and if then 3 .... Q×P; 4 Kt—QB3 followed by P—K4, realizing his strategic ambition.

No. 19

Queen's Gambit. White threatens to
get the better center with P×P.

In reply to 3 P×P, Black has nine feasible defensive moves, which are inspired by four types of defensive ideas:

1. *Maintain a strong point in the center by retaining a Pawn at Q4.* (2 .... P—K3—Orthodox and allied defenses; 2 .... P—QB3—Slav Defense.)

2. *Liquidate the center.* (2 .... P×P—Queen's Gambit Accepted; 2 .... P—QB4.)

3. *Counter-attack.* (2 .... P—K4—Albin's Counter Gambit; 2 .... Kt—QB3; 2 ....B—B4.)

4. *Permit White to set up the strong center in the hope that it will prove vulnerable.* (2 .... Kt—KB3; 2 .... P—KKt3.)
In all cases Black must attempt to liberate himself by either .... P—QB4 (most common) or .... P—K4.

The first deserves most attention because it is by far the best and therefore the most important. Perhaps most of the others, or all, are playable if followed up properly. Experience has,

however, indicated that, except for 2 .... P—K3 and 2 ....
P—QB3, only 2 .... P×P can be recommended. There is no
theoretical reason that makes the others wholly unsound. It
is simply the case that the normal sequence leads to the better
of it for White.

While it is unlikely that the present analysis, as far as these
unusual defenses are concerned, will be radically changed at
some time in the future, it should not be supposed that such
a possibility is wholly out of the question. However, since they
are all strategically simple, though tactically complicated, the
lines are much more easily understood, so that we shall only
touch upon them briefly.

2 .... P—K3: ORTHODOX AND ALLIED DEFENSES

For the time being White must concentrate on development,
the effectiveness of which is increased by threatening as much
as possible. Thus we get the main line: 3 Kt—QB3, Kt—KB3;

No. 20

Position after 6 .... O—O in the
Orthodox Defense.

4 B—Kt5! (with a view to P×P, P×P, B×Kt, splitting
Black's Pawns), QKt—Q2; 5 Kt—B3 (renewing the threat),
B—K2; 6 P—K3, O—O (*Diagram No. 20.*)

Here we come to a many-pronged fork in the road, so that it

is wise for White to stop and get a clear picture of what lies ahead.

In view of the many normal possibilities at each turn, it is not feasible to set up one ideal position. However, we do know this much: White's game is freer, which means that he must either attack or transform his temporary superior mobility into a permanent advantage.

There are five primary types of superiority which White may strive to turn his temporary plus into. These are illustrated in *Diagram No. 21*. One must not make the mistake of thinking that they are mutually exclusive: if one alone is strong, two together are fortissimo.

In 21A we have the *Q-side bind*. Here White's advantage lies on the Q-side. By the eventual advance P—Kt5, he will weaken Black's Q-side Pawns, enter with his Rook or minor piece, sooner or later secure something tangible. Black's defenses in the present position are at best palliatives; it is likely that he is already lost against exact play. There is one good way to counteract such a set-up: don't let it happen. If Black is prepared to react with .... P—K4 the moment White tries P—B5, the Q-side bind can never become effective. Another

TYPICAL ADVANTAGES FOR WHITE IN THE QUEEN'S GAMBIT DECLINED

No. 21A

No. 21B

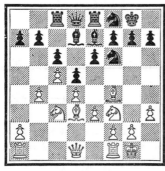

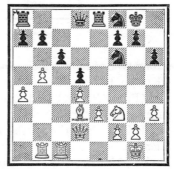

Q-side Bind.

Minority Attack.

TYPICAL ADVANTAGES FOR WHITE IN THE
QUEEN'S GAMBIT DECLINED

No. 21C

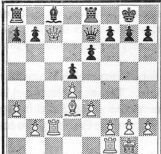

Superior Development.

No. 21D

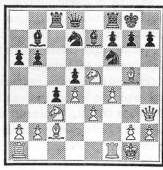

K-side Attack with Pieces.

No. 21E

K-side Attack with Pawns.

strong type of reply which is occasionally available is . . . . P—
QKt3 on P—B5, and if then P—QKt4, P—QR4; P—QR3,
RP×P; P×P, P×P; KtP×P, B—R3 or . . . . Q—R4 with
superior development.

21B is an instance of the *minority attack*. Black is in a
dilemma because he cannot avoid a fatal weakening of his
Pawns. If . . . . P×P; R×P (or even P×P) with pressure on
the QKtP and the QP. If . . . . R—K3; P×P, P×P; Kt—K5,

R—B1 and Black is saddled with a backward Pawn on an open file. Again once things have reached such a point nothing can be done about it, though Black's chances of holding out are a bit better than in 21A. The best defense, as so often, is a counter-attack against the White K-side.

An analogous type of superiority occurs where Black tries to prevent the White march by .... P—QKt4. He then has a backward QBP on an open file, which reduces the mobility of his pieces, regardless of whether it can be held or not.

21C is nothing but *superior development.* Here Black cannot develop his B, nor can he afford to exchange Queens. The win for White may be long and tedious, but it is clear that such a position is wholly undesirable. Black can only avoid it by being more careful with the exchanges which he permits. An analogous inferiority occurs where Black weakens himself too much on the White squares on the Q-side. E.g., from *Diagram No. 20*, 7 R—B1, P×P?; 8 B×P, P—B4; 9 O—O, P—QKt3; 10 Q—K2, B—Kt2; 11 B—QR6 with a clear plus for White.

In 21D we have the *King-side attack with pieces.* White already has a frightful threat: Kt×Kt, followed by Q×P mate. Black cannot avert serious loss. His defense against such a set-up is a proper system of exchanges earlier.

Finally, 21E illustrates the *King-side attack with Pawns.* The threat P—Kt5 forces the opening of a file, when the White assault can hardly be halted. It is customary for White to castle long when he has such a plan in mind, for otherwise the Pawn advance may weaken his own K-position too much. However, such an offensive with the King, say, at KR2 is by no means impossible. As usual, it is too late for Black to start defending now. At an earlier stage he should have instituted a vigorous counter-attack long before this position arose.

There is one feature which all the Black positions have in common in the above diagrams: they are all cramped. Further, the defender in four cases has not tried to free himself with .... P—QB4, while in the one where he has he did not follow it up properly. It is not hard to see why the necessary counterplay could always have been secured by a break with the QBP. In fact, we may set up the useful practical rule: *If Black can play .... P—QB4 in the Orthodox Defense without being punished immediately he has secured an even game.*

Returning now to *Diagram No. 20*, we find that White cannot lead into a positive advantage directly (of the types mentioned). E.g., 7 P—B5? would be answered by 7 .... Kt—K5. If, then, as normally, 8 B×B, Q×B; 9 B—Q3, Kt×Kt; 10 P×Kt, P—K4 and Black has much the better of it.

In the absence of any concrete superiority, White can do no better than prevent Black from liberating his game. We already know that *the* freeing move is .... P—QB4. It follows that the strongest 7th move for White will be that which best eliminates .... P—QB4 for the time being. It turns out that that move is 7 R—B1.

Now it will be most useful to jump ahead in order to view the various alternatives as branches of one main line: 7 .... P—QB4 (in answer to 7 R—B1) would be refuted by 8 P×BP, P×P; 9 P—B6!, Kt—Kt3; 10 Kt—K5. So Black must try to liberate himself in another way: exchange of pieces. To prepare that, 7 .... P—B3 is most useful. Thus the main normal line from *Diagram No. 20* runs as follows: 7 R—B1, P—B3; 8 B—Q3, P×P; 9 B×P, Kt—Q4; 10 B×B, Q×B; 11 O—O, Kt×Kt; 12 R×Kt, P—K4; 13 P×P, Kt×P; 14 Kt× Kt, Q×Kt; 15 P—B4, Q—K5!; 16 B—Kt3, B—B4; 17 Q—R5, P—KKt3; 18 Q—R4, QR—Q1 with equality.

Partly from the discussion so far, we may set up two important principles for the treatment of this variation:

1. Black must free his game by exchanges. His problem really boils down to that of the satisfactory development of his QB.

2. In order to secure an advantage White must retain as many pieces as possible.

In the latter part of the main line (from move 14 on) the problems are tactical: White is ahead in development, would like to build up an attack, just cannot find a way to do so. The second principle may, however, be used earlier to try to find an improvement. One such try is 13 Q—B2 (instead of 13 P×P) but against it both 13 .... P×P and 13 .... P—K5, though not devoid of difficulties, are both adequate.

Most promising at the present writing is 13 B—Kt3, for if then 13 .... P×P; 14 P×P, Kt—B3; 15 R—K1, Q—Q3; 16 Kt—K5 is not easy to meet, while on 13 .... P—K5; 14 Kt—Q2, Kt—B3; 15 Q—B2 White's pressure against the center and Q-side continues.

Still, the advantage that White has above is of a most dubious nature, which is why there have been attempts to do better at an earlier stage. All are based on our second principle, but have not proved convincing because Black always finds a way to break loose. E.g., 11 Kt—K4 (instead of 11 O—O in the main line) is met by 11 .... KKt—B3; 12 Kt—Kt3, P—K4!; 13 O—O, P×P; 14 Kt—B5, Q—Q1; 15 KKt×P, Kt—K4 with nothing to fear.

On Black's 8th move in the main line there is an interesting try which involves playing for .... P—QB4 at an early stage: 8 .... P—KR3; 9 B—R4, P×P; 10 B×P, P—QKt4; 11 B—Q3, P—QR3; 12 O—O!, P—B4; 13 P—QR4! and Black's Pawns are somewhat too weak. It is worth our while to observe that 7 .... P—KR3 is essential for the above, for if 8 .... P×P; 9 B×P, P—QKt4; 10 B—Q3, P—QR3; 11 B×Kt!, B×B (or 11 .... Kt×B; 12 O—O and .... P—B4 is bad); 12 Q—B2! gains a vital tempo to keep the Black QBP permanently backward.

Yet we must (regretfully, perhaps) conclude that 8 B—Q3 leads to nothing lasting because Black can compel too much blood-letting. If we try to discover why 8 B—Q3 petered out we come to the conclusion that it is because it loses a tempo. I.e., Black is going to free his game by exchanging his QP for the White BP, and White will then have to recapture with his B. Accordingly, if White can make some other useful move, postponing the development of his B, he will be a move ahead of the main line and it stands to reason—if nothing else happens

—that he would then secure a marked superiority. The most common alternative is 8 Q—B2, chiefly because the Q is frequently useful on the B file anyhow.

It is at once evident (*Diagram No. 22*) that after 8 Q—B2 the freeing maneuver beginning with 8 .... P×P will not work. For after 8 .... P×P; 9 B×P, Kt—Q4; 10 B×B, Q×B; 11 O—O, Kt×Kt; 12 Q×Kt, P—K4? is impossible because the White Queen is now covering the square K5. There remains the possibility of getting the B out via the Q-side by means of .... P—QKt3, but this weakens the White squares

No. 22

Position after 8 Q—B2 in the Orthodox Defense.

in Black's camp. Besides, White can play his KP up and secure a strong Pawn center. The strategy which should guide his further play is to prevent the complete liberation of the Black game, either by exchanging the Black B, or by preparing to secure possession of an open file. While White's advantage in this variation is slight, it is nevertheless real.

Because the exchange of his QP does not liberate the game sufficiently, Black can also try to temporize, make some other move in order to postpone the capture of the White QBP until White's B has moved. The most common is 8 .... P—QR3, which is strong because it is more than a mere tempo move: it also prepares the advance of the Black QKtP. This introduces a new element into the fight, for Black now has the choice of two liberating maneuvers. That this choice is only apparent is due to the fact that the plan of the main line (with exchange of a number of minor pieces on the K-side) is almost always inferior when White's Q is at B2 because the Q will prevent the advance of the KP, while .... P—QR3 obviously has no connection with the KP. Thus Black has shifted his intentions: he is not going to free himself by exchanging minor pieces on the K-side, but by advancing Pawns on the Q-side.

To prevent this new liberating threat White has the choice of one of three lines: he can stall around for a while, making noncommittal moves in the hope that his superior development will net him something (this is known as "the struggle for a tempo"), or he can exchange in the center in order to play for a minority attack on the Q-side, or he can block the Q-side by playing his P to B5.

The exchange variation is not quite as strong here as at other times; it will be considered independently in any case. 8 P—B5, as usual, is foiled by 8 .... P—K4.

There remains the struggle for a tempo. White again reasons that since Black is going to play .... P×P anyway, he might as well postpone the development of his B. Furthermore, he might eventually want to try for an attack against the Black K-position. This explains 9 P—QR3 (after 8 .... P—QR3 in *Diagram No. 22*). Now Black has only one good tempo move, 9 .... R—K1, whereupon White continues with 10 P—KR3, when Black's tempi are exhausted. But after 10 P—KR3 Black just manages to free himself by 10 .... P—KR3; 11 B—R4, P×P; 12 B×P, P—QKt4; 13 B—R2, P—B4; 14 P×P, Kt×P; 15 B—Kt1, QKt—Q2, etc.

After 9 P—QR3 above, 9 .... P—QKt4! is another excellent choice. 9 P—B5 could be met, as usual, by 9 .... P—K4, while 9 P×P, BP×P leaves Black's game perfectly solid: the QB file and square QB5 will be good springboards for his pieces.

Still another excellent defensive line in *Diagram No. 22* is

8 .... Kt—K5!, to release the pin. Then the simplification 9 B×B, Q×B; 10 Kt×Kt (or 10 B—Q3, P—KB4), P×Kt; 11 Q×P, Q—Kt5ch is all that Black can ask.

Before leaving this variation it is essential to find out what happens against inferior defensive play. The most common mistake is to allow a backward QBP, which may lead to decisive loss of material early. E.g., 8 .... R—K1 (*Diagram No. 22*); 9 B—Q3, P×P; 10 B×P, P—QKt4?; 11 B—Q3, P—QR3? and now 12 Kt—K5! wins a Pawn, for on 12 .... B—Kt2; 13 Kt×Kt, Q×Kt; 14 B×Kt and 15 B×Pch.

Summing up, we find four types of liberating maneuver for Black in the above variations:

a) .... QP×BP, followed by .... Kt—Q4, exchange of minor pieces on the K-side, eventually by .... P—K4. By avoiding too many exchanges White can get a slight, though theoretically doubtful, superiority.

b) .... QP×BP followed by .... P—QKt4, ... P—QR3, eventually .... P—QB4. Black must be sure that he will not be saddled with a backward QBP. On occasion Black may also try .... P—QKt3, followed by .... B—Kt2, eventually .... P—QB4, though the danger of becoming too weak on the White squares (White may play for B—QR6) is acute here. The type of advantage for White would then be that in 21C, discussion.

c) .... P—QR3 followed by .... P—QKt4.

d) .... Kt—K5.

Because of the wealth of choice, alternatives to 7 .... P—B3 in the main line cannot be recommended. E.g., 7 .... P—QKt3 (the older reply) yields White a strong attack of the type of 21D: 8 P×P, P×P; 9 B—Q3, B—Kt2; 10 O—O, P—B4; 11 Q—K2, P—B5; 12 B—Kt1, P—QR3; 13 Kt—K5, P—Kt4; 14 P—B4, Kt—K5 (essential); 15 B×Kt, P×B; 16 Kt×Kt, Q×Kt; 17 B×B, Q×B; 18 P—B5! and Black's artificially isolated KP is a serious weakness. The only good defenses are those which utilize one of the four ideas above.

Despite the enormous amount of research and practical

investigation devoted to 7 R—B1, no worthwhile advantage has ever been conclusively demonstrated for White. On the other hand, Black always has a cramped game, can at best hope for a draw. Again, as in some other major openings (compare the Ruy Lopez) both sides want better.

Of the alternatives on White's 7th move (instead of 7 R—B1 in *Diagram No. 20*) none has ever held the stage for more than a brief spell because none can prevent .... P—QB4, though the proper time may vary.

In the most popular, 7 Q—B2, there is no adequate reply to 7 .... P—B4. The obvious intention is to saddle Black with an isolated QP: 8 BP×P, BP×P; 9 Kt×P, Kt×P; 10 B×B, Q×B (10 .... Kt×B is also playable); 11 Kt×Kt, P×Kt; 12 B—Q3, Q—Kt5ch; 13 Q—Q2 etc., but though White has a little edge, it is not enough to win. On 7 .... P—B4; 8 R—Q1 is sometimes seen, with a view to preserving the tension. 8 .... P—KR3; 9 B—R4, Q—R4; 10 B—Q3, BP×P; 11 KP×P, P×P; 12 B×P, Kt—Kt3; 13 B—QKt3 leaves White with a freer game, though whether this should mean anything in the long run may well be doubted. Besides, 10 .... Kt—Kt3; 11 P×QP, QKt×P is also pretty good.

Otherwise, the ideas do not differ essentially from those previously discussed. On alternatives such as 7 B—Q3 (in *Diagram No. 20*) it is advisable to play 7 .... P×P; 8 B×P, P—B4, later developing the QB at QKt2. On 7 .... P—B4 at once, if Black goes through with his plan of giving White an isolated QP, he may find himself subjected to a strong attack. E.g., 7 B—Q3, P—B4; 8 O—O, BP×P; 9 KP×P, P×P; 10 B×P, Kt—Kt3; 11 B—Kt3!, B—Q2; 12 Q—Q3, QKt—Q4; 13 Kt—K5, B—B3; 14 QR—Q1 and Black's game is not easy.

THE EXCHANGE VARIATION: BP×QP

The Exchange Variation is one of the most complex and difficult to judge in the entire realm of opening theory. In part this is due to the varied circumstances under which it may be played, in part to the many unsolved tactical problems.

Since White may try P×P at almost any time between the 3rd and 9th moves, we must concentrate on the general problems involved.

First we must observe that on P×P, KP×P or BP×P, most of the freeing maneuvers mentioned above, which begin with .... P×P, are no longer available to Black. On the other hand, the threat P—B5 is not at White's disposal any more. Thus White must try to get an advantage by the minority attack (*Diagram No. 21B*) or by a K-side attack (*Diagram No. 21D,E*) or by superior development (*Diagram No. 21C*). Black can liberate himself with .... Kt—K5 or some other appropriate exchange or—at times—he may institute a counter-attack.

To make the discussion most valuable, we shall assume that Black is at liberty to recapture in one of three ways: with the KP, BP or KKt. Then the ensuing position must be considered in the light of one or more of the following questions:

1. If Black recaptures with the KP (*Diagram No. 23A*)

a) Can White castle long and storm the enemy K-side with his Pawns, or is Black's counter-attack too strong?

b) Can White castle short and push the minority attack to a successful conclusion?

2. If Black recaptures with the BP (*Diagram No. 23B*)

a) Can White maintain a better-developed position by play on the QB file?

b) Can White build up a K-side attack with his pieces?

3. If Black recaptures with the Kt (*Diagram No. 23C*)

Can Black avoid the fixation of his center Pawn without being constricted too much or does he merely transpose into previous formations?

1. Recapture with the KP: There is first of all the question in 1a above. From *Diagram No. 23A* the normal line would be in White's favor because he can sidestep the enemy attack, while Black can not do so quite as easily. For both sides the primary consideration in defensive play is to prevent the opening of a file near the King. E.g., ... P—KR3 by Black would be bad because after 8 B—KB4, P—KKt4 eventually will force the KKt file open. Thus we get as the main line: 8 Q—B2, O—O; 9 KKt—K2 (better than 9 Kt—KB3), R—K1; 10 P—KR3, Kt—B1 (see comment at end); 11 O—O—O, P—QKt4; 12 P—KKt4, P—QR4; 13 Kt—Kt3, P—R5; 14 K—Kt1, Q—R4; 15 QKt—K2! and Black cannot pry a file open. Relatively best for Black is to force a few exchanges: 10 .... Kt—K5 (instead of 10 .... Kt—B1); 11 B×B, Q×B; 12 B×Kt, P×B; 13 P—KKt4, Kt—B3; 14 Kt—Kt3, P—KR3, etc. While White's game is still a bit better Black has freed himself considerably and is much better off than in the previous case.

Another defensive idea which is occasionally useful is that of postponing castling to bring about a few favorable shifts or exchanges first.

All told this line is quite strong for White, though not wholly without its risks, as is always the case with attacks.

Against the minority attack (*Diagram No. 21 B*) Black has a somewhat harder time. His chief defense is a counter-attack against White's K-side, but in the normal line White's prospects are superior: (from *Diagram No. 23 A*) 8 Q—B2, O—O; 9 Kt—B3, R—K1; 10 O—O, Kt—B1; 11 Kt—K5, Kt—Kt5 (see comment); 12 B×B, Q×B; 13 Kt×Kt, B×Kt; 14 Kt—K2, Q—R5; 15 Kt—Kt3, and White's Pawns will soon march, while Black's attack is blocked. However, 11 .... Kt—K5! (instead of 11 .... Kt—Kt5) is more logical and may be better. The Pawn obviously cannot be taken, which gives Black's counterplay a somewhat brighter appearance.

One little-known idea for the hard-pressed defender is that of playing .... P—KR3 followed by .... Kt—K1. E.g., 8 Kt—B3, O—O; 9 O—O, P—KR3; 10 B—R4, Kt—K1; 11 B—Kt3, B—Q3; 12 Q—B2, B×B; 13 RP×B, Kt—Q3 with *almost* even chances. The Kt at Q3 is excellent for both attack and defense; under certain circumstances .... P—QKt4 to block the advance and prepare .... Kt—B5 may even be tried.

2. Recapture with the BP: Here things shape up differently.
White has an advantage in terrain, but if he does not play aggressively it will soon be dissipated.

First (*Diagram No. 23B*) we must observe that White can-

THE EXCHANGE VARIATION

No. 23A

No. 23B

No. 23C

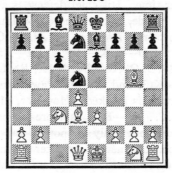

not derive any lasting profit from an immediate concentration
on the QB file, i.e., the answer to 2a is in the negative. For
Black is not so far behind in development that he cannot recoup. E.g., 8 Kt—B3, O—O; 9 O—O, P—QR3; 10 P—QR4,
P—QKt3; 11 Q—K2, B—Kt2; 12 QR—B1, Kt—K5! with a
satisfactory position: Black can get all his pieces out and
neutralize White's slight pull.

On the other hand, 2b provides the solution to White's problem because Black is compelled to avoid a crushing attack: 8 Kt—B3, O—O; 9 O—O, P—QR3; 10 R—B1, P—Kt4; 11 Kt—K5, B—Kt2; 12 P—B4, P—R3 (otherwise Black will be overwhelmed); 13 B—R4, Kt×Kt; 14 BP×Kt, Kt—K5; 15 B×B, Q×B; 16 B×Kt and Black's B is weak in conjunction with so many Pawns on Black.

This idea of a Kt vs. a bad B frequently occurs in the Queen's Gambit: Black so often has a number of Pawns on White squares, which leaves his B too little scope.

Note in the above variation that White combines the motif of an attack with that of pressure on the QB file and that of leaving his opponent with a bad B.

3. Recapture with the Kt: This (3) is rarely seen but normally has no independent value because it transposes into one of the customary lines. In 23C after 7 .... Kt×P; 8 B×B, Q×B; 9 Kt×Kt it is obvious that we get back to one of the former lines. If, however, 8 .... Kt×B here (after 8 B×B) to force a variation, 9 Kt—B3, O—O; 10 O—O is in White's favor because of his better center which cannot easily be neutralized (10 .... P—QB4; 11 Q—B2, P—KR3; 12 KR—Q1 with superior development).

Summing up, we may draw three worthwhile conclusions:

1. Despite its simplifying character, the Exchange Variation in many cases strengthens White's bind.

2. The two chief types of advantage which White may secure with it are the minority attack and the better endgame because of Black's bad QB, which is hampered by the many Pawns on White.

3. Black's best counter in virtually all variations is an early .... Kt—K5 followed, if possible, by a counter-attack.

Improvements for Black: The main lines of the straight Orthodox (including the Exchange Variation) are not wholly satisfactory for Black. He need not lose by force, but for a long while he is necessarily subjected to a cramped position and must always play with the greatest accuracy to escape ignominious defeat. It is chiefly for this reason that masters have resorted to so many different defenses.

If we analyze White's bind in the main lines above we find that it rests principally on two factors: a) the pin of the KKt by White's QB and b) the difficulties arising from the attempt to develop Black's QB properly. Once Black has played .... P—K3, he can do nothing but try one of the liberating maneuvers given above to get his QB out. *However, he can attempt to break the force of the pin at a number of points*, by getting his Q out of the way, or by removing his Kt, or by creating a diversion in some other part of the board. It is this idea which is at the basis of virtually all alternatives within the framework of the Orthodox.

Working backwards from the main line, we find that the first important variant for Black is the *Cambridge Springs Defense*. 1 P—Q4, P—Q4; 2 P—QB4, P—K3; 3 Kt—QB3, Kt—KB3; 4 B—Kt5, QKt—Q2; 5 P—K3, P—B3; 6 Kt—B3, *Q—R4* (*Diagram No. 24*). This Q sortie not only releases the pin, thus preventing the normal continuation, but also threatens .... Kt—K5 and (when White's QB is undefended) .... P× P. In addition it pins the White QKt, with all the benefits deriving from that.

It should first be observed that White cannot disregard Black's last move and go his own way. For if 7 B—K2, Kt— K5; 8 R—B1, P×P costs White a Pawn for which he cannot find adequate compensation.

To reply to his opponent's threats White has one of three choices (*Diagram No. 24*): 7 Kt—Q2 (his turn to break a pin!), 7 B×Kt (to avoid any combinations which may arise should this B remain inadequately defended: the most common is 7 B—Q3?, Kt—K5; 8 O—O??, Kt×B; 9 Kt×Kt, P×P and wins a piece) and 7 P×P (to clarify the situation in the center).

I. 7 Kt—Q2: White releases the pin of his QKt. 7 .... Kt—K5 now would fail of its purpose because after 8 KKt× Kt, P×Kt; 9 B—R4 Black's game is still cramped and he has weakened his Pawn structure. Instead, Black can play for

.... P—K4 or .... P—QB4 at an early stage. Tactical considerations determine which of the two is superior. Thus on 7 .... P—K4 at once 8 Kt—Kt3 leaves Black's Pawn position hopelessly weak. Similarly 7 .... P—B4 would block the KB. Consequently either 7 .... B—Kt5, to get this B doing something useful, or 7 .... P×P, to force the exchange of White's QB, is best. In the further course of the game, ... P—K4 is

No. 24

Cambridge Springs Defense.

normally not quite adequate (e.g., 7 Kt—Q2, B—Kt5; 8 Q—B2, O—O; 9 B—K2, P—K4; 10 O—O, KP×P; 11 Kt—Kt3, Q—B2; 12 KKt×P and Black's position is far from easy) but tactics must decide. However, by exchanging White's QB and preparing .... P—QB4 Black can almost always equalize without much trouble. Thus a major line is 7 .... B—Kt5; 8 Q—B2, P×P; 9 B×Kt, Kt×B; 10 Kt×P, Q—B2 (10 .... B×Ktch is also all right); 11 P—QR3, B—K2; 12 P—KKt3, O—O; 13 B—Kt2, B—Q2; 14 P—QKt4, P—QKt3, etc.: .... P—QB4 cannot be prevented in the long run. Another good idea for the defense here is .... Kt—Q4, to get rid of White's QKt and at the same time ease Black's position. The two B's are always a potential advantage.

II. 7 B×Kt simplifies too much: by normal development White cannot prevent an early and favorable .... P—QB4.

III. 7 P×P is the line most often seen nowadays: its leading idea is the weakening of the Black center. It also avoids the traps arising from the exposure of White's QB.

A recapture with a Pawn would deprive the Q sortie of all meaning since at best Black could only transpose into an inferior branch of the Exchange Variation. So 7 .... Kt×P is virtually forced.

Again Black will try to free himself with either .... P— K4 or .... P—QB4 and again some hair-raising complications may ensue. This time .... P—B4 is usually inferior to .... P—K4, though once more tactical considerations must prevail. White can defend his Kt with either 8 Q—Kt3 or 8 Q—Q2. On 8 Q—Kt3, B—Kt5; 9 R—B1, P—K4! Black can sacrifice a Pawn for the sake of quick development, while on 8 Q—Q2, QKt—Kt3; 9 R—B1 White gives up a Pawn to get his pieces out quickly. In neither case do the complications lead to any decisive result with best play: it is as a rule wisest to decline the Pawn and continue with one's own idea. Thus on 8 Q— Kt3, B—Kt5; 9 R—B1, P—K4; 10 B—QB4! is best, while on 8 Q—Q2, B—Kt5 is preferable. We have passed over these variations rather cursorily because they contain no essentially new ideas.

One of the chief drawbacks to the Cambridge Springs is that White can evade it. On his 6th move in the main line (1 P— Q4, P—Q4; 2 P—QB4, P—K3; 3 Kt—QB3, Kt—KB3; 4 B—Kt5, QKt—Q2; 5 Kt—B3, P—B3) he may try 6 P×P, transposing into the Exchange Variation, or 6 P—QR3, or even 6 P—K4!, which is the most novel. Here the idea is to compel an early liquidation of the Black center, in the conviction that White's better development will tell in the long run. White's chief hope is that he may be able to sacrifice a Pawn to secure a strong attack, or that Black may open his position too early. E.g., 6 P—K4, P×KP; 7 Kt×P, B—K2 (or 7 .... Q—Kt3; 8 B—Q3!?); 8 Kt—B3, O—O; 9 Q—B2, P—K4; 10 O—O—O with good prospects.

The Manhattan Variation arises after 1 P—Q4, P—Q4; 2

P—QB4, P—K3; 3 Kt—QB3, Kt—KB3; 4 B—Kt5, QKt—Q2;
5 Kt—B3, *B—Kt5* (*Diagram No. 25*).

It is evident that Black's idea is counter-attack. All such
lines, to have any meaning, must sooner or later continue with
.... P—QB4 or .... Kt—K5 or both. The strength of
Black's play is that both these moves will soon be available.

No. 25   No. 26

Manhattan Variation.   Lasker's Defense.

Unfortunately, however, he will find himself unable to refute
normal development.

White's first thought is to lock the center with 6 P×P, P×P
(almost always a good idea when Black varies). Then he may
simply continue his development, taking due care to answer the
threats that come up: 7 P—K3, P—B4; 8 B—Q3, Q—R4; 9
Q—B2, P—B5; 10 B—B5, O—O; 11 O—O, R—K1; 12 P—
QR3 with advantage because of his more solid Pawn position.

Lasker's Defense: The basic idea here is *unpinning* with an
early .... Kt—K5, although it may be played at a number of
points; its strength is that it frees Black by exchanges. Since
it does no harm, Black is well advised to precede the Kt sortie
with .... P—KR3, B—R4. Then the main line would be:
1 P—Q4, P—Q4; 2 P—QB4, P—K3; 3 Kt—QB3, Kt—KB3; 4
B—Kt5, B—K2; 5 P—K3, O—O; 6 Kt—B3, P—KR3; 7 B—
R4, Kt—K5 (*Diagram No. 26*).

White is compelled to submit to several exchanges. He then usually tries to get an advantage by securing the better Pawn center, for he is justified in assuming that any Black Q-side majority will be nullified for a long time to come: 8 B×B, Q×B; 9 P×P, Kt×Kt; 10 P×Kt, P×P; 11 Q—Kt3! (something must be done against .... P—QB4). 11 .... Q—Q3 and if 12 P—B4, P×P; 13 B×P, Kt—B3! is now the quickest way to equalize, though 11 .... R—Q1 is also playable. What Black must guard against is that White may hold the center solid and develop strong pressure against the Q-side.

Another idea which White may use is that of merely maintaining superior development, with the alternative of transposing into the Exchange Variation. For this he must keep the QB file open, so he plays 8 B×B, Q×B; 9 Q—B2. Now 9 .... Kt×Kt leads to much the same kind of play as in the Orthodox: Black will have a little difficulty freeing himself. Instead, 9 .... Kt—KB3! is surprisingly good: now the exchange variation is inferior because an early .... P—QB4 cannot be prevented, while on straight development .... P—QB4 will be possible quite early. All things considered, Lasker's Defense is one of the major good defenses at Black's disposal. Its chief drawback is that it is not good for more than a draw, even against poor play.

Of the variants for White on his fourth move (after 1 P—Q4, P—Q4; 2 P—QB4, P—K3; 3 Kt—QB3, Kt—KB3, instead of 4 B—Kt5) 4 Kt—B3 is the only one that need concern us seriously here. Against other moves, such as 4 B—B4, or 4 P—K3, after the normal .... P—QB4 Black no longer has any opening problems.

We come then to *Diagram No. 27*. Of course, transposition into other lines is quite easy, but there are several independent and fascinating features if Black chooses to vary.

The most obvious reply is 4 .... P—B4. There is a widespread misconception that this is a variation of the Tarrasch Defense. True, it may transpose into the Tarrasch but the two are distinct because of the all-important difference that Black need not submit to an isolated Pawn. A normal reaction such as 5 P—K3 (after 4 .... P—B4) would be met by 5 .... Kt—B3 with a perfectly symmetrical position where an early draw can be expected. Instead, White can try to get an advantage in one of two ways: 5 BP×P, to get the better center, or 5 B—Kt5, to maintain the pressure on the center and force Black to some clarification which, it is hoped, will be unfavorable.

After 5 BP×P, Kt×P! (5 .... KP×P; 6 P—KKt3 transposes into the Rubinstein refutation of the Tarrasch Defense);

No. 27

Position after 4 Kt—B3 in the Queen's
Gambit Declined.

6 P—K4 is indicated. A forced series of moves (Black has the more cramped game, so he is glad of a chance to exchange) now ensues: 6 .... Kt×Kt; 7 P×Kt, P×P; 8 P×P, B—Kt5ch; 9 B—Q2, B×Bch!; 10 Q×B, O—O. Here White has the better Pawn center, but the exchanges have already freed Black's game considerably. The Pawn structure dictates the further plans: White with his freer position will undertake a K-side attack, Black, with the majority of Pawns on the Q-side, will head for the endgame, though he must not be oblivious of the dangers lurking on the other wing. A typical continuation is 11 B—B4, Kt—B3; 12 O—O, P—QKt3; 13 KR—Q1, B—Kt2; 14 Q—B4, R—B1 (or 14 .... Q—B3!); 15 P—Q5, P×P;

16 B×P, Q—K2; 17 Kt—Kt5!, Kt—K4!; 18 B×B, Kt—Kt3 with about even chances. An interesting idea for White is that of playing his B to QKt5 in order to weaken the enemy Q-side. It is quite strong when Black makes the mistake of not exchanging his KB immediately, or when Black tries .... P—QR3; .... B—R4, P—QKt4; B—B2 only to be met by an early P—QR4, but ineffective if Black simply continues with the normal .... P—QKt3, etc. Another thought which is often useful for White is P—K5!, to keep Black cramped. Despite the abandonment of the central square Q4 to Black it may lead to a strong attack. E.g., in the above, 11 P—K5 (instead of 11 B—B4), Kt—Q2? (11 .... Kt—B3; 12 B—Q3, Q—R4 with equality is correct); 12 B—Q3, Kt—Kt3; 13 O—O, Kt—Q4; 14 Kt—Kt5, P—KKt3; 15 Kt—K4 with powerful pressure which Black probably cannot resist.

The other alternative for White involves further pressure with 5 B—Kt5 (after 4 .... P—B4). Then 5 .... BP×P is forced, when 6 KKt×P leaves Black with a better Pawn center, but inferior development (some lines are extremely complicated) while 6 Q×P gives White the better Pawn position but frees Black's position completely. A model line runs 6 Q×P, B—K2! (6 .... Kt—B3; 7 B×Kt! gives White the better of it); 7 P×P, P×P; 8 P—K3, Kt—B3; 9 B—Kt5!, O—O; 10 Q—QR4, B—Q2 with about even chances.

Another enterprising try for Black in *Diagram No. 27* is the Ragosin Variation, 4 .... B—Kt5, which is a counter-attack without the major drawback of the Manhattan Variation. I.e., this time normal development does not lead to an advantage for White. For if 5 P—K3, P—B4 transposes into a variation of the Nimzoindian Defense which is good for Black: 6 B—Q3, QP×P!; 7 B×BP, O—O; 8 O—O, Kt—B3 with a more than satisfactory game (page 178). Nor is 5 P×P, P×P any better for White: 6 B—Kt5, P—KR3; 7 B×Kt, Q×B etc. It should be recalled that when Black's QB is at liberty to move where it pleases the Exchange Variation loses much of its force because Black can get rid of White's powerful KB. Consequently, after 4 .... B—Kt5, the chief independent attempt at refutation is 5 Q—R4ch, Kt—B3; 6 P—K3 (or 6 Kt—K5, B—Q2), O—O; 7 B—Q2. Now comes an interesting and unusual feature: Black gives up the center in order to be able to clarify the situation with .... P—K4: 7 .... P—QR3!; 8 Q—B2, P×P; 9 B×P, B—Q3!; 10 P—QR3, P—K4! with adequate counterplay.

Other alternatives for Black offer few important new ideas. On 4 .... QKt—Q2; 5 P×P, P×P; 6 B—B4!, to play for attack with P—K3, B—Q3, O—O, P—KR3, Kt—K5, B—R2, P—KB4, is rather unusual, but not quite sufficient. The variant 4 .... Kt—K5 leads into positions similar to the Dutch Defense and Stonewall.

The reader may have noticed that the possibility of transpositions has occurred more frequently in the last ten or fifteen pages. By concentrating on ideas and essential Pawn structures one will be much more alive to such eventualities and will master them far more easily.

The Tarrasch Defense: There has never been a Homer to sing the great battle of Tarrasch vs. the world. To the day of his death Tarrasch stoutly maintained that his defense was by far the best, that the others were merely being "orthodox" by sticking to horse-and-buggy misconceptions. Despite his Herculean labors, however, today we believe that he was wrong.

The Defense occurs after 1 P—Q4, P—Q4; 2 P—QB4, P—K3; 3 Kt—QB3, P—QB4 (*Diagram No. 28A*). Tarrasch's idea was to secure free development for his pieces, for he held that that would amply compensate any weakness in the Pawn position that might ensue. It is this point which is the bone of contention. For in the best variations Black, it is true, does have ample scope for his pieces but that does not turn out to be sufficient compensation for the debilitating weakness of his Pawn structure. The Achilles' heel is the isolated QP, which reduces Black's freedom of action and yields White the important central square Q4 as well as—in most cases—the subsidiary QB5.

The refutation by which the whole defense stands or falls is the Rubinstein Variation, which is designed to saddle Black with an isolated QP. It runs (from *Diagram No. 28A*): 4 BP× P, KP×P; 5 Kt—B3, Kt—QB3; 6 P—KKt3, Kt—B3; 7 B—

<table>
<tr><td align="center">No. 28A</td><td align="center">No. 28B</td></tr>
<tr><td>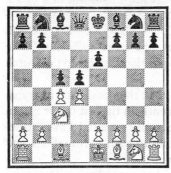</td><td>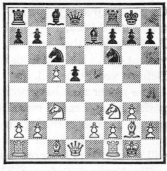</td></tr>
<tr><td align="center">Tarrasch Defense.</td><td align="center">Tarrasch Defense, Rubinstein Variation. White has a marked advantage.</td></tr>
</table>

Kt2, B—K2; 8 O—O, O—O and now the strongest is 9 P×P (*Diagram No. 28B*).

So far both sides have merely completed their development. Now however Black is faced by a difficult choice: shall he recapture and submit to positional inferiority, or sacrifice and play for the attack?

The positional line runs 9 .... B×P; 10 Kt—QR4!, B—K2; 11 B—K3. It is clear why this line is so powerful for White: he has absolute control of Q4, temporary control of QB5. On 11 .... Kt—K5; 12 Kt—Q4! at once is best. In the further course of the game White will be anxious to solidify his hold on the QB file and to play for the ending, where Black's QP and bad B are well-nigh fatal weaknesses. Black can do little but ward off White's threats as they arise. Almost nobody has been willing to defend this position in a serious tournament test, which is a sufficient indication of its inferiority. The best that Black can do is draw with infinite difficulty.

In the sacrificial line (from *Diagram No. 28B*) 9 .... P—Q5, the refutation, is, as so often, tactical. For quite a while it was believed that 10 Kt—QR4, B—B4 gives Black enough, but this belief has been abandoned because of the crushing, though simple, 11 B—B4!, which completes White's development and prepares further valuable exchanges, especially of Black's crucial QP. 11 .... Kt—K5; 12 P—QKt4!, Kt×QKtP (or 12 .... B—B3; 13 P—Kt5, Kt—K2; 14 B—K5); 13 Kt×P, B—Kt3; 14 R—Kt1!, P—QR4; 15 P—QR3, Kt—QB3; 16 Kt×Kt, P×Kt; 17 R—Kt7 should win for White.

In the face of these annihilating variations, all research and improvements necessarily center around Black's game.

For White, 9 B—Kt5 (instead of 9 P×P in the main line) is worth a try, though it is not quite as good. In the so-called normal variation 4 P—K3 (in *Diagram No. 28A*, instead of 4 BP×P) the perfect symmetry should occasion Black no difficulty, though there are some traps to be avoided. A good rule for Black to follow is that an early transposition into the QGA is desirable.

Improvements for Black are all designed to take the sting out of the Rubinstein Variation. Some have enjoyed a short vogue of popularity, but all have been discarded sooner or later. The three main tries (numbers refer to the main line above) are 7 .... B—Kt5, 6 .... P—B5 (the Folkestone Variation) and 6 .... BP×P (the von Hennig-Schara Gambit).

7 .... B—Kt5 is played with a view to weakening White's hold on the center. But 8 B—K3 retains the bind, while 8 Kt—K5! gives up a P temporarily for a crushing attack: 8 .... P×P; 9 Kt×B, P×Kt; 10 Kt×Ktch, Q×Kt; 11 P×P, Q× Pch; 12 B—Q2, Q—B3; 13 O—O!, R—Q1; 14 Q—Kt3! and Black is in a bad way.

6 .... P—B5 (the Folkestone Variation) is somewhat more complicated. Here Black avoids the isolani once and for all, but releases the pressure on White's center. The natural reaction in such cases is the break P—K4. It turns out that this is strongest if played at once: 7 P—K4!, P×P; 8 Kt—KKt5, Q×P; 9 B—B4!, P—KR3; 10 KKt×KP, Q×Qch; 11 R×Q, B—K3; 12 Kt—QKt5 and Black is lost.

4 .... BP×P (*the von Hennig-Schara Gambit*) is refuted by the in-between move 5 Q—R4ch! (on 5 Q×P at once 5 .... Kt—QB3 gains important time for Black though White can try it anyhow), B—Q2; 6 Q×QP, P×P; 7 Q×QP, Kt—KB3; 8 Q—Kt3, etc. With straight development Black does not have enough for the Pawn.

Coming back to the main line (1 P—Q4, P—Q4; 2 P—QB4, P—K3; 3 Kt—QB3, Kt—KB3, etc.—see page 104) we find a wide variety of alternatives for Black, few of which have shown any promise.

I. 3 .... P—QR3 (*Janowski's Defense*) is designed to force an early clarification in the center. Its weakness is that Black is forcing White to make good moves: after 4 P×P, P×P; 5 B—B4, etc. straight development gives White the better of it, for we have a branch of the Exchange Variation where Black has played the useless .... P—QR3.

II. 3 .... P—QKt3 is tried with a view to solving the perennial headache of the Black QB. By fianchettoing at such an early stage Black avoids the attack with Kt—K5, etc. which comes up later because the Kt can be driven away. To date no theoretical refutation has been found. White's best is undoubtedly 4 P×P, P×P; 5 P—KKt3, for the counter-fianchetto deprives Black's of its force. Early breaks with P—K4 have not turned out well in practise.

III. 2 .... P—QB4 aims at an early liquidation of the center. The idea is admirable, for later Black must sweat mightily to play .... P—QB4, but White's plus in development is too great: 3 BP×P, Q×P; 4 Kt—KB3, P×P; 5 Kt—B3, Q—QR4; 6 Kt×P, Kt—KB3; 7 Kt—Kt3, Q—B2; 8 P—Kt3, etc. with advantage.

IV. 2 .... P—KKt3 is another move designed to keep the

way free for the Black QB. 3 Kt—QB3, Kt—KB3 transposes
into the Gruenfeld, but 3 P×P is stronger. On 3 .... Q×P;
4 Kt—QB3, Q—QR4; 5 Kt—B3 White's development is much
superior.

V. 2 .... Kt—QB3 (*Tchigorin's Defense*) is another instance
of an immediate counter-attack. To continue properly Black
must give up his QB. That is why Tchigorin favored the line,
for he was firmly convinced that a Kt is always better than a B.

In order to have a reasonably playable game Black must
concentrate on quick development. After 3 Kt—KB3 (3 Kt—
QB3 is also good), e.g., 3 .... P—K3?; 4 Kt—B3, Kt—B3; 5
B—Kt5, B—K2; 6 P—K3 Black has merely deprived himself
of his main liberating move so that White has a clear positional
superiority.

Black consequently tries to hit at the White center: 3 Kt—
KB3, B—Kt5; 4 Q—R4! (to evade the pin and compel the ex-
change of Black's QB), B×Kt; 5 KP×B, P—K3; 6 Kt—B3,
B—Kt5 (to relieve the pressure on his center); 7 P—QR3,
B×Ktch; 8 P×B: White's two Bishops are a telling ad-
vantage.

VI. 2 .... Kt—KB3 is probably the best of Black's alternatives on the second move. It is not, strictly speaking, a wholly
independent variation because it can transpose into a variety of
other lines, e.g., on 3 Kt—QB3, P—KKt3, we have the Gruenfeld, on 3 Kt—KB3, P—B3, we have the Slav. The crucial
question about the defense is whether there is an adequate
answer to 3 P×P. White must not be too hasty: after 3 ....
Kt×P; 4 P—K4, Kt—KB3; 5 B—Q3, P—K4!; 6 P×P, Kt—
KKt5 Black recovers his P with an adequate position. But
by proceeding slowly White can accomplish the same thing
without permitting the break: 3 P×P, Kt×P; 4 Kt—KB3,
B—B4; 5 P—K3, Kt—QB3; 6 QKt—Q2, Kt—Kt3 (or 6 ....
Kt—B3; 7 Q—Kt3); 7 P—K4, B—Kt5; 8 P—Q5, etc.

VII. 2 .... B—B4 is designed to solve the eternal problem of
the proper development of the Black QB. It fails only because
the Q-side turns out to be too weak. After 3 Kt—KB3, P—

K3; 4 Q—Kt3! Black is already at a loss for a good move. Most usual is the counter-action 4 Q—Kt3, Kt—QB3; 5 P—B5!, R—Kt1; 6 B—B4. White retains his marked superiority by an early advance against the Black Q-side. Worthy of note here is that after 3 Kt—KB3, P—QB3 is Black's best bet, to transpose into the Slav Defense. On 4 Kt—B3, P—K3! is correct, and not 4 .... Kt—B3?; 5 P×P, P×P; 6 Q—Kt3! etc. (page 134).

Again returning to the main line, we must consider an important deviation on White's third move: 1 P—Q4, P—Q4; 2 P—QB4, P—K3; 3 Kt—KB3. In modern chess the order of moves is constantly increasing in importance. While this is due chiefly to the greatly enlarged possibilities of transpositions, in some cases it is also based on the desire of one player to stick to a certain variation and allow no deviation from it. In the present line there is a combination of these motifs. Quite often the position arises because White does not wish to allow the Nimzoindian: 1 P—Q4, Kt—KB3; 2 P—QB4, P—K3; 3 Kt—KB3, P—Q4, etc. At other times White chooses the line because he wishes to develop his QKt at Q2. Frequently it is played automatically and has no special significance.

Black's simplest reply is 3 .... Kt—KB3 (after 3 Kt—KB3) when there are two ways in which White can deviate from the main lines of the QGD. The first is that where he develops his QKt at Q2, the second that where he shuts in his QB, but avoids the normal line of the Tarrasch Defense.

The only advantage which can accrue from posting the QKt at Q2 rather than at QB3 is that on .... QP×BP the Kt may recapture instead of the B, thus making the liberating .... P—K4 virtually impossible. As we know, however, the main freeing move is not .... P—K4, but .... P—B4. Further, the lack of pressure against White's center makes Black's game easier. For all these reasons this form of the gambit cannot be recommended. After 3 .... Kt—KB3; 4 B—Kt5, QKt—Q2; 5 P—K3, O—O; 6 QKt—Q2 Black can equalize with either 6

.... B—Q3 and an early .... P—K4, or 6 .... B—K2 and an early .... P—B4. All that he must guard against is giving up the center for insufficient reason.

The other alternative for White, where he shuts in his QB, is more promising. It is, however essential to avoid the symmetrical normal position of the Tarrasch Defense. Since this line is even only because of the symmetry it is sufficient for White to wait one move: 3 Kt—KB3, Kt—KB3; 4 Kt—B3, B—K2 (or 4 .... QKt—Q2, or 4 .... P—B3—of course, Black can transpose into other lines with 4 .... P—B4 or 4 .... B—Kt5) and now 5 P—K3. It turns out that normal development would give White the better of it: Black can play .... P—B4, but White secures the square K5 for his Kt. Thus: 5 P—K3 (after 4 Kt—B3, B—K2), O—O; 6 B—Q3, P—B4; 7 P—QKt3, P—QKt3; 8 O—O, B—Kt2; 9 B—Kt2, QKt—Q2; 10 Q—K2, QP×P; 11 KtP×P, P×P; 12 P×P, etc. The hanging Pawns need not be feared by White because of his excellent development. Once the Kt is securely posted at K5, a K-side attack almost automatically ensues. It is advisable for Black to avoid the entire line by transposing into the QGA at an early stage. Thus 4 Kt—B3, B—K2; 5 P—K3, P×P; 6 B×P, P—B4, etc.

In view of the eased situation in the center Black may also vary on his fourth turn: 3 Kt—KB3, Kt—KB3; 4 B—Kt5 and now either 4 .... B—Kt5ch or 4 .... P—KR3.

4 .... B—Kt5ch (the Vienna Variation) can lead to some exciting complications in the main line: 5 Kt—B3, P×P; 6 P—K4, P—B4; 7 P—K5, P×P; 8 Q—R4ch, Kt—B3; 9 O—O—O, B—Q2; 10 Kt—K4, B—K2; 11 P×Kt, P×P; 12 B—R4, R—QB1!; 13 K—Kt1, Kt—R4; 14 Q—B2, P—K4; 15 Kt×QP, P×Kt; 16 R×P, Q—Kt3; 17 R×B! with an unclear position. Black can avoid the complications with 6 .... P—KR3; 7 B×Kt, Q×B, but White has no choice once he has started.

4 .... P—KR3 (the Duras Variation) yields White control of the center in return for the two Bishops. With energetic play

White can make his plus in terrain tell: 4 B—Kt5, P—KR3; 5 B×Kt, Q×B; 6 Q—Kt3, P—B3; 7 QKt—Q2, Kt—Q2; 8 P—K4, P×KP; 9 Kt×P, Q—B5; 10 B—Q3, P—K4; 11 O—O, B—K2; 12 KR—K1 and Black's game is difficult. In other lines White may emerge with the slight theoretical advantage of a better center Pawn. (Compare French Defense, page 68.)

SLAV DEFENSE: 1 P—Q4, P—Q4, P—QB4, P—QB3

It has become clear how the pressure which White is enabled to exert in the Queen's Gambit is due to one or more of three factors. These are:

1. The Black QB cannot be developed normally and gets in the way of the other Black pieces.

2. The Pawn position offers White numerous targets (especially the minority attack in the Exchange Variation), which are frequently converted into permanent weaknesses.

3. The pin of the Black KKt by B—Kt5 cramps the Black position; the second player must go to a great deal of trouble to neutralize or destroy the pin.

While no defense as yet discovered has succeeded in eliminating all three of these drawbacks, the one which comes nearest is the Slav, so-called because it was first played by Slavic masters (notably Alapin). Although the opening had been known as long ago as 1910 and earlier, its great strength was not fully recognized until Euwe adopted it in many important tournament and match games in the early 1930's.

It is obvious that Black's second move (*Diagram No. 29*) will permit him to develop his QB and will avoid any unbalance in the Pawn structure. While the pin is not prevented, it has all the teeth taken out of it because B—Kt5 at present does not tie the Kt to its post. Naturally, if all this continued to be true regardless of how White continued, the Queen's Gambit would soon have to be retired to the nearest museum. The trouble (from Black's point of view) is twofold: normal development by White will soon make the realization of all of Black's plans impossible, and the removal of the QB frequently leaves the Q-side dangerously weak—Black must always make sure that he has an adequate defense to any action undertaken there. These basic principles hold for all variations of the Slav.

On his third move (*Diagram No. 29*) White has the choice of four different lines of play, each motivated by a different strategical idea. He has 3 P×P (the Exchange Variation) where he relies solely on his extra move. Then there is 3 Kt—KB3, non-committal development where White is going to make up his mind later as to exactly what policy he will adopt.

<table>
<tr><td align="center">No. 29</td><td align="center">No. 30</td></tr>
</table>

Slav Defense.   Position after 5 .... B—B4 in the Slav Defense.

Next comes 3 Kt—QB3, based on some complicated traps, which is designed to put the heat on the Black center immediately. And finally, he may try 3 P—K3, again straight development in the hope that the extra move will tell, but this time retaining the tension in the center.

I. The Exchange Variation: 3 P×P, P×P. This received a good deal of attention a few years ago, when Purdy maintained that it provided a complete refutation of the Slav. While his analysis contained some good ideas, Purdy's opinion has remained unsubstantiated. On the contrary, the exchange leaves Black with fewer problems to solve than would otherwise be the case.

But despite the mild and benevolent look on White's pieces when they make their moves, Black must exercise some care. The great danger in this (as in all other symmetrical variations) is that Black will keep on copying White's moves too long. Thus after 3 P×P, P×P; 4 Kt—KB3, Kt—KB3; 5 Kt—B3, Kt—B3; 6 B—B4, the simplest line is 6 .... P—K3 (rather than 6 .... B—B4, which endangers the Q-side). After 6 .... B—B4; 7 P—K3, P—QR3 the new move 8 Kt—K5! gives White the better of it. On 6 .... P—K3, however, 7 P—K3, B—Q3! leads to exchanges which are easily sufficient for equality, e.g., 8 B×B, Q×B; 9 B—K2, O—O; 10 O—O, P—QR3 and so on. Here 7 .... B—K2 (instead of 7 .... B—Q3) is weak because after 8 B—Q3, O—O; 9 P—KR3! White avoids exchanges and maintains the pressure, e.g., 9 .... B—Q2; 10 O—O, P—QR3; 11 R—B1, B—K1; 12 B—Kt1 and Black is at a loss for good moves.

II. 3 Kt—KB3 is by far the most important line in the Slav and accordingly both players and analysts have devoted the greatest amount of attention to it. After the normal 3 .... Kt—KB3, 4 Kt—B3 Black finds himself compelled to modify his original plan: he cannot both preserve Pawn equilibrium and get his B out. For on 4 .... B—B4; 5 P×P, P×P? (5 .... Kt×P is a bit better but not enough for equality); 6 Q—Kt3, Q—Kt3 (or 6 .... B—B1; 7 Kt—K5); 7 Kt×P, Kt×Kt; 8 Q×Kt, P—K3; 9 Q—Kt3 Black does not have enough for the Pawn.

Consequently, to get his B out Black must give up the center with .... P×P. As usual, the struggle then centers around whether White can force P—K4 under favorable circumstances or not. According to best available information at present Black cannot prevent P—K4 permanently, but can take the sting out of it. In line with our general theories, which teach us that the two Pawns abreast in the center are strong if and only if they cramp the enemy pieces, Black's objective should be to exchange pieces or to get rid of the White QP or both.

After 3 .... Kt—B3; 4 Kt—B3, P×P the usual normal line runs 5 P—QR4 (to prevent the support of the Black QBP), B—B4 (*Diagram No. 30*) and now White may choose to prepare P—K4 in one of two ways: 6 P—K3 or 6 Kt—K5.

With 6 P—K3 he envisages straight development followed by Q—K2 and P—K4 eventually. To prevent this Black keeps a sharp eye on White's K4: 6 P—K3, P—K3; 7 B×P, B—QKt5!; 8 O—O, O—O; 9 Q—K2 (on other moves .... P—QB4 would be a more than adequate rejoinder) and now there are two replies to the White threat: 9 .... B—Kt5 and 9 .... Kt—K5. 9 .... B—Kt5 is safer: it allows P—K4, but soon compels a break in the White center. Thus: 10 R—Q1 (not 10 P—K4 because of 10 .... B×Kt), QKt—Q2; 11 P—R3, B—KR4; 12 P—K4, Q—K2 (threatening .... P—K4); 13 P—K5, Kt—Q4; 14 Kt—K4, P—KR3! (to prevent an annoying pin) with complete equality because the break .... P—KB3 cannot be prevented. 9 .... Kt—K5 in the main line (instead of 9 .... B—Kt5) is a bit doubtful because of the interesting sacrifice 10 B—Q3!, first seen in the Euwe-Alekhine match in 1937. The move sacrifices a P to cramp Black's game: 10 .... B×Kt; 11 P×B, Kt×QBP; 12 Q—B2, B×B; 13 Q×B, Kt—Q4; 14 B—R3, R—K1; 15 QR—Kt1 with strong pressure.

Summarizing, we find that the leading ideas for both sides in this crucial variation are the following:

1. White wishes to force P—K4 under favorable circumstances. Against weak play on Black's part this will yield him an advantage.

2. Black can prevent P—K4 only by .... B—QKt5 and then occupying the square with his Kt at the appropriate moment. In that event he must always be on guard against a sacrifice beginning with B—Q3.

3. Black can take the sting out of the advance by .... B—KKt5, followed by preparing the break .... P—K4. Should White advance P—K5, the break .... P—KB3 would equalize.

4. Against weak play by White or some unusual variant the liberating idea for Black is .... P—QB4.

Returning now to *Diagram No. 30*, we find the alternative 6 Kt—K5 for White, which envisages recapturing the BP with the Kt and setting up the center with P—B3 and P—K4, or with the fianchett of the KB. In reply, Black's best choice is to pin the White QKt and break the White center with an early .... P—QB4. The other line, where he tries 6 .... QKt—Q2; 7 Kt×P(B4), Q—B2, to force .... P—K4, is refuted by 8 P—KKt3, P—K4; 9 P×P, Kt×P; 10 B—B4, KKt—Q2; 11 B—Kt2, P—B3; 12 O—O, R—Q1; 13 Q—B1, B—K3; 14 Kt—K4!, B—QKt5; 15 P—R5, O—O; 16 Kt×Kt, Kt×Kt; 17 Kt—B5 with an overwhelming position. The leading idea all along here, of course, has been how White can take advantage of the clumsy lack of coordination of the Black pieces. Other important thoughts were that of holding Black's three Pawns on the Q-side with White's two, and that of securing the two Bishops.

However, 6 .... P—K3 (instead of 6 .... QKt—Q2 after 6 Kt—K5) is more adequate, although a new sacrificial possibility has strengthened the line for White. The main variation is 7 P—B3, B—QKt5; 8 P—K4!, B×P!; 9 P×B, Kt×P; 10 B—Q2! (the improvement), Q×P; 11 Kt×Kt, Q×Ktch; 12 Q—K2, B×Bch; 13 K×B and White has the better endgame although whether he can win is a dubious matter. The older line 8 Kt×P (B4), instead of 8 P—K4!, leads only to equality.

Finally, one idea for Black against inferior play is worth noting: if White hesitates too long about recapturing the BP, Black may sacrifice his KP to hold on to the BP, in which case the Q-side majority is often a valuable asset. E.g., 6 Kt—R4 (in *Diagram No. 30*), B—B1; 7 P—K3 (7 Kt—B3 is best), P—K4!; 8 P×P, Q×Qch; 9 Kt×Q, B—Kt5ch; 10 B—Q2, B×Bch; 11 K×B, Kt—K5ch; 12 K—K1, B—K3 with advantage.

White, of course, can choose not to prevent .... P—QKt4.

While this carries less punch as a rule, in some cases it has led to brilliant victories. Its main virtue is that it leads Black to weaken his Q-side. The main line runs 5 P—K3, P—QKt4; 6 P—QR4, P—Kt5; 7 Kt—R2, P—K3; 8 B×P, QKt—Q2 (the point is that Black cannot prevent P—K4 permanently but can take the sting out of it by .... P—B4 at the right time); 9 O—O, B—Kt2; 10 Q—K2, P—B4; 11 R—Q1 and now 11 .... P×P is undoubtedly best to avoid the sacrificial line 11 .... Q—Kt3; 12 P—K4! etc. The idea for White is to take advantage of Black's temporarily cramped position by an early attack. This entire variation may bear watching.

The second main line of the Slav here occurs where Black decides to shut in his QB with .... P—K3. Thus: 3 Kt—KB3, Kt—B3; 4 Kt—B3, P—K3; 5 P—K3, QKt—Q2; 6 B—Q3 (*Diagram No. 31*).

In order to free himself, Black may now pursue one of three plans: 1) 6 .... P×P followed by an advance on the Q-side; 2) 6 .... B—Q3 followed by .... P—K4; or 3) 6 .... B—K2 followed by development on the Q-side. Of the three, the first is the most promising, and now considered theoretically sound, the second is safest but unattractive, the third is by far too timid.

I. The Meran Variation: 6 .... P×P; 7 B×BP, P—QKt4; 8 B—Q3, P—QR3. Black hopes to be able to play .... P—B4 early, develop his B at QKt2, his other pieces normally, after which he would actually have the better of it. An example of such an eventuality is 9 O—O, P—B4; 10 P—QR4, P—Kt5; 11 Kt—K4, B—Kt2; 12 QKt—Q2, B—K2; 13 Q—K2, O—O; 14 R—Q1, P—QR4 and Black's game leaves little to be desired. In this line Black must be on guard against a possible P—R5, fixing his RP, or P—K4, with advantage in the center.

But White has no reason to be satisfied. Black has not only weakened the Q-side, he has also laid his center bare. Consequently an advance there is indicated. In reply to 9 P—K4! (after 8 .... P—QR3) there is a long series of complications which were once considered favorable for White, but have since had the real sting taken out of them: 9 .... P—B4; 10 P—K5, P×P; 11 Kt×KtP, P×Kt! (an old move recently rehabilitated); 12 P×Kt, Q—Kt3!; 13 P×P (best), B×P; 14 P—QKt4, O—O; 15 O—O, P—B4; 16 Q—K2, P—K4! and although Black's game is slightly inferior he can probably hold it.

In the above variation, if 11 .... Kt×KP (instead of 11 .... P×Kt); 12 Kt×Kt, P×Kt; 13 Q—B3!, B—Kt5ch; 14 K—K2, R—QKt1; 15 Q—Kt3! with a strong pull for White.

No. 31

Position after 6 B—Q3 in the Slav Defense.

Black should not try .... P—QKt4 without the follow-up .... P—QB4; he would simply be saddled with a backward Pawn on an open file, while .... QP×BP without .... P—QKt4 would merely concede his opponent the better center without adequate compensation.

II. 6 .... B—Q3 is safer but is likewise not entirely adequate. It is true that after 7 O—O, O—O the break 8 P—K4 is not favorable, since neither 8 .... P×BP; 9 B×P, P—K4 nor 8 .... P×KP; 9 Kt×P, Kt×Kt; 10 B×Kt, P—QB4 is sufficient to give White an adequate advantage. But by referring to the normal position of the Tarrasch Defense we see that Black cannot set up the symmetry required for equality there. Consequently, on 7 O—O, O—O; 8 P—QKt3 would be most logical. The threat 8 .... P—K4 could be answered by 9 BP×P, BP×P; 11 Kt—QKt5, B—Kt1; 12 P×P, Kt×P; 13 B—K2 with a slight but certain superiority because of Black's isolated Pawn. White's idea, if Black does not break, is to set up a Kt at K5 followed by a K-side attack, as in the variation of the QGD where he shuts in his QB (see page 131). White's motivating thought here is that exchanges would merely liberate Black's cramped position, so that the temporary inferiority in the center would soon be neutralized.

III. 6 .... *B—K2* is entirely too timid and has no positive merit. True, again the early break is not too bad: 7 O—O, O—O; 8 P—K4, P×KP; 9 Kt×P, P—QKt3; 10 Q—K2, B—Kt2; 11 R—Q1, Q—B2; 12 B—Kt5, P—B4; 13 P×P, P×P leaves White with only a minimal advantage. (For this type of position, compare the French Defense, page 68 and *Diagram No. 14A*). But the restraining 8 P—QKt3 (instead of 8 P—K4) leaves Black badly cramped without any immediate possibility of freeing himself. Against normal play White's idea is the usual one of Kt—K5 followed by a K-side attack.

The conclusion we must necessarily come to is that the entire line beginning with .... P—K3 is theoretically unsatisfactory for Black.

Other alternatives illustrate some new ideas. Improvements are really significant only for Black, but in view of the fact that analytical results here have varied so widely at times it is well to be aware of a few other choices. On Black's 5th move, after 3 Kt—KB3, Kt—B3; 4 Kt—B3, P—K3; 5 P—K3, P—QR3 may be tried to mobilize the Q-side immediately, perhaps develop the Kt at QB3. It is refuted by P—B5!, P—QKt3; 7 P×P, QKt—Q2; 8 Kt—QR4!, Kt×P; 9 B—Q2 and Black will not be able to get rid of his QBP, which is backward on an open file.

A stronger alternative—though rarely seen—is the Stonewall 5 .... Kt—K5. Then 6 B—Q3, P—KB4; 7 Kt—K5,

Q—R5!; 8 O—O, B—Q3; 9 P—B4, O—O leads to a complicated game with the chances only slightly in favor of White.
White may attack on the Q-side (with P—B5, P—QKt4
eventually) or on the K-side (with R—B3, R—R3, etc.).
What both sides must avoid is to be left with a bad B (the QB
for both sides because the Pawns are on those respective colors)
against a Kt. This variation should be compared with the
Dutch Defense (page 205).

For White we should mention 6 Kt—K5 (instead of 6 B—Q3
in the line leading to the Meran Variation, *Diagram No. 31*).
The idea is to avoid the Meran by preparing a K-side attack,
but there is no adequate refutation of the natural .... P—
QB4 at an early stage. A good possibility is 5 B—Kt5 (after
3 Kt—KB3, Kt—B3; 4 Kt—B3, P—K3) to transpose into
a favorable line of the QGD (where .... P—QB3 early is
bad as a rule). If then 5 .... P×P; 6 P—K4, P—QKt4;
7 P—K5, P—KR3; 8 B—R4, P—KKt4; 9 Kt×KKtP, P×Kt;
10 B×KtP, QKt—Q2!; 11 P×Kt! is hard to meet.

In summing up, we find that Black can equalize by giving up
the center temporarily with .... P×P, but that the alternative
of shutting in his QB is not theoretically sufficient. Under
these circumstances, we must once more expect attempted improvements for both sides. Those for Black have already been
treated in the course of the discussion; now we come to White's
tries.

After 3 Kt—KB3, Kt—B3, a line which attracted a good deal
of attention some seven or eight years ago is 4 P—K3. White
expects 4 .... B—B4, for 4 .... P—K3 is, as just mentioned,
inferior for Black. On 4 .... B—B4 White then hopes to get
an advantage by an early attack against the weakened Black
Q-side, especially by exerting pressure along the QB file.
While this line has much to recommend it, by taking suitable
precautions and defending against the threats as they come
along Black can hold his ground. One interesting trap is 4
P—K3, B—B4; 5 P×P, P×P; 6 Q—Kt3, when 6 .... Q—B2!
is best. On 6 .... Q—B1; 7 B—Q2, P—K3; 8 Kt—R3! (White

has reserved the development of this Kt in order to keep the QB file open), Kt—B3; 9 R—B1, Kt—K5? loses (9 .... Kt—Q2 is essential): 10 Kt—K5, Kt×B; 11 K×Kt, B—Kt5ch; 12 K—Q1, B—K2; 13 B—R6! and White will win. Another trap is 4 P—K3, B—B4; 5 P×P, P×P; 6 Kt—B3, P—K3; 7 Kt—K5, when 7 .... QKt—Q2? is refuted by 8 P—KKt4!, B—Kt3; 9 P—KR4, etc. 7 .... KKt—Q2!, however, is adequate.

Another idea for White is that of exchanging the Black QB for his KKt in order to secure the two Bishops. Thus: 4 P—K3, B—B4; 5 Kt—B3, P—K3; 6 Kt—KR4. Against inaccurate play White can then also get a stronger center which, in conjunction with the B's, would be quite formidable. But the proper reply 6 .... B—Kt5; 7 Q—Kt3, Q—Kt3!; is hard to meet: after 8 P—KR3 (carrying out the original idea), B—R4; 9 P—Kt4, B—Kt3; 10 Kt×B, RP×Kt; 11 B—Kt2, B—Kt5!; 12 B—Q2, QKt—Q2; 13 O—O—O, B×Kt!; 14 B×B, Q×Q; 15 P×Q, Kt—Kt3! White must block the position, which deprives his B's of their value.

Straight development for White is meaningless once Black has posted his B at B4. E.g., 4 P—K3, B—B4; 5 B—Q3, P—K3; 6 Kt—B3, B×B; 7 Q×B, QKt—Q2; 8 O—O, B—Kt5, etc. with equality.

Should Black shut in his B with 4 .... P—K3 in answer to 4 P—K3, White should continue as in the main line above (page 139) when Black's game remains cramped. Otherwise .... P—QB4 would equalize quite easily for Black. An interesting alternative for Black is the Stonewall Variation, 4 P—K3, P—K3; 5 QKt—Q2 (or 5 Kt—B3), Kt—K5, which has been discussed above (page 139). It makes no essential difference whether the White Kt is at QB3 or at Q2.

It should be mentioned that if Black takes the BP on his third move (3 Kt—KB3, P×P) it will be recaptured by means of 4 P—K3, P—QKt4; 5 P—QR4, B—Kt2; 6 P×P, P×P; 7 P—QKt3 with the better game because of the stronger center Pawns.

III. 3 Kt—QB3: The reason why Black can develop his QB

with impunity in most variations of the Slav is that his center does not have much pressure exerted against it. One idea behind 3 Kt—QB3 is to create this pressure in order to make . . . . B—B4 impossible or inferior. And, in point of fact, after 3 . . . . B—B4; 4 P×P, P×P; 5 Q—Kt3 wins a Pawn at once. Likewise if 3 . . . . Kt—KB3; 4 P—K3, B—B4; 5 P×P, P×P; 6 Q—Kt3!, B—B1! (virtually forced); 7 Kt—B3 followed by Kt—K5, P—KB4, etc. gives White an overwhelming game. And though 3 . . . . Kt—KB3; 4 P—K3, P—K3 is possible, we already know that it would merely transpose into a line which must be considered inferior for Black.

So we come back to the crucial variations, to see whether Black is really forced to transpose into this inadequate defense or not.

First, there is 3 . . . . P×P; 4 P—K4! Now 4 . . . . P—QKt4; 5 P—QR4, P—Kt5; 6 Kt—R2, Kt—B3; 7 P—K5, Kt—Q4 is almost even though Black's K-side may turn out to be weak. 4 . . . . P—K4! (instead of 4 . . . . P—QKt4) leads to great complications after 5 Kt—B3, P×P; 6 B×P!? The consensus of opinion is that Black can accept the sacrifice: 6 . . . . P×Kt; 7 B×Pch, K—K2; 8 Q—Kt3, Kt—B3; 9 B—K3, Q—R4; 10 O—O—O, Q—KKt4!, etc. However, White has a more promising line where he only sacrifices a Pawn: 6 Kt×P (instead of 6 B×P), for if then 6 . . . . B—QB4; 7 B—K3, Kt—Kt5; 8 Kt×P!, Q×Qch; 9 R×Q, Kt×Kt; 10 B×B with the better of it. This variation will undoubtedly receive more attention in the future.

The second crucial variation is the unsolved problem (if indeed a solution is possible) of the theoretical refutation of Winawer's Counter-Gambit: 3 . . . . P—K4. The best try is 4 P×QP, BP×P; 5 P—K4!, P×KP; 6 B—Kt5ch, B—Q2; 7 P×P, B×B; 8 Q×Qch, K×Q; 9 Kt×B, B—Kt5ch. Black's game is inferior, but he may be able to hold it.

IV. 3 P—K3 really has no independent status but is merely a prelude to one of a number of lines. Whatever strength it has lies in transpositions. Thus on 3 . . . . Kt—B3?; 4 Kt—QB3

Black must choose the inferior 4 .... P—K3, since 4 .... B—B4?; 5 P×P, P×P; 6 Q—Kt3 would now lead back to a variation already rejected. However, 3 .... B—B4 and if 4 Kt—B3, P—K3, is sufficient.

ALBIN COUNTER GAMBIT: 1 P—Q4, P—Q4; 2 P—QB4, P—K4

In this gambit Black gives up a Pawn in order to secure freedom for his pieces and a bind on the enemy position by means of a powerful center Pawn. It fails for the usual simple tactical reason that White can return the P at the appropriate moment to secure an overwhelming positional advantage.

The main line begins 3 QP×P, P—Q5. Now the entire play of both sides revolves about this QP: its strength is shown by the fact that 4 P—K3? would be refuted by 4 .... B—Kt5ch; 5 B—Q2, P×P! and if 6 B×B, P×Pch; 7 K—K2, P×Kt (Kt)ch and wins. Instead, however, 4 Kt—KB3 (after 3 QP×P, P—Q5) retains the pressure: the normal continuation is then 4 .... Kt—QB3 (on 4 .... P—QB4; 5 P—K3 would be strong because Black has no check with the B); 5 QKt—Q2, B—K3 (or 5 .... B—KKt5; 6 P—KR3, B×Kt; 7 Kt×B when White already has the advantage of the two Bishops); 6 P—KKt3, B—QB4; 7 B—Kt2, (7 P—QR3 is really a waste of time here because Black will have to play .... P—QR4 sooner or later anyhow), KKt—K2; 8 O—O, P—QR4; 9 P—Kt3, O—O; 10 B—Kt2, Kt—Kt3; 11 Kt—K4, B—R2; 12 P—B5 with a clear advantage. Black can regain his P with 6 .... Q—Q2 (instead of 6 .... B—QB4) the idea of which is to reinforce the QP, but then White can build up adequate pressure against the enemy Q-side: 7 P—QR3, KKt—K2; 8 Q—R4, Kt—Kt3; 9 B—Kt2, B—K2; 10 O—O, O—O; 11 P—QKt4 etc. The idea to remember is that by a K-fianchetto plus quick development White will always get enough counterplay against the enemy Q-side if Black sets out to recover his P.

QUEEN'S GAMBIT ACCEPTED: 1 P—Q4, P—Q4; 2 P—QB4, P×P

Since so many of Black's troubles in the Queen's Gambit can be traced to a cramped game, offhand it looks as though it would be good policy to get free play for the pieces, even at the cost of giving up the center temporarily. This is the leading motif of the Queen's Gambit Accepted: a more comfortable game gets priority, equality in the center will come later. Naturally, White is anxious to play P—K4, as in all variations of the QG. By removing the Pawn barrier Black makes the struggle to see whether White can force a favorable advance or not all the more acute.

White must regain his Pawn, but also prevent the liberating .... P—K4, which would follow, e.g., on 3 P—K3. Consequently 3 Kt—KB3 is most natural. Perhaps it should be mentioned that Black cannot afford to try to hold on to the P: if now 3 .... P—QKt4?; 4 P—QR4, P—QB3; 5 P—K3, B—Kt2; 6 P×P, P×P; 7 P—QKt3 with the better game. Thus Black is compelled to play positionally.

It is to be expected, of course, that the defender will insert .... P—QB4 at an early stage. White will then be faced by the crucial problem of the QGA: whether to play QP×BP, banking on speedier development, or to leave the status quo untouched, allowing the isolated P with .... BP×QP, KP×P.

As a rule, the better development which comes after QP×BP is useless if the Queens are exchanged because it can only be exploited by an energetic attack. E.g., 3 Kt—KB3, Kt—KB3; 4 P—K3, P—K3; 5 B×P, P—B4; 6 O—O, Kt—B3; 7 Kt—B3, B—K2; 8 P×P, Q×Q; 9 R×Q, B×P; 10 P—QR3, K—K2; 11 P—QKt4, B—Kt3; 12 B—Kt2, R—Q1 with equality, despite the fact that Black lost a move with his KB. However, as we shall see, if White had been able to avoid the exchange of Queens he could have retained a marked superiority in view of Black's loss of time.

It follows that for Black there is a constant sparring for position from the very beginning. He must not allow loss of time with his KB, for he is rarely certain of being able to exchange Queens. Thus Black, after the preliminaries, can either crystallize the position in the center (with .... BP×QP) or concentrate on developing his Q-side first, especially since he can get his QB out via QKt2. White meanwhile will hasten to mobilize his K-side.

This leads us to the first normal line: 3 Kt—KB3, Kt—KB3; 4 P—K3, P—K3; 5 B×P, P—B4; 6 O—O, P—QR3 (*Diagram No. 32*).

White is anxious to get his Q out of the way in order to be able to take prompt advantage of a move of the Black KB, so he plays 7 Q—K2, with which he also threatens an eventual

No. 32

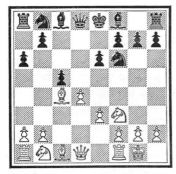

Position after 6 .... P—QR3 in the Queen's Gambit Accepted.

No. 33

Position after 6 .... P×P; 7 P×P in the Queen's Gambit Accepted.

P—K4. In particular, should Black advance on the Q-side, this center thrust would be annoying.

Black continues with his plan: 7 .... Kt—B3; 8 R—Q1 (White is still waiting for Black to commit himself) but now Black can afford to continue on the Q-side for tactical reasons: 8 .... P—QKt4; 9 B—Kt3, P—B5; 10 B—B2, Kt—QKt5!; 11 Kt—B3, Kt×B; 12 Q×Kt, B—Kt2; 13 P—Q5!, Q—B2!; 14 P—K4, P—K4 with equality.

Consequently an improvement is called for. It is found in the rejection of 8 R—Q1 (in the main line), which had not turned out well. Instead, 8 Kt—B3! creates a difficult problem. 8 .... P—QKt4; 9 B—Kt3, P—B5; 10 B—B2, Kt—QKt5; 11 B—Kt1 would not exchange pieces, and P—K4 would be inevitable, yielding White a powerful center. Similarly, 8 .... P—QKt4; 9 B—Kt3, P×P; 11 R—Q1, B—K2; 12 P×P, O—O; 13 P—Q5 is bad for Black, while 8 .... P×P (instead of 8 .... P—QKt4); 9 R—Q1, B—K2; 10 P×P, O—O; 11 P—Q5, P×P; 12 Kt×P, Kt×Kt; 13 B×Kt, Q—B2; 14 B—Kt5 is again inferior. Finally, on 8 .... P—QKt4; 9 B—Kt3, B—K2 White carries out his plan: 10 P×P, B×P; 11 P—K4, P—Kt5; 12 P—K5! with an overwhelming game. In this connection it may be pointed out that when the R is at Q1, the idea of P×P, B×P; P—K4 is much inferior to the present case because Black can reply .... Kt—KKt5, compelling the R to retreat.

Should Black postpone the development of his KB with 9 .... B—Kt2 (instead of 9 .... B—K2 in the last variation above) White may find occasion to make use of another idea which is often quite effective in this status quo set-up: the break with P—Q5. Thus: 10 R—Q1, Q—Kt3; 11 P—Q5!, P×P; 12 P—K4!, P×P; 13 Kt×KP and should win.

The reaction to the above improvement for White is one for Black. Most of his troubles arise from allowing the possibility of P—Q5, which in turn is due to placing the Kt at QB3. So let us try .... QKt—Q2. This would work out satisfactorily, if it were not for a King Pawn advance: 7 Q—K2, P—QKt4; 8 B—Kt3, B—Kt2; 9 P—QR4!, QKt—Q2; 10 P—K4!, P×QP; 11 P×P, Q—Kt3; 12 P—K5 with a powerful attack. A similar sacrificial advance of the KP is also possible in other variations.

All these variations are so strong for the first player that it seems advisable for the defender to exchange .... BP×QP at an early stage (see p. 147).

The proper handling of the line where there is an exchange of QP for BP without any real hope of securing an advantage is worth mentioning. To secure any real winning chances, White must either keep Black badly cramped or get the upper hand on the Q-side or both. He usually tries to do so with P—QR3,

P—QKt4, B—Kt2, etc. (In view of the symmetrical Pawn situation P—K4 would mean little.) Black should counter symmetrically, but break as early as possible, i.e., ... P—QKt5 if he gets the chance, if not, ... P—QR4 after White has played P—QKt4. If the Queens are exchanged, the King should be kept in the center. Finally, the QB5 squares are important strong points for both sides.

The other major Pawn skeleton can also arise from the main line leading to *Diagram No. 32* if Black tries 6 .... P×P instead of 6 .... P—QR3. Thus: 3 Kt—KB3, Kt—KB3; 4 P—K3, P—K3; 5 B×P, P—B4; 6 O—O, P×P; 7 P×P (*Diagram No. 33*).

The isolani determines the further course of battle. Black's long-range plan is to head for the endgame, where his superior Pawn structure will tell. White will concentrate on preparations for an attack in the center and on the K-side. More specifically, Black's strong point is his Q4, where he will endeavor to place a Kt (Kt's are always best in the center). Secondarily, he will try to secure play on the Q-side, chiefly with the R on the QB file and a Kt at QB5. Exchanges will always be welcome. White, on the other hand, will post a Kt at K5, if possible at QB5 too, then build up threats against the Black K, usually with P—KB4—B5. Exchanges should be avoided for him.

From *Diagram No. 33* these ideas work out in a typical instance as follows: 7 .... B—K2; 8 Q—K2, Kt—B3; 9 R—Q1, P—QR3; 10 Kt—B3, Kt—QKt5; 11 B—KKt5, O—O; 12 Kt—K5, QKt—Q4; 13 QR—B1, R—K1; 14 B—Q3, P—R3; 15 B—R4, B—Q2; 16 B—Kt1 with chances for both sides. .... P—QKt4 is none too good for Black: it opens QB5 to the White Kt's.

In view of the indecisive results in the main lines White would be glad to find some improvement.

We may recall that Black's game is fairly easy because he can always play .... P—QB4 at an early stage. Thus if

White could prevent this liberating move he might be able to secure an advantage. That is the idea behind 4 Q—R4ch (after 3 Kt—KB3, Kt—KB3—*Diagram No. 34*).

Of the many possible replies, none has proved wholly adequate in practise, although Black need not loose by any means. It is worth our while to consider them in some detail.

A. 4 .... Q—Q2 is designed to simplify by forcing an early exchange of Queens. In this Black succeeds. While White's plus in terrain remains, even without Queens, Black manages to bleed the position so much that he can reduce his disadvantage to a minimum: 5 Q×BP, Q—B3; 6 Kt—R3! (or 6 P—K3, B—K3!), Q×Q; 7 Kt×Q, P—K3; 8 P—QR3, P—B4; 9 B—B4, Kt—B3; 10 P×P, B×P; 11 P—QKt4, B—K2; 12 P—Kt5, Kt—QKt1; 13 Kt—Q6ch, B×Kt; 14 B×B and now 14 .... Kt—K5; 15 B—B7, P—QR3 gets rid of so much wood that there is little left to start a fire.

B. 4 .... B—Q2 aims to compel an early .... P—QB4 but Black must distort his development to do so: 5 Q×BP, P—K3; 6 Kt—B3, Kt—R3 (this is the hitch); 7 P—K4, P—B4; 8 B—K2, P×P; 9 Kt×P, R—B1; 10 Q—Q3, Kt—QKt5; 11 Q—Kt1 with advantage.

C. 4 .... P—B3 is played with a view to developing the QB early, but the normal strength of such a line is sapped to some extent by the fact that White can force an early P—K4. Thus: 5 Q×BP, B—B4; 6 Kt—B3, QKt—Q2; 7 P—KKt3!, P—K3 (much better is 7 .... Kt—K5 to compel exchanges, which deprives White's center of its value: 8 B—Kt2, Kt×Kt; 9 P×Kt, Kt—Kt3; 10 Q—Kt3, B—K5! etc.); 8 B—Kt2. Now the normal continuation is 8 .... B—Q3, to advance the KP. White can then counter with 9 Kt—KR4, B—Kt3; 10 P—K4, when he still controls more terrain.

D. 4 .... QKt—Q2 is straight development to play .... P—B4 early. After 5 Kt—B3, P—K3; 6 P—K4, P—B4; 7 P×P (7 P—Q5 is inferior because of the neat combination 7 .... P×P; 8 P—K5, P—QKt4), B×P; 8 B×P, when White's game remains slightly freer.

All in all, A is simplest, though it can at best lead to a draw, while D holds most promise for the future.

Q—R4ch may also be tried a move earlier: 3 Q—R4ch (instead of 3 Kt—KB3), when Black would be faced with substantially the same problems.

Two alternatives for Black are worth mentioning. 3 Kt—KB3, P—QR3 (instead of 3 .... Kt—KB3), to bring out the QB. It is a perfectly sound alternative if White plays passively, though Black must prepare .... P—K4 rather than

No. 34

Position after 4 Q—R4ch in the
Queen's Gambit Accepted.

.... P—QB4: 4 P—K3, B—Kt5; 5 B×P, P—K3; 6 P—KR3, B—R4; 7 Kt—B3, Kt—KB3; 8 O—O, Kt—B3!; 9 P—R3, B—Q3, etc. However, 6 Q—Kt3 (instead of 6 P—KR3) may enable White to exploit Black's weakened Q-side.

Finally, 3 .... P—QB4 (after 3 Kt—KB3) has never been refuted: if 4 P—Q5, P—K3; 5 P—K4, P×P; 6 P×P, Kt—KB3; 7 B×P, B—Q3 Black's game is perfectly solid. Here Black gets rid of the problem of the center (White's QP is none too strong) but the development of the QB still remains.

QUEEN PAWN GAME WITH 1 P—Q4, P—Q4 WHERE WHITE DOES NOT PLAY THE QUEEN'S GAMBIT

We have already pointed out that 2 P—QB4 is by far the strongest continuation for White. In fact, the difference between it and other moves is so great that it may justifiably be said that when White omits the advance of the QBP there is no real theoretical problem because Black can equalize in a variety of ways. Still, there are many difficult questions that may come up, chiefly in relatively unexplored regions. Besides, even in theoretically even positions one must be familiar with the ideas for both sides in order to continue properly.

White, then, resorts to a number of unusual lines. For him principles will vary quite widely. Black, however, has quite an easy time of it in the beginning. For .... P—QB4 is almost always possible, and always good. It will be recalled that in the QGD Black had to fight to get this move in, whereas here it is handed to him on a silver platter. That explains the early theoretical equality.

One point for White should not be overlooked: there is no law forbidding P—QB4: he merely chooses not to play it. Consequently, if opportunity knocks, he may be able to advance his QBP and transpose into a favorable line of the QG or QP opening. This possibility must always be borne in mind by Black.

We can further consider, by way of introduction to the openings themselves, that when Black plays .... P—QB4, while White does not (which is nearly always the case in this division) we have in effect a Queen's Gambit with colors reversed where White is a move to the good compared with the normal line. Most of the time this fact makes all the difference in the world; at other times it is of no moment. Incidentally, this motif of playing openings with colors reversed is quite common in modern chess.

It would be impossible to consider all the tortuous and irregular lines which White might conceivably excogitate. Fortunately, it is also unnecessary. General principles are sufficient to indicate Black's plan of campaign against a wholly unexpected debut: after .... P—QB4, development, preparation of .... P—K4. Thus we need consider only those lines where White has some definite idea in mind.

COLLE SYSTEM: 1 P—Q4, P—Q4; 2 Kt—KB3, Kt—KB3; 3 P—K3,
               P—B4; 4 P—B3

This is the most promising try for White in the present section. White is in effect playing a Slav Defense with colors reversed and with a move to the good. Though the variation is not one of the best for Black in the Slav (see page 137) the extra move gives it a punch which is otherwise absent.

The first and most obvious counter for Black is to develop quickly and prepare for .... P—K4 early. Then Black's main problem is whether to post his QKt at QB3 or at Q2. It so happens that .... QB3, which looks more natural, is in reality inferior. Thus: 4 .... P—K3; 5 QKt—Q2, Kt—B3; 6 B—Q3, B—Q3; 7 O—O, O—O; 8 P×P! (essential to avoid an isolated P), B×P; 9 P—K4, P—K4; 10 P×P, Q×P; 11 Q—K2, B—KKt5; 12 Kt—K4 and White stands much better. The possibilities of a K-side attack and superior development have been White's trump cards. With exact play, however, Black can make his opponent's plus virtually insignificant: 9 .... Q—B2 (above, instead of 9 .... P—K4); 10 Q—K2, B—Q3; 11 R—K1, Kt—KKt5!; 12 P—KR3, KKt—K4; 13 Kt×Kt, Kt×Kt; 14 P×P, P×P; 15 Kt—B3, Kt×B; 16 Q×Kt, Q—B5; 17 R—Q1, Q×Q; 18 R×Q, R—Q1, etc.

Nevertheless, in the normal line where both sides adhere to general principles most strictly White gets the better of it. Reason?—the extra move. E.g., it may have been noted that the break with P—K4, which Black must work so hard for in the normal QGD, is easy here for White (whose role corresponds to that of the defender in the QGD). One great strength of the Colle System is that many natural moves work out badly for Black.

Analysis of the above variation reveals that the center thrust is strong for White only because he can precede it with QP× BP, avoiding an isolated Pawn. Consequently, ... QKt—Q2, to recapture with the Kt and thereby prevent the execution of the plan, comes to mind. It does in point of fact compel White to revise his system somewhat, but Black is still subjected to a

strong attack: 4 .... P—K3; 5 QKt—Q2, QKt—Q2; 6 B—Q3,
B—Q3; 7 O—O, O—O; 8 R—K1 (instead 8 P—K4, BP×P;
9 BP×P, P×P; 10 Kt×P, Kt×Kt; 11 B×Kt, Q—Kt3 merely
saddles White with an isolated P), Q—B2 (8 .... P—K4; 9
P—K4! will be in White's favor); 9 P—K4, BP×P; 10 BP×P,
P×P; 11 Kt×P, Kt×Kt; 12 R×Kt, R—K1; 13 R—R4! with
excellent attacking chances. Another instance of a typical
assault is 8 .... R—K1 (in the previous line, instead of 8 ....
Q—B2); 9 P—K4, QP×P; 10 Kt×P, Kt×Kt; 11 B×Kt,
P×P?; 12 B×Pch!, K×B; 13 Kt—Kt5ch, K—Kt3; 14 P—
KR4, R—R1; 15 R×Pch!! and wins. Any early thrust in the
center by Black with .... P—K4 would be met by P—K4,
when the liquidation of Pawns would be in White's favor because of his better development.

It is instructive to examine why the Colle System can offer
such attacking possibilities while its analogue in the Slav Defense is at best mediocre. Of course it is the "extra move" but
what are the magic qualities which inhere in one such lowly
move? If we go back to the other line, we find that an early
P—K4 by White (thus the plan which Black follows here)
merely frees the defender's game and that the best is the slow
line with .... P—QKt3. Here, however, the slow line would
be inferior because of the break with P—K4 (which the defender does not have in the Slav at such an early date). In
other words, the extra move deprives Black of what would
otherwise be the best line and adds force to White's attack.

The significant point is that White's "secret weapon" is an
attack against the Black K position. It follows that if the defender safeguards that corner properly he will have nothing to
fear. The most tenable type of K position (against a relatively
poorly developed opponent) is that with the K fianchetto.
Thus the defense with .... P—KKt3 suggests itself and does
indeed work out quite well: 4 .... P—KKt3 (instead of 4 ....
P—K3); 5 QKt—Q2, QKt—Q2; 6 B—Q3, B—Kt2; 7 O—O,
O—O and now 8 P—QKt4 is the only way for White to
equalize. On 8 P—K4, e.g., there would follow 8 .... QP×P;

9 Kt×P, P×P; 10 Kt×P, Kt—K4; 11 Kt×Ktch, B×Kt; 12 B—K2, B—Q2 with the better of it. 8 P—QKt4 abandons the break in the center and concentrates on the Q-side, after which neither side can hope to achieve much. Black maneuvers to get a Kt to QB5 as soon as possible. This line is one of the reasons why the Colle System is so seldom seen in master chess. An analogue to it in the QGD is the Catalan Opening, where the strongest defense is .... P—QB4, whereas here White has played only P—QB3.

Another idea for Black is to try for .... P—K4 without a preliminary .... P—K3. This is sound enough strategically, but fails for tactical reasons: 4 .... QKt—Q2 (instead of 4 .... P—K3); 5 QKt—Q2, Q—B2; 6 Q—R4!, P—KKt3; 7 P—B4!, B—Kt2; 8 BP×P, Kt×P; 9 P—K4, Kt—Kt3; 10 Q—B2 with the better chances.

A simple way to secure immediate complete equality when White intends to play the Colle System is the early development of the Black QB: 1 P—Q4, P—Q4; 2 Kt—KB3, Kt—KB3; 3 P—K3, and now either 3 .... B—B4 or 3 .... B—Kt5. .... P—QB4 can come in later, or perhaps, after Black is completely developed, ... P—K4 may be superior. The weakening of the Q-side is of no consequence here because the absence of open files make it impossible for White to do anything and because Black's center is solid. A typical line is 3 .... B—B4; 4 B—Q3, P—K3; 5 B×B, P×B; 6 Q—Q3, Q—B1; 7 P—QKt3, Kt—R3; 8 O—O, B—K2; 9 P—B4, O—O; 10 Kt—B3, P—B3; 11 B—Kt2, Kt—K5 with an easy game.

Turning to *Diagram No. 35*, we find some other ideas for White. 4 QKt—Q2 aims to play the QGA in reverse. And, to be sure, if he is permitted to carry out his plan he will get the better of it. E.g., 4 .... QKt—Q2; 5 P—QR3, P—K3; 6 P×P, B×P; 7 P—QKt4, B—K2; 8 B—Kt2, O—O; 9 P—B4, P—QKt3; 10 B—Q3 and White's game is freer. (Compare page 137 in the Slav Defense.) When faced by such a problem, a player must consider the various possible transpositions to solve it correctly. 4 .... P×P; 5 P×P, P—K3 would transpose into a form of the Caro-Kann (with the right colors!) where Black is badly off because he cannot develop his QB properly and because White can sink a Kt at K5. However, there is one significant improvement possible: 4 .... P×P; 5 P×P, P—KKt3! instead of 5 .... P—K3. Then the QB can develop and we have a variation of the Caro-Kann which is quite all right for Black. Thus this type of analysis has already given us one equalizing line without even examining the merits and demerits of the specific position. A striking illus-

No. 35

Position after 3 .... P—B4 in the
Queen Pawn Game.

tration of the importance of transpositions in contemporary chess!

4 .... QKt—Q2; 5 P—QR3, Q—B2; 6 P—B4 would be like the analogous line in the Colle; it is certainly not bad on general principles, but it does not work out well: 6 .... P—KKt3; 7 P×QP, Kt×P; 8 Q—Kt3, KKt—Kt3; 9 P—QR4, etc.

Another line which general principles and transposition suggest is 4 .... QKt—Q2 (White was threatening to take the P); 5 P—QR3, P—KKt3. After 6 P×P, Kt×P; 7 P—QKt4, QKt—Q2; 8 B—Kt2, B—Kt2, the two B's will soon neutralize one another.

Again coming back to *Diagram No. 35*, 4 P—QKt3 is designed to build up an attack by settling a Kt at K5, a motif which is similar to Nimzovitch's attack (see page 227). This is also the analogue of the fianchetto defense for Black, which is none too good because it does not have a sufficiently direct influence on the center. By developing normally, Black can secure equality fairly easily; it should be noted that he has a ready target on White's Q-side: 4 .... P—K3; 5 B—Kt2, Kt—B3; 6 B—Q3, B—Q3; 7 O—O, O—O; 8 QKt—Q2, Q—K2; 9 Kt—K5, P×P; 10 P×P, B—R6 with a good game.

After 1 P—Q4, P—Q4; 2 Kt—KB3, Kt—KB3 moves other than those already mentioned have virtually nothing to offer but variety.

3 B—B4, P—B4; 4 P—K3, Kt—B3; 5 P—B3 is a variation of the Slav with colors reversed. Either 5 .... P—K3, to continue with .... B—Q3, or 5 .... B—Kt5, or 5 .... Q—Kt3, with normal continuations in each case, is quite sufficient. White's set-up lacks punch.

On 3 B—Kt5, P—K3 is probably best, when White can transpose into a QGD. If he does not, the natural line with .... P—QB4, ... QKt—Q2, ... P—K3, ... B—Q3, ... Q—B2, eventually .... P—K4 will equalize at least. The QB should be fianchettoed for Black. This line is strong for White if he can post his Kt at K5, but Black can normally prevent him from doing so. An example of the type of attack he can build up is 3 B—Kt5, P—K3; 4 P—K3, P—B4; 5 P—B3, B—K2 (he can also get out of the pin with .... QKt—Q2 and .... Q—Kt3); 6 B—Q3, Kt—B3 (6 .... QKt—Q2 is preferable); 7 QKt—Q2, P—KR3; 8 B—R4, O—O; 9 O—O, P—QKt3 (9 .... Q—B2 was much better); 10 Kt—K5!, Kt×Kt (and here 10 .... B—Kt2; 11 P—KB4 was preferable); 11 P×Kt, Kt—Q2; 12 B—Kt3, B—R5; 13 B×B, Q×B; 14 P—KB4, etc.

3 P—KKt3 is interesting as the first historical instance of the now popular Catalan Opening, though it has no force without P—QB4. Normal development by Black is quite adequate.

Variants for Black are possible, but rarely good. On 1 P—

Q4, P—Q4; 2 Kt—KB3, P—QB4 is tempting, but 3 P—B4!
forces Black into inferior lines: 3 .... P—K3 is the Tarrasch
Defense to the QGD, 3 .... BP×P; 4 P×P, Q×P; 5 Kt—B3
loses valuable time.

A logical but tactically insufficient idea is 2 Kt—QB3 after
1 P—Q4, P—Q4. It is designed to compel an early P—K4, but
suffers from the obvious drawback of leaving Black a free hand
to develop. The normal 2 .... Kt—KB3; 3 B—Kt5, B—B4 is
quite good for the defender. 4 P—K3, P—B3, followed by an
eventual .... Q—Kt3 should even give Black the upper hand.
4 P—B3, which is more consistent with the spirit of the opening, should be met by 4 .... P—B3, when White must give up
his powerful QB to force P—K4, which leaves his Pawns too
fragile. The idea of playing the Q to QKt3 for Black is powerful in all lines.

The *Stonewall Variation* can be a steamroller if it is not met
properly. The idea is to hold the center with Pawns at QB3,
Q4, K3, KB4, plant a Kt at K5, shift the heavy pieces to the
K-side and begin a murderous assault there. White's ideal
position could arise as follows: 1 P—Q4, P—Q4; 2 P—K3, Kt—
KB3; 3 B—Q3, P—B4; 4 P—QB3, Kt—B3; 5 P—KB4, P—
K3; 6 Kt—B3, B—Q3; 7 O—O, O—O; 8 Kt—K5, Q—B2; 9
Kt—Q2, R—K1; 10 P—KKt4 with a crushing attack.

There are three things wrong with Black's play above: he
voluntarily shut in his QB, he allowed Kt—K5 without further
ado, and he made no effort to occupy his K5 with his own Kt.
He cannot really prevent Kt—K5 by White permanently but
he can take the poison out of its fangs by correcting the other
two errors. Thus the normal defensive line would be 1 P—Q4,
P—Q4; 2 P—K3, Kt—KB3; 3 B—Q3, P—B4; 4 P—QB3,
Kt—B3; 5 P—KB4, B—Kt5; 6 Kt—B3, P—K3; 7 QKt—Q2,
B—Q3; 8 P—KR3, B—R4; 9 P—QKt3, P×P; 10 BP×P, R—
QB1 and Black has no great troubles any more.

An alternate defensive plan is to try to exchange the White
KB, without which White's attack is virtually meaningless.
Thus: 2 P—K3, Kt—KB3; 3 B—Q3, Kt—QB3, threatening

both .... P—K4 and .... Kt—QKt5, either one of which is sufficient to equalize. E.g., 4 P—KB4, Kt—QKt5; 5 Kt—KB3, Kt×Bch; 6 P×Kt, P—KKt3; 7 Kt—B3, B—Kt2; 8 O—O, O—O etc. However, this line is not always available because White may choose 3 P—KB4 in preference to 3 B—Q3. The main general defense which is sufficient for equality is the development of the QB.

Chapter V

QUEEN PAWN OPENINGS
PART II

DEFENSES WHERE BLACK DOES NOT
PLAY .... P—Q4

The openings to be treated in this chapter are undoubtedly by far the most difficult to understand. Even masters have been known to make serious positional errors in them. One reason is that the ideas are somewhat more complicated than in other debuts; another is that transpositions are almost always vital. Then too, subtle traps endow the order of moves with an importance which is absent elsewhere. Nonetheless, these openings can be grasped and mastered by a systematic application of the method which we have followed up to now.

This chapter comprises all regular openings where White begins with 1 P—Q4, but Black does not reply 1 .... P—Q4 early (he may do so at a later stage). We already know that after 1 P—Q4, White wishes to continue with P—K4 to secure the better Pawn center. Any reasonable Black defense must therefore block the advance of the White KP or have something in mind to nullify the effects of such an advance when it occurs.

Though the matter has already been touched upon in Alekhine's Defense and on other occasions, it is essential to dispel a confusion about the center which has affected many players.

In many Hypermodern openings we find that Black permits, often encourages, White to advance his Pawns in the center and form what appears to be a powerful phalanx there. Then Black deftly attacks and White's structure collapses like a house of cards. This has led to the idea that several Pawns in the center are bound to be weak and that it is better to control the center from the sides. Consequently, it is sometimes said, Black's idea in these openings is to deliberately induce White to form a strong Pawn center.

Nothing could be further from the truth. Other things being equal, a Pawn in the center is a decided advantage. It is a disadvantage only when it cannot be held there.

Thus the crucial question is: Are other things equal? Or Black may ask: If I allow him to set up a powerful center phalanx can I then shatter that structure or must I further submit passively?

In other words, in all these openings, we find two paramount questions for Black and two for White:

1. Can a strong Pawn center be set up for White? (normally Pawns at QB4, Q4, K4)

2. If it can, can it be maintained?

We can push it one step further back by recalling that the strength of a Pawn center lies in the fact that it cramps the enemy's game. Then the one fundamental question is: Can Black, once he has begun by not placing a Pawn in the center, manage to free himself all the same?

The answers to these and the subsidiary questions they involve determine the theoretical status of virtually all the openings in this chapter.

This line of reasoning helps us to see why in practise only one move stands out as of major theoretical value: 1 .... Kt—KB3, and that because it does not merely develop a piece normally, but also prevents the march of the enemy KP. There are two other replies which are regular and independent: 1 .... P—QB4 (The Benoni Counter Gambit) and 1 .... P—KB4 (The Dutch Defense). Besides, there are four moves which have some independent features, but will normally transpose into a more standard line: 1 .... P—K3, 1 .... P—QB3, 1 .... P—Q3 and 1 .... Kt—QB3. Everything else is irregular because Black must make some effort to block White's immediate P—K4.

THE INDIAN DEFENSES: 1 P—Q4, Kt—KB3

The name is derived from the fact that the game played in India does not have the initial double Pawn move, so that the slower type of development which is so characteristic of this group is seen there much more often.

All these defenses have three important features in common:

1. The struggle centers about whether White can manage to play P—K4 or not.

2. If Black allows P—K4, he must secure compensation in one of three ways: a) an effective attack on the White Pawn center with his pieces; b) a break with .... P—KB4; c) a solidification of the Pawn structure which will make White's temporary control of more terrain meaningless.

3. A delayed .... P—Q4 by Black is often most effective.

We have already mentioned the fact that transpositions are of so much more moment here than in the KP. We shall point out the most significant transpositions as we come to them. To help the reader grasp the close interrelationship of all these defenses we have set up a genealogical diagram (see page 161).

A. THE NIMZOINDIAN-Q-INDIAN COMPLEX: 1 P—Q4, Kt—KB3; 2 P—QB4, P—K3

In this group of openings Black's main thought is prevention rather than cure: P—K4 will not be allowed.

One significant psychological feature should not be overlooked: Black often adopts the above sequence of moves in order to transpose into an easier line of the QGD. For many masters, reluctant to permit the Nimzoindian Defense, play out the KKt first, when 3 .... P—Q4 brings about a variation of the QGD which does not have as much of a sting as the normal lines (page 130).

It would be useless to catalogue all the possible kinds of Pawn positions that may come up. Six, however, are so fundamental that they deserve a little more attention.

36A occurs when Black exchanges his KB for White's QKt.

FAMILY TREE OF THE INDIAN DEFENSES

1 P—Q4, Kt—KB3
2 P—QB4:

A. Nimzoindian-Q-Indian Complex

2 ... P—K3

1. 3 Kt—QB3, B—Kt5—Nimzoindian
2. 3 Kt—KB3
   a. 3 ...: P—QKt3—Queen's Indian
   b. 3 ...: B—Kt5ch—Bogoljuboff Variation
   c. 3 ...: P—B4; 4 P—Q5, P—QKt4—Blumenfeld Counter-Gambit
3. 3 Kt—QB3, P—Q4 or 3 Kt—KB3, P—Q4 or 3 P—K3, P—Q4 transpose into the QGD.

B. K-Indian-Gruenfeld Complex

2 ... P—KKt3

1. 3 Kt—QB3, B—Kt2; 4 P—K4 or 3 Kt—KB3, P—Q3—K—Indian (possibly double fianchetto)
2. 3 Kt—QB3, P—Q4—Gruenfeld
3. 3 Kt—KB3, P—Q4—K—Indian with delayed .... P—Q4
4. 3 Kt—KB3, P—KKt3; 4 P—KKt3 transposes into lines analogous to Reti's Opening. 3 Kt—KB3, P—QB3; 4 Kt—B3, P—Q4 transposes into a line which may also come from the Slav Defense. Cannot transpose into the QGD.

C. Old Indian

2 ... P—Q3

1. 3 Kt—QB3, P—K4—Old Indian or Tchigorin
2. 3 Kt—QB3, P—KKt3; 4 P—K4—K—Indian (Only transpositions possible that into double fianchetto or a variation of the Ruy Lopez)

D. Unusual Alternatives

A. 2 ....: P—K4—Budapest Defense (may transpose into French Defense)

B. Irregular

White's Pawn position is technically inferior, but he usually has control of more terrain, especially if he can play P—K4 and P—KB4 (or P—KB3). It is essential for him not to weaken his Pawns further by P—Q5 or QP×KP, unless he has no choice in the matter. On the other hand, Black should not play .... P—Q4 because that would give White an opportunity to dissolve his doubled Pawns. White's play lies on the K-side, where he should try to build up an attack, Black's on the Q-side where he should hit at the exposed White Pawns. This Pawn position is normally slightly favorable for Black, but White's attacking possibilities must not be underestimated.

36B may come out of 36A if Black advances .... P—Q4 and White captures. Here Black's counter-attack on the Q-side is much slower because he has no tangible objective. White, on the contrary, can push up in the center quickly and effectively with P—B3 and P—K4, when his attack assumes menacing proportions very quickly. Black should not let White's steamroller get started. Normally favorable for White.

36C is due to passive play on Black's part. White has command of the center and can exploit it in a variety of ways. Usually the most effective is to play on the Q-side, though if he has fianchettoed his KB, a K-side attack may also be in order. Note that if Black takes .... KP×QP, we have a familiar type of positional advantage for White: P at K4 vs. P at Q3. (Compare page 21 in the Ruy Lopez.) The break with .... P—KB4 for Black would expose his center P's too much. His best plan is .... P—QB3, ... Q—B2, if possible .... QKt—Q2—KB1—K3—KB5 or Q5. White must never play QP×KP: that would dissipate his entire advantage. Similarly, P—Q5 should be avoided unless it leads to a clear superiority. 36C is always favorable for White.

36D can come out of 36C if White plays P—Q5. The solidification of the center crystallizes the plans for both sides. White will advance on the Q-wing with P—QKt4 and an eventual P—QB5 (after due preparation). Black will break on the K-wing with .... P—KB4. Somewhat favorable for

PAWN POSITIONS IN THE NIMZOINDIAN-Q-INDIAN COMPLEX

No. 36A

Slightly favorable for Black.

No. 36B

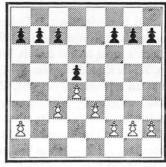

Normally favorable for White.

No. 36C

Always favorable for White.

No. 36D

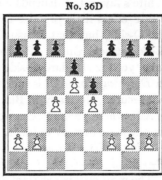
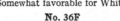

Somewhat favorable for White.

No. 36E

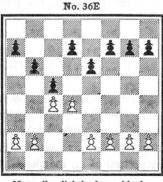

Normally slightly favorable for White; initiative is important.

No. 36F

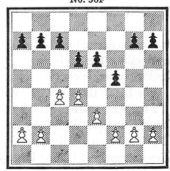

Normally favorable for Black.

White, but depends to a certain extent on who has the initiative.

36E is obviously a Q-Indian set-up. The struggle for the center is still unresolved. White's play lies along the Q-file, Black's must be cut to suit White's. If he has a chance to do so, White should advance P—Q5; the gain in terrain then yields him an advantage. If not, P×P is weak, especially in conjunction with P—K4? because he thereby yields his square Q4 to Black. Should White threaten P—Q5, Black will reply . . . . P×P, when the evaluation of the resultant position depends on whether . . . . P—Q4 can be forced or not. If it can, the game is even, if not White has the better of it. Normally somewhat in White's favor, but depends entirely on who has the initiative.

36F offers little promise for White. He has some play on the Q-side, but that is usually more than offset by Black's K-side attack. On . . . . P—K4, P×P? would be a definite mistake, yet the standard Q-side attack with P—Q5, P—QB5 (as in *Diagram No. 36D*) is much less effective because the QP is not secure. Normally in Black's favor.

After these preliminaries we can turn to the variations with an adequate armory of ideas.

Nimzoindian Defense: 1 P—Q4, Kt—KB3; 2 P—QB4, P—K3; 3 Kt—QB3, B—Kt5.

The most striking characteristic of this defense is that it is a fighting line: it does not merely prevent P—K4, but it also opens counter-attacking possibilities.

White's continuation is dictated by the need for development, the desire to get P—K4 in and, in many cases, the idea of compelling the exchange of the Black KB for White's QKt under favorable circumstances.

For Black there are four main ideas interwoven in his play:

First, the counter-attack with . . . . P—QB4. This usually breaks up the White center but the reply QP×BP leaves Black's Pawn position weak because of the backward QP. Consequently it is now largely discredited as an independent line, though it retains its value in conjunction with .... P—QKt3, sometimes with .... P—Q4.

Second, the counter-attack with .... P—Q4. This and the next are Black's major weapons nowadays. The idea is clear enough: compel an early collapse of the White center. Its tactical execution is far more complicated.

Third, counterplay with .... P—Q3 and .... P—K4. In the older lines, where Black developed his QKt at Q2, this system gave him much too cramped a game. The improvement of playing the QKt out to QB3 early has considerably enhanced the value of the whole counter-action.

Fourth, counterplay with .... B×Ktch and an attack on the Q-side against White's P at QB4. Usually Black does not adopt this line unless he can gain a tempo (normally when White plays P—QR3) though it has its merits when tried independently too.

A fifth idea which occurs in a few variations is that of an attack against the White K-side. Normally, such a plan can be successful only if White has weakened his K-position seriously. 36F is the type of Pawn position where it is most promising.

Unlike other branches of the QP game, the continuations for White on his 4th move here (from *Diagram No. 37*) do not fall into any regular pattern. Any two will be found to have some elements in common and some elements that differ.

The major lines are based on varying specific ideas. They are: a) 4 Q—B2 and 4 Q—Kt3—to compel the exchange of Black's KB for White's Kt; b) 4 P—QR3—to solidify the center and build up a K-side attack; c) 4 P—K3—quick development with overtones of a K-side attack; d) 4 Kt—B3—straight development. All these lines are playable, though 4 Q—B2 and 4 P—K3 are considered best.

I. 4 Q—B2 has retained its popularity longest. Its main idea, as mentioned above, is to defend the Kt in order to be able to compel the exchange of the Black KB for the White QKt

without weakening the White Q-side Pawns. Thus White will
secure the two Bishops, an advantage which is relatively slight
yet notoriously persistent. It is chiefly for this reason that
masters have come back to it again and again.

It might be thought that one of the main ideas behind 4 Q—
B2 is the preparation of P—K4. Yet, despite the obvious fact
that 4 Q—B2 does make P—K4 possible, it would be a mistake
to think that that is one of its main objectives. For P—K4 at
present could leave White's center dangerously weak in view of
his lack of development. E.g., if 4 .... O—O; 5 P—K4, P—
B4!; 6 P—Q5? (6 P—QR3 is better, but leads only to equality),
B×Ktch; 7 P×B, P×P; 8 KP×P, R—K1ch and Black
has all the play. Of course, all this does not mean that P—K4
may not be good at some future date. If he wishes to set up a
solid center White must make sure that it will be permanent:
that is always the criterion.

In reply to 4 Q—B2, Black has two major continuations:
4 .... P—Q4 and 4 .... Kt—B3. Other lines either lose too
much time or saddle him with a permanent weakness. E.g., on
4 .... B×Ktch White can answer either 5 Q×B, with the advantage of the two B's—thus attaining one of his major objectives at no cost—or 5 P×B, followed by P—K4, B—Q3,
Kt—K2, with a strong attack. Likewise, on 4 .... P—B4,
after 5 P×P Black will be saddled with a backward P on an
open file (on 5 .... B×P; 6 Kt—B3, P—Q4; 7 B—Kt5! leads
to complications which are dubious for Black). E.g., 5 ....
Kt—B3; 6 Kt—B3, B×P; 7 B—Kt5, P—QKt3; 8 P—K3,
B—Kt2; 9 B—K2, B—K2; 10 O—O, R—QB1; 11 QR—Q1,
etc. The position is analogous to that in the Sicilian Defense
where Black allows P—QB4.

We come then to the first main line: 4 Q—B2, P—Q4 (from
Diagram No. 37). After 5 P—QR3 the position becomes
extremely complicated. The most recent analysis indicates
that White can get an advantage after 5 .... B×Ktch; 6
Q×B, Kt—K5; 7 Q—B2, P—QB4; 8 QP×P, Kt—QB3!; 9
P×P! (rather than 9 P—K3, Q—R4ch; 10 B—Q2, Kt×B with
equality), P×P; 10 Kt—B3, B—B4; 11 P—QKt4. Here 11

POSITIONS IN THE NIMZOINDIAN DEFENSE

No. 37

Nimzoindian Defense.

No. 38A

Position after 5 .... Q×P in the
4 Q—B2 Line.

No. 38B

Position after 8 P—QKt4 in the
Milner-Barry Variation.

No. 38C

Position after 7 B—Q2 in the 4 Q—
Kt3 Line.

No. 38D

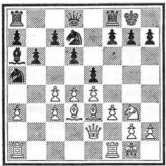

No. 38E

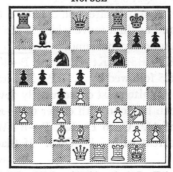

Ideal Positions for White in the Saemisch (4 P—QR3) and Rubinstein (4 P—K3)
Lines.

.... O—O; 12 B—Kt2, B—Kt3; 13 P—K3 is good for White, but Black can try 11 .... P—Q5; 12 Q—B4, Q—B3.

Straight development with 5 P—K3 or 5 Kt—B3 would allow .... P—B4, when Black would equalize without any trouble—always the case in the QP openings when Black can play both .... P—Q4 and .... P—QB4 with impunity. One interesting point here is that after 5 P—K3, P—B4 we have a line which can also arise from the Ragosin Variation of the QGD (page 124).

Thus there remains only 5 P×P.

We can see that if Black replies 5 .... P×P he will have the same inherently weak Pawn structure as in the Exchange Variation of the QGD (*Diagram No. 23, page 116*). Black must therefore have some reason to assume that he can secure counterplay which he does not have in the exchange line. Since his QB is free to develop early, that is one form of compensation. Another is his attack on the Q-side. Together they improve his game, but do not yield full equality. 6 B—Kt5 or even 6 P—K3 followed by normal development (with P—QR3 inserted at an appropriate point) give White somewhat the better of it.

Consequently Black's best is surely 5 .... Q×P (5 .... Kt×P has rarely been tried, may be worth some investigation).

Our main line thus far, from *Diagram No. 37*, runs 4 Q—B2, P—Q4; 5 P×P, Q×P.

Again White would like to try his main threat 6 P—QR3 and again a move which is strategically sound turns out to be tactically unsound. Thus: 6 P—QR3, B×Ktch; 7 Q×B, Kt—B3!; 8 Kt—B3 (or 8 P—K3, P—K4 with equality) Kt—K5 followed by .... P—K4, freeing Black's game completely.

White must consequently develop and defend his KP. That can be done with either 6 P—K3 or 6 Kt—B3 (*Diagram No. 38A*). On 6 P—K3, P—B4 White can finally carry out his threat with 7 P—QR3. If Black plays carelessly, White will be able to set up two Pawns at QB4 and Q4 and secure strong attacking chances. E.g., 7 P—QR3, B×Ktch; 8 P×B, QKt—Q2; 9 Kt—B3, P—QKt3; 10 P—B4, Q—Q3; 11 B—-Kt2, B—Kt2; 12 B—K2, R—QB1; 13 O—O, B—K5; 14 Q—B3, O—O; 15 QR—Q1, KR—Q1; 16 P—Q5!, etc. But an exchange of BP for QP at an early stage frees Black's game and thereby demolishes White's hopes of an attack. Thus: 6 P—K3, P—B4; 7 P—QR3, B×Ktch; 8 P×B, O—O; 9 Kt—B3, P×P!; 10 BP×P, P—QKt3; 11 B—B4, Q—B3 with easy equality. Another illustration of the familiar principle that a strong Pawn center is useless if the opponent is well developed.

The alternative 6 Kt—B3 (*Diagram No. 38A*) is designed to avoid the weakening of the Pawn position and secure the two B's "pure." In this White succeeds, but Black can develop so easily that his slight disadvantage fades off into nothingness. 6 Kt—B3, P—B4; 7 B—Q2, B×Kt; 8 B×B (8 P×B transposes into the other line), P×P; 9 Kt×P, P—K4; 10 Kt—B3, Kt—B3; 11 R—Q1, Q—B4 etc.—Black has no particular difficulties, although the two B's may retain their force for a long time to come.

The salient features of the above lines are that White tries to get an advantage by setting up a strong Pawn center and securing the two B's, while Black equalizes by a break in the center (.... P—QB4, also .... P—K4 whenever possible) and exchanges.

In the other main line in reply to 4 Q—B2, Kt—B3 (the Zurich or Milner-Barry Variation) Black takes a different tack. Here he will evidently not try .... P—Q4, since his QKt would then be out of place: his projected Pawn set-up will rather begin .... P—Q3 and .... P—K4, his goal will be a position like 36F, with a Pawn at K4. It is, however, essential for him to prevent White from playing P—K4 early, or at any rate to have an adequate counter ready, for if he does not, White's anchor at Q5 will be secured and he can pursue his Q-side counterplay.

Thus the ideas and plans for both sides shape up as follows: White wishes to secure the two B's, advance on the Q-side, will be content to hold in the center. Black is anxious to advance in the center, exploit his somewhat superior development (White will have to lose time to get the two B's) and build up an attack against the K-side.

It should be added that the entire variation is relatively new, but that practise has favored Black to a certain extent.

After 4 .... Kt—B3; 5 Kt—B3 is somewhat better than 5 P—K3, for on the latter move 5 .... P—K4 may be played at once. This brings up another significant idea here: White's first objective is to force Black to postpone .... P—K4 as long as possible. Similarly, we shall see later how Black may also try to prevent or postpone the execution of White's plan.

Thus far the second main line runs 4 Q—B2, Kt—B3; 5 Kt—B3. Now 5 .... P—Q3, preparing .... P—K4. 6 P—QR3, B×Ktch; 7 Q×B, O—O; 8 P—QKt4 (*Diagram No. 38B*) gives us one crucial position. White has carried out the first part of his plan (secured a favorable position for the further advance on the Q-side) but at a considerable cost in development. While the sacrifice 8 .... P—K4 is now unsound (9 P×P, Kt—K5; 10 Q—Kt2, P×P; 11 Kt×P, Kt×Kt; 12 Q×Kt, R—K1; 13 Q—Kt2!) simple development with 8 .... R—K1, threatening .... P—K4, compels White to modify his scheme. For 9 P—Kt5, Kt—Kt1; 10 P—Kt3, P—QR3! accentuates Black's development too much. Consequently the simple 9 P—K3 (after 9 .... R—K1) is necessary, when 9 .... P—K4; 10 P×P, (10 P—Q5 is not so good because the Pawn structure cannot be maintained), P×P; 11 B—K2 leaves White with a minimal plus which does not mean much.

It is instructive—and important—to see what would happen if either side should play badly. If Black plays too passively and allows White to set up a strong Pawn phalanx with Pawns at QR3, QKt4, QB4, Q5, K4, KB2, KKt3, KR2, the thrust P—B5 will eventually disrupt his position. To obviate this possibility he must not let White's "anchor"—the Pawn at Q5—be fortified by a Pawn at K4. Thus .... P—KB4 must be played early if possible, while if White does manage to get P—K4 in, he must break with .... P—KB4. (A fuller discussion of the proper handling of this type of P position will be found under the K-Indian Defense, page 189.) E.g., 4 Q—B2, Kt—B3; 5 Kt—B3, P—Q3; 6 B—Q2, B×Kt; 7 B×B, P—QKt3?; 8 P—K4, B—Kt2; 9 P—KKt3, Q—K2; 10 B—Kt2, P—K4; 11 P—Q5, Kt—QKt1; 12 P—QKt4, O—O; 13 O—O, Kt—K1; 14 Kt—Q2, P—Kt3; 15 P—B4! and White has all the play.

On the other hand, White would also be in a bad way if Black could carry out his plan. E.g., 4 Q—B2, Kt—B3; 5 Kt—B3, P—Q3; 6 P—QR3, B×Ktch; 7 Q×B, P—QR4; 8 P—KKt3 (8 B—Kt5 is safer), Kt—K5; 9 Q—B2, P—B4; 10 B—Kt2, O—O; 11 O—O, P—K4; 12 B—K3, Q—K2; 13 P×P, P×P; 14 Kt—Q2, Kt—B3; 15 Kt—Kt3?, P—R5; 16 Kt—B1, Kt—KKt5 and this time Black has the upper hand.

Recapitulating, we find that on 4 Q—B2, the two main defensive lines are 4 .... P—Q4 and 4 .... Kt—B3. In both, one of White's major objectives is to secure the two B's. Further, in the first White wishes to set up a strong Pawn center, in the second to attack on the Q-side. Black's central idea in the first is to equalize by exchanges and a break in the center, in the second, to set up a Pawn at K4 and build for a K-side attack.

II. 4 Q—Kt3 as we have already pointed out, is closely allied to the 4 Q—B2 line and transposes into it in many cases. The chief significant difference is that Black must do something about his B right away so that .... P—Q4 is no longer feasible.

There are again two main defensive lines: 4 .... Kt—B3 and 4 .... P—B4. 4 .... Kt—B3 is substantially the same as against 4 Q—B2. However the position of the White Q makes it even more favorable for Black than in the previous case be-

cause on 5 Kt—B3, P—QR4!; 6 P—QR3, P—R5 Black gains a
tempo. Otherwise it is all the same where White's Q is, so
that only .... P—B4 need concern us here.

After 4 .... P—B4; 5 P×P the situation differs from that in
the previous case because Black's KB is en prise and because
White's Q is on another square. The effect of these differences
will soon be clear.

Strategically, after 4 Q—Kt3, P—B4; 5 P×P the problem is
exactly the same as in the previous case: Can Black's QP be
forced to remain backward, and if so, can Black secure compensation elsewhere? Tactically, it will be somewhat easier for
Black to maneuver this time because White's Q often turns out
to be somewhat awkwardly placed. Nevertheless, with best
play Black again cannot rid himself of his backward QP, which
means that the entire variation is theoretically inadequate.

In what follows, the main ideas for White are to keep the
Black QP backward and to build up a K-side attack. Black
will base his play on quick development, advance of the QP if
possible, and a counter-attack against the enemy K, usually on
the K-side, but on occasion on the Q-side too.

The main line runs 4 Q—Kt3, P—B4; 5 P×P, Kt—B3; 6
Kt—B3, Kt—K5; 7 B—Q2 (White cannot afford a tripled
QBP), when there are now two main variations for Black (*Dia-
gram No. 38C*).

First there is 7 .... Kt×B; 8 Kt×Kt, P—B4; 9 P—K3,
B×P; 10 B—K2, O—O; 11 O—O—O (if he castles short
Black's counter-attack will be much stronger), P—QKt3; 12
Kt—B3. White has achieved his aim in the opening: kept
Black's QP backward, while Black's counterplay will prove to
have little force. Furthermore, White has good attacking
chances on the K-side (P—KKt4 properly prepared will
eventually open a file).

The other main line (from *Diagram No. 38C*) begins 7 ....
Kt×QBP and is designed to take advantage of the White Q-
position. There are some traps to be avoided (chiefly an early

.... P—Q4) but with solid play White secures a lasting advantage. It is best for White to fianchetto his KB because otherwise Black will be able to build up a strong attack against the White King. E.g., 7 .... Kt×QBP; 8 Q—B2, P—B4; 9 P—K3, O—O; 10 P—QR3, B×Kt; 11 B×B, P—QKt3; 12 P—QKt4, Kt—K5; 13 B—Q3?, Kt×B; 14 Q×Kt, B—Kt2; 15 O—O, Kt—K2; 16 B—K2 (note sad necessity), Q—K1; 17 KR—Q1, R—Q1; 18 P—QR4, P—B5 and Black's attack is overwhelming.

Once he fianchettoes his KB, however, White automatically takes the sting out of the diagonal of Black's QB, when he can continue with his Q-side play. Thus the chief variation would be: 7 .... Kt×QBP; 8 Q—B2, P—B4; 9 P—KKt3, O—O; 10 B—Kt2, P—Q3; 11 R—Q1, P—K4; 12 P—QR3, B×Kt; 13 B×B with a clear superiority. Incidentally, the continuation here is easy for White because there is a tangible object for his attack (P at Q3). Another point worth noting in the above line is that the order of moves must be watched carefully to make sure that Black will not be able to sneak in .... P—Q4. Thus after 7 .... Kt×QBP; 8 Q—B2, O—O the correct move is 9 P—QR3! but not 9 P—KKt3? for then 9 .... P—Q4! is much too strong, e.g., 10 P×P, P×P; 11 P—QR3, P—Q5! etc.

It should be mentioned that there is a significant improvement possible for Black in the above variations: after 4 Q—Kt3, P—B4; 5 P×P, Kt—B3; 6 Kt—B3 simply 6 .... B×P, instead of the time-consuming Kt foray. Then 7 B—Kt5 is essential to prevent .... P—Q4, when 7 .... P—KR3 virtually compels the exchange. Black does not get rid of his backward QP but does manage to reduce material to such an extent that that weakness cannot be exploited properly. 6 B—Kt5 instead of 6 Kt—B3 is an interesting break from routine: it prevents .... P—Q4 and avoids the more hackneyed lines.

Recapitulating, we find that 4 Q—Kt3 is most effective against 4 .... P—B4, when the motif of keeping the Black QP backward is White's major preoccupation. Black can then never fully equalize, though he may well reduce White's plus to a minimum. However, 4 .... Kt—B3 is a much more forceful reply for Black. It compels a transposition into lines previously considered in answer to 4 Q—B2.

III. 4 P—QR3 (The Saemisch Variation) is a forceful but two-edged line. White is willing to compromise his Pawn position on the Q-side in order to solidify his center and attack on the K-side. It is obvious that such tactics will lead to a sharp struggle.

The reply 4 .... B×Ktch; 5 P×B is forced. Black may then continue with either .... P—Q3, to keep White's Pawns doubled (though at the cost of a cramped position for himself) or .... P—Q4 to capitalize on his superior development. Either idea is all right if followed up properly, but should Black misplay his hand the consequences may well be fatal. The great strength of both the Saemisch and 4 P—K3 is derived from this.

It is essential for the theory of the whole opening to understand just what White is driving at. We can best grasp his objectives from an examination of two ideal positions.

In the first, 38D, we see that White has a powerful P center, that he will continue with P—B4 and a K-side attack. The position is already very hard for Black to defend: the counterplay against the White QBP, which is his only trump card, takes too long to develop and is not conclusive even if it should succeed: the stakes on the other wing are much higher.

In the second ideal position (*Diagram No. 38E*), White again has a powerful P center, while the threatened P—K4, which can no longer be stopped, will soon blast the roads open for a decisive attack. Again Black's counterplay on the Q-wing is much too slow and much too insignificant.

From these two ideal positions, which White would like to approximate and Black would like to prevent, the great majority of variations in both the Saemisch and Rubinstein (4 P—K3) lines take their cue. It will also be found that this type of ideal is present in other branches of the Nimzoindian as well.

There are various ways in which Black can avoid the ideal positions. Essentially they boil down to two: to break up the White center by early thrusts or to secure adequate compensation in the attack against the QBP. There is still another type of defense which may best be described as a palliative: to prevent the advance P—K4 as long as possible in the hope that White will have to dislocate his game in order to force it, a hope which is rarely realized. Incidentally, it should not be forgotten that White's Pawn structure is inherently weaker than Black's, so that if White's plans miscarry he may find that he has a lost endgame on his hands.

One vital point is sometimes overlooked: proper timing may make all the difference in the world here. It is essential for both sides to play with precision.

If we now turn to the variations we find that they are simple applications of the above principles.

After 4 P—QR3, B×Ktch; 5 P×B, the first major line runs 5 .... P—B4, to begin the process of breaking up White's center. Then 6 P—B3 (to prepare P—K4), P—Q4!; 7 P—K3, O—O; 8 BP×P (now necessary because of the threat of .... Q—B2! in reply to 8 B—Q3?), Kt×P! An essential point: in the good defenses Black always manages to recapture with a piece at Q4 and continue the break-up of the White P center with .... P—K4. Thus here: 9 B—Q2 (on 9 P—B4, Kt—B6 is too strong), Kt—QB3; 10 B—Q3, P×P; 11 BP×P, P—K4! and once his P center is shattered White has nothing.

The second major line exemplifies the best defense when Black plays .... P—Q3, rather than .... P—Q4. It will be recalled that his counterplay here consists of an attack against the White QBP. Since there's no time like the present White's chief concern must be what to do if Black carries out his plan immediately. E.g., 4 P—QR3, B×Ktch; 5 P×B, P—Q3; 6 P—B3, P—B4; 7 P—K4, Kt—B3; 8 B—K3, P—QKt3; 9

B—Q3, P—K4 (not essential: 9 .... Kt—QR4 may be played, though Black must then consider the possibility of P—K5); 10 Kt—K2, Kt—QR4 (not 10 .... B—R3??; 11 Q—R4). Now the threat is .... B—R3, so White cannot afford to develop normally, for if 11 O—O, B—R3; 12 Kt—Kt3, O—O! or even 12 .... Q—Q2 compels White to ruin his P position, perhaps lose a P in the long run, without any compensation. One little-known but valuable idea for Black is to castle on the Q-side: with the P position blocked his K can be defended there much more easily than on the K-side. If White blocks the center by advancing P—Q5, one possibility Black must not overlook is that on P—KB4 he may be able to reply .... KP×BP and settle a Kt at K4.

Mistakes by Black will be punished by the realization of the most important preliminary element in White's plan: setting up an unchallenged strong Pawn center.

IV. 4 P—K3 (The Rubinstein Variation) is closely related to the Saemisch. In both cases the ideal positions are the same, 38D and 38E. Frequently the two transpose into one another.

Though the ideal positions for White are structurally the same as in the Saemisch, there is one important difference: White has an extra tempo because he has not advanced P—QR3. We have already noted of how much importance timing and an extra move may be. It stands to reason that a line in the Saemisch where everything depended on a tempo would be so much stronger for White. Our "reason" is borne out by practise. For the main variation there where everything hung by a hair was that where Black plays .... P—Q3, keeps the P position blocked and speeds to the attack against the White QBP. It turns out here that that line is not adequate for Black because White has ample time to both defend the BP and develop his attack.

Since the block defense is unsatisfactory, Black must resort to a more open game where he tries to crack the White center early. Thus 4 .... P—Q4 is in order. Now there are two alternatives for White: 5 P—QR3, to transpose into a line of the Saemisch, or 5 B—Q3, straight development. The strength of the former (5 P—QR3) lies in the fact that P—K3 has been played instead of P—B3; consequently on an eventual BP× QP, if in reply .... Kt×QP (as in a variation of the Saemisch), P—QB4 is feasible. This variation is a serious problem for Black at the moment, though it will probably be solved soon. E.g., after 5 P—QR3, B×Ktch; 6 P×B, P—B4; 7 P×QP, Q×P! may be tried. On 7 .... KP×P instead, 8 B—Q3, O—O; 9 Kt—K2, P—QKt3; 10 O—O, B—R3; 11 B×B! is White's plan: 11 .... Kt×B; 12 Q—Q3!, so that if 12 .... Kt—B2; 13 P×P, P×P; 14 P—QB4, leaving Black with a crippled Pawn position, while if 12 .... Q—B1; 13 P—B3 will eventually force P—K4 and the "steamroller" attack.

Where White chooses straight development Black must again tread carefully, but if he stops the P—B3, P—K4 steamroller before it gets started, he should have no real difficulties. The method to adopt is that of liquidating the center Pawns and transposing into the P structure of the QGA. The main line runs: 4 P—K3, P—Q4; 5 B—Q3, O—O. Now White must decide whether to develop his Kt at K2 or at B3. In the former case, 6 Kt—K2, P—B4; 7 O—O Black must exchange in the center immediately (.... QP×P and then .... B×P) because otherwise White may reverse the roles and transpose into a QGA type of position which is favorable to him! Thus if 7 .... Kt—B3; 8 P×QP, KP×P; 9 P×P, B×P; 10 P—QR3, B—K3; 11 P—QKt4 and White has the better of it because Black cannot build up an attack by using his Q4 as a fulcrum, the main counterplay in that sort of position (see page 147). However, the double P exchange in the center will equalize easily enough, especially since White's KKt is ineffectually posted (it should be at KB3) for a QGA set-up. One other idea is worth mentioning here: if White plays P—QR3 at a later date, Black should not reply .... B×Kt, but should liquidate in the center and then retreat with his B. E.g., after 4 P—K3,

P—Q4; 5 B—Q3, O—O; 6 Kt—K2. P—B4; if 7 P—QR3, the best is 7 .... QP×P; 8 B×P, P×P!; 9 P×P, B—K2: if White captures the B at any point his P position on the Q-side will be quite weak. Where White develops his KKt at KB3, Black need not be in any hurry to exchange his BP for the White QP. Thus: 4 .... P—Q4; 5 B—Q3, P—B4; 6 Kt—B3, O—O; 7 O—O, QP×P; 8 B×P, Kt—B3!; 9 P—QR3, B—R4! with equality.

In other defenses (alternatives to 4 .... P—Q4) the principle holds that Black equalizes if and only if he breaks in the center properly. E.g., on 4 .... P—B4; 5 Kt—K2, P×P?; 6 P×P, P—Q4; 7 P—B5 is bad, while 5 .... P—Q4 will be good enough in the long run. An idea for White in these variations is to develop his Kt at K2 early in order to continue with P—QR3 and relieve the pressure on his Q-side. This plan is feasible only if Black delays the center break. Timing is all-important here.

V. Alternatives on White's Fourth Move: Besides those mentioned, there are at least half a dozen lines for White which have been tried at one time or another. We cannot afford to devote too much space to them because they introduce little that is new: they are largely attempts to recast the old ideas.

The most interesting is 4 Kt—B3. Here 4 .... B×Ktch (*Diagrams No. 36A, 38D*) is inferior because White can defend his QBP with his Kt and build up a powerful center quickly. He intends the maneuver Kt—Q2 and, if necessary because of the pressure against his QP, Kt—QKt3. One advantage of having his Kt at QKt3 is that Black then cannot try the attack with .... Kt—QR4. We thus have the same experience as in the Rubinstein Line: White has not lost a tempo with P—QR3 and as a result .... B×Ktch is not good. The alternative 4 .... P—QKt3 is however easily enough to equalize: if then 5 P—K3, B—Kt2; 6 B—Q3, Kt—K5; 7 Q—B2, P—KB4; 8 O—O, B×Kt; 9 P×B, O—O may be tried (for now the steamroller will take long to prepare and will have little force, e.g., 10 Kt—K1, P—Q3; 11 P—B3, Kt—KB3; 12 P—K4, P×P; 13

P×P, P—K4 with at least equality) or simply .... O—O, ...
P—Q4 and .... P—B4 as in the Rubinstein Variation.

Q-Indian Defense: 1 P—Q4, Kt—KB3; 2 P—QB4, P—K3;
3 Kt—KB3, P—QKt3.

We have already pointed out the close relationship between
this and the Nimzoindian. The ideas are in many cases the
same, frequently the variations are too. Then there is the important psychological consideration that White often plays his
KKt out first in order to avoid the Nimzoindian and that Black
must accordingly have an adequate knowledge of both.

The Pawn structures which may come up and the ideal
positions which White has in mind are not essentially different
from those seen before. We shall point out what is new as it
comes along.

It will be recalled that the fundamental struggle hinges on
P—K4 for White: the attacker would like to play it, the defender to prevent it. The method which Black has chosen this
time is that of the fianchetto—control from a distance. On
general principles the best way to deprive an opponent's
fianchettoed B of its claws is to fianchetto your own B on the
same diagonal.

The Q-Indian is much more closely knit than the Nimzoindian. From the major concern for both sides—forcing or
preventing P—K4—a group of minor or subsidiary ideas arise,
chiefly in connection with the method of reaching one's goal.
For White the most important is P—Q5 at an appropriate
moment, for once he can block the diagonal of Black's QB he
will have no trouble advancing his KP. Another thought is the
exchange of B's, though here he must not forget that all exchanges help Black free his game. For Black there are more
branches. He can prevent P—K4 by occupation of the square
with a piece, usually with the Kt, though sometimes the B will
do too. Or he can control the square with a P, either .... P—
Q4 or (once his KKt has moved) .... P—KB4. In the former
case he blocks his QB, often a serious drawback, in the latter
he occasionally facilitates a White P—Q5. Black may also try

a counter-attack with .... P—QB4: if he does he must make sure that P—Q5 is not possible and that he will not be saddled with a backward QP.

With this background it is easy enough to understand the main line (unlike the Nimzoindian there is one major variation here by which the whole defense stands or falls). Development and a wary eye on K4 are the watchwords: 4 P—KKt3, B—Kt2; 5 B—Kt2, B—K2; 6 O—O, O—O (*Diagram No. 39*).

In the position reached there are a number of ways in which P—K4 may be prepared. The most obvious is 7 Kt—B3, which continues the major line. Then 7 .... P—Q4 would allow 8 Kt—K5, blocking the diagonal of Black's B, e.g. 8 .... QKt—Q2; 9 P×P, P×P; 10 Q—R4! and 10 .... Kt—Kt1 is forced. Or on 8 Kt—K5, P—B3; 9 P—K4 will eventually lead to a P position favorable to White: P at Q4 vs. P at QB3 as in some variations of the QGD and French Defense. At bottom this method of exploiting .... P—Q4 (by an early P—K4) is a resurrection of one of White's basic positional motifs in the QGD: to play P—K4 after 1 P—Q4, P—Q4.

Since .... P—Q4 is inadequate, Black resorts to the occupational method: 7 .... Kt—K5 (in reply to 7 Kt—B3). Now an obvious line such as 8 Kt×Kt, B×Kt; 9 B—B4, P—Q3; 10 Kt—K1, B×B; 11 Kt×B, P—KB4 frees Black's game considerably. So 8 Q—B2 comes to mind, to compel the Black Kt to go away. Black exchanges 8 .... Kt×Kt; 9 Q×Kt, P—KB4 and again prevents P—K4. On 10 B—K3, B—KB3; 11 Q—Q2, B—K5 White will sooner or later have to resort to the exchange of B's: then 12 Kt—K1, B×B; 13 Kt×B, Kt—B3 (not 13 .... P—Q3; 14 Kt—B4, Q—K2; 15 P—Q5 and White plants a Kt at K6) and Black has enough counterplay on the K-side and in the center to compensate for his theoretical inferiority on the Q-side.

Thus Black succeeds in his main purpose, though he does not equalize the effect of White's QBP and QP completely. White will always retain endgame chances on the Q-side. However, as in some variations of the Nimzoindian, since the anchor at

Q5 is not secure, the White advance will be much less effective. White has little reason to be satisfied with the situation: the advantage is either non-existent or negligible.

It is well to remember that .... P—Q4 for Black is not bad on principle, but only because in most cases it blocks the B and allows an unfavorable P structure. If these conditions do not hold, ... P—Q4 is excellent since it helps to break up White's center. E.g., on 7 Q—B2 (instead of 7 Kt—B3 in *Diagram No. 39*) B—K5; 8 Q—Kt3 (if 8 Q—Q1, B—Kt2!), P—Q4!, or 7 ....

No. 39

Crucial Position in the Q-Indian
Defense.

Kt—B3; 8 Kt—B3, P—Q4!; 9 P×P, Kt—QKt5 is sufficient because the subsequent break .... P—QB4, which will liquidate the center completely, cannot be prevented.

On 7 Q—B2, another good reply is 7 .... P—B4. Then 8 P×P is met by 8 .... P×P!, when the backward QP does not matter much because it is easily defended and because Black has sufficient counterplay on the QKt file. In this variation P—K4? is a mistake for White (after QP×P, P×P) since it yields the square Q4 to Black without getting anything in return.

Finally, White may prefer not to make any direct effort to force P—K4, but to develop simply with 7 P—Kt3. Then the

break in the center is called for and turns out well: 7 ....
P—Q4; 8 Kt—K5, P—B4; 9 P×BP, KtP×P; 10 P×P, P×P;
11 Kt—QB3, QKt—Q2 with equality.

Under the circumstances it is not surprising to find many
attempted improvements for both White and Black. White
would like to get a clearer superiority, while Black would like to
force a more complete liquidation of the center and secure a
freer game.

On his 5th move in the main line there are several interesting
alternatives for Black.

First there is 5 .... B—Kt5ch, on the theory that exchanges
always free a cramped game. The only trouble is that Black
will have to exchange a developed piece for an undeveloped one,
which will help his opponent. Thus after 5 .... B—Kt5ch;
6 B—Q2 (best), B×Bch; 7 Q×B, O—O; 8 Kt—B3, 8 ....
Kt—K5? is now refuted by 9 Q—B2, Kt×Kt; 10 Kt—Kt5!,
winning the exchange. This combination is not possible in the
other line because once White has castled Black has the in-
between move .... Kt×KPch. Consequently, on 8 Kt—B3,
Black must resort to either 8 .... P—Q4; 9 Kt—K5, or 8 ....
P—Q3; 9 Q—B2, Q—K2; 10 O—O, P—B4; 11 QR—Q1, P×P;
12 Kt×P with the usual inferior P structure in both cases. An
interesting point here is that the recapture with the QKt (7
QKt×B instead of 7 Q×B) is not so good because the QKt is
badly placed at Q2, from where it exerts no pressure against the
Black center. 7 .... P—Q4, or even 7 .... P—B4 (for P—Q5
is no longer possible) is adequate. Likewise, on 6 QKt—Q2
(instead of 6 B—Q2) White gets nowhere because of an early
break in the center with .... P—Q4 and .... P—QB4.
White's QKt belongs at QB3 in all these variations in order to
keep the square Q5 under surveillance.

Thus 5 .... B—Kt5ch, while superficially plausible, in
reality hastens White's development.

Another alternative on Black's 5th turn is 5 .... P—B4,
again to dissolve White's center. The drawback here is that
White can reply 6 P—Q5! and cramp Black's game perma-

nently: 6 .... P×P; 7 Kt—R4, Q—B2; 8 P×P, P—Q3; 9 O—O, QKt—Q2; 10 Kt—QB3, P—QR3; 11 P—K4. White has a violent attack which is hard to meet.

An important consideration on 5 .... P—B4 is that after 6 O—O, P×P; 7 Kt×P, B×B; 8 K×B, P—Q4 is refuted by 9 Q—R4ch, Q—Q2; 10 Kt—Kt5, or 8 .... B—K2 (instead of 8 .... P—Q4); 9 Kt—QB3, O—O; 10 P—K4 with advantage to White.

These variations lead us to some significant generalizations about .... P—QB4 in a Q-Indian type of position. Black's intention in playing .... P—QB4 is to free himself. As long as White retains his QP, he can do so only by advancing both BP and QP. Consequently .... P—QB4 is good only as a prelude to .... P—Q4. In other words the move is strong only if .... P—Q4 can eventually follow (often preceded by .... BP×QP). There are thus two maneuvers against .... P—QB4 which Black must watch: the advance P—Q5 and the advance P—K4. If either of these occurs, he will get a cramped game or a backward QP. This analysis must be changed somewhat if White tries QP×BP in answer to .... P—QB4. Then .... P—Q4 might conceivably expose the Black Pawns and be weak; instead Black could secure counterplay on the QKt file.

All this leads to the natural question of what will happen if Black tries the alternative 5 .... P—Q4 (in the main line, after 4 P—KKt3, B—Kt2; 5 B—Kt2). 6 Kt—K5 would then block the diagonal, while 6 P×P, P×P would fix the Pawn position in a mold which is normally good for White. However, these slight drawbacks are much less significant than the objections to 5 .... B—Kt5ch and 5 .... P—B4.

One of the most intriguing variants for Black is 5 .... Q—B1 (again in the main line). The idea is that now .... P—QB4 can no longer be refuted by P—Q5 because the B is defended and that further after .... P—QB4, ... BP×QP White will have to retake with the Q (thus losing time) because of the attack on the QBP. There is no good way out of the dilemma for White: on 6 O—O, P—B4; 7 P×P releases the tension as usual, while on the natural 7 P—Kt3, P×P; 8 B—Kt2, B—K2; 9 Kt×P, B×B; 10 K×B, P—Q4 has equalized.

Alternatives for White before the sixth move have at least the virtue of novelty to recommend them. All, of course, are based on the idea of forcing P—K4 more quickly.

The first thought that comes to mind (after the initial moves) is 4 Kt—B3, to continue with Q—B2. Then 4 .... B—Kt5 transposes into a variation of the Nimzoindian which is theoretically sufficient. 4 .... B—Kt2 is also playable, however. Then on 5 Q—B2, B—Kt5 prevents P—K4 and leads to variations analogous to the Zurich line in the Nimzoindian (page 170). E.g., 6 P—QR3, B×Ktch; 7 Q×B, Kt—K5; 8 Q—B2, O—O; 9 P—KKt3, P—KB4, etc. Another thought for White is to try 5 B—Kt5 (after 4 Kt—B3, B—Kt2) to threaten P—K4, but both 5 .... B—Kt5 and 5 .... P—KR3 are sufficient: the latter may transpose into a variation of the QGD (page 131). On 5 .... B—Kt5; 6 Q—B2 will eventually force P—K4, though at a slow pace which will deprive it of some of its value.

A promising line for White is that where he prevents the pin with P—QR3. E.g., 4 Kt—B3, B—Kt2; 5 P—QR3, B—K2; 6 B—B4, O—O; 7 Q—B2, Kt—R4; 8 B—Q2, P—KB4; 9 P—K3, P—Q3; 10 B—Q3 and P—K4 to follow.

In all these cases Black always has the alternative of an early center break with .... P—QB4 or .... P—Q4. As long as he has not fianchettoed his KB, White can then hold open the possibility of a favorable transposition into some lines of the QGD.

All in all, these alternatives for White offer a welcome break from routine, though their theoretical value is still a matter of dispute.

Q-Indian Defense on the 2nd Move: 1 P—Q4, Kt—KB3; 3 Kt—KB3, P—QKt3, or 2 P—QB4, P—QKt3.

Here we have much the same situation as in the Queen's Pawn Game where White omits P—QB4: one side avoids the theoretically best line for the sake of variety. Consequently little importance attaches to these variations, though some interesting ideas may come forth.

After 1 P—Q4, Kt—KB3; 2 Kt—KB3, P—QKt3 the best is 3 P—QB4, when 3 .... P—K3 gives us the regular Q-Indian. If he does not wish to be a "regular" fellow, White may try one of two things: an early development of his QB, or a Colle set-up.

An instance of the first is 3 B—Kt5, which is designed to cramp Black's game. 3 .... P—K3 is possible, but in such cases where White has exposed his QB it is usually a good thought to try to exchange it. E.g., 3 B—Kt5, Kt—K5; 4 B—R4, B—Kt2; 5 P—K3, P—KR3; 6 QKt—Q2, P—KKt4; 7 B—Kt3, Kt×B with equality.

We have already seen that the Colle System is none too strong against a K-fianchetto and—on occasion—a Q-fianchetto. The same conclusion holds even where Black has not played .... P—Q4. The trouble is that an early P—K4 (usually feasible when Black omits .... P—Q4) leaves White's center position rather shaky and usually yields Black the two B's. E.g., 3 P—K3, B—Kt2; 4 QKt—Q2, P—K3; 5 B—Q3, P—B4! (essential); 6 O—O, Kt—B3; 7 P—B3, B—K2; 8 P—K4 and now 8 .... P×P; 9 Kt×P (or 9 P×P, Kt—QKt5; 10 B—Kt1, B—R3), O—O; 11 Q—K2, Kt—K4!; 12 B—B2, Q—B1!; 13 P—KB4, B—R3 and Black has all the play. Black will never have any difficulties if he prevents a favorable P—K4.

In the line beginning with 1 P—Q4, Kt—KB3; 2 P—QB4, P—QKt3 White may vary by attempting a very early P—K4. In this he can succeed, but blood-letting will deprive his center phalanx of value. E.g., 3 Kt—QB3, B—Kt2; 4 P—B3, P—Q4; 5 P×P, Kt×P; 6 Kt×Kt, Q×Kt; 7 P—K4, Q—Q2; 8 B—QB4, P—K3; 9 Kt—K2, B—Kt5ch and the Pawns have no serious cramping effect.

Bogoljubow Variation: 1 P—Q4, Kt—KB3; 2 P—QB4, P—K3; 3 Kt—KB3, B—Kt5ch.

This line is strategically a branch of the Q-Indian (see the

variation 5 .... B—Kt5ch on page 182), though it may differ
from it in some significant respects.

Again 4 B—Q2 is best (4 Kt—B3 transposes into a weak
branch of the Nimzoindian), but this time the evaluation of the
continuations differs. After 4 .... B×Bch; 5 Q×B, P—Q4!
is excellent because the QB has not been fianchettoed so that
its diagonal cannot be blocked. We then have a QGD in effect, without black Bishops. The same ideas hold: to force an
early .... P—Q4 or .... P—K4.

On the other hand, since the pressure against Black's Q4 does
not mean anything, there is no longer any reason to suppose
that the Kt is necessarily better placed at QB3. Thus on 4
B—Q2, B×Bch; 5 QKt×B may be tried. Then on 5 .... P—
Q4 the B file will be open to the Rook, so that Black will have
a much harder time playing .... P—QB4. On 5 .... P—Q3
(in answer to 5 QKt×B) a hasty P—K4 would be useless because Black can break the White center with .... P—KB4.
The fianchetto of the KB is again best: it increases the eventual
pressure against Black's Q-side.

B. K-INDIAN—GRUENFELD COMPLEX

The distinguishing feature in this group is the fianchetto of
the King's Bishop. This time, however, Black makes little or
no real effort to stop P—K4: instead he allows the move and
then tries to get compensation.

It is not fruitful to discuss the two branches of this complex
together—they have too little in common. In the Gruenfeld
we need consider only those P positions where Black plays
.... P—Q4, while in the K-Indian we are concerned almost
exclusively with variations with .... P—Q3. Nevertheless
one vital idea does unify the two: White is allowed a strong P
center because such a center sets up targets and allows lively
counterplay. In both Black concentrates on quick development of pieces, while White must watch his P center lest it fall
apart.

The major Pawn skeletons which can come up here are

shown in *Diagram No. 40*. There are some other important ones not given here because they have already been discussed in other connections; they will be referred to. 40A-D occur in the K-Indian Defense chiefly, 40E-F in the Gruenfeld.

K-Indian Defense: 1 P—Q4, Kt—KB3; 2 P—QB4, P— KKt3.

Here Black makes no effort at all to stop P—K4; his only concern is to get compensation for it. This compensation must necessarily be a break with .... P—KB4. Thus the problem for White in almost all lines (there are some unusual exceptions which prove the rule) is what to do about an eventual .... P— KB4. It is a safe general rule that White cannot get an advantage unless he plays KP×BP.

To turn to the diagrams: In 40A we have the most obvious case, where both sides have completed their preliminaries. It is always favorable for White. He should be satisfied to keep it intact because then .... P—KB4 could be met by a double P exchange which would leave Black's Pawns badly exposed. On occasion Black tries to get counterplay here with an attack on the KP; such counterplay is normally hopelessly ineffective. The P structure which ensues after .... KP×QP is one which we have seen time and again (page 8 ff.): White with his strong

PAWN POSITIONS IN THE K-INDIAN-GRUENFELD COMPLEX

No. 40A   **No. 40B**

Always favorable for White.   Strong for White.

PAWN POSITIONS IN THE K-INDIAN-GRUENFELD COMPLEX

No. 40C

Normally favorable for Black.

No. 40D

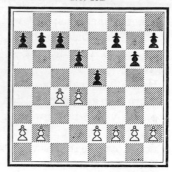

Normally somewhat in Black's favor.

No. 40E

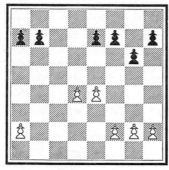

Always favorable for Black.

No. 40F

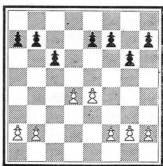

Always favorable for White.

P at K4 vs. the weak P at Q3 has a clear advantage. Another possible variant comes up when White tries P—Q5. Then White envisages an eventual Q-side attack with P—QKt4, P—QB5, etc. (*Diagram No. 36D* and discussion). This too should be in his favor provided he is prepared to reply to .... P—KB4 properly.

In *Diagram No. 40B* we see an ideal set-up for White against best defensive play. In 40A the QP has been advanced to Q5. Then on .... P—KB4, the reply was KP×BP, KtP×P, P—

KB4, P—K5. It is true that Black now has counter-chances on the KKt file, but the attack can usually be parried quite easily. In the meantime White can proceed with his devastating advance on the Q-side. Good for White unless Black has the initiative. On KP×BP Black may recapture with a piece: then the square K4 becomes a powerful anchorage for White's pieces, while P—KB4 again shakes the Black position. Ultimately, the Q-side advance is the conclusive weapon in both cases.

These two Pawn structures, together with the related 36D, are of such vital importance that it is worth our while to consider them a bit more fully.

40A is the original position. It is to White's advantage, as we have mentioned, to keep the center unstable as long as possible. To get some counterplay, Black then frequently resorts to .... KP×QP, in the hope that White's KP may prove weak. This hope is doomed to failure if White does not exchange pieces without good reason. For we know that the strength of the P at K4 derives from its cramping effect on the enemy pieces.

If Black plays passively instead of exchanging, White has various plans at his disposal. One is to continue with P—KB4, eventually an attack along the KB file. For this reason it is better to develop the KKt at K2 rather than at KB3. Another plan begins with P—Q5 (36D—it makes no difference whether the Black KKtP is at KKt3 or at KKt2). Sometimes White is virtually compelled to advance his QP because of counter-attacking possibilities; at other times he chooses it voluntarily.

Whatever the reason has been, once White's Pawn is at Q5 in 40A, the lines are sharply drawn. Positionally, his play lies on the Q-side, where he can base it on the favorable Pawn chain, P's at Q5, K4, vs. Black P's at Q3, K4. The attack against such a Pawn chain is directed at its base, here Black's QP. I.e., White will play P—B5 as soon as feasible.

Against a purely passive defense, the advance of the BP (P—B5) will compel a fatal weakening of the Black Pawn structure. If he captures .... QP×BP, the recapture will leave the Black QBP exposed on an open file. If he does not take, White will pile up his heavy artillery on the QB file, continue with BP×QP, eventually break into the Black camp via QB7 and secure a decisive gain of material. Thus White has a fairly simple, direct long-range plan, the execution of which will net him a winning advantage if he is not crossed.

That is why Black is compelled to undertake some counter-action. Most common is that where he posts his Kt at QB4, holds it with .... P—QR4 and seeks to build up counterplay in the center. White must drive Black's Kt away from QB4 with P—QKt3, P—QR3, P—QKt4. Then on .... RP×KtP, White may be able to use the QR file; otherwise he will proceed with his attack on the Pawn chain, though this time he must prepare P—QB5 more carefully.

One point is important in this Pawn chain attack: White's play is "anchored" in the Pawns at K4 and Q5 and neither should be exchanged or weakened without good reason. If the KP goes, the QP may turn out to be just as weak as Black's QBP, which will deprive White's play of its point.

An alternative long-range plan for White after P—Q5 involves holding the center, castling long and storming the enemy K-side. With Black's Pawn at KKt3, the KR file can normally be opened. Black will, of course, try to build up a counter-attack on the Q-side. Again purely passive play would favor White. He could continue with B—K3, Q—Q2, O—O—O, B—KR6, P—KR4, P—KR5, eventually opening the KR file.

It is abundantly clear that Black cannot afford to sit back quietly. He must counter-attack, with .... P—KB4. Without this move he has no real offensive prospects of any kind.

On .... P—KB4 White must take notice. He must consider whether he can afford to disregard Black's threats and proceed with his own Q-side action. The answer depends entirely on the element of time. Black's attack, after all, affects White's King directly, while White's aims at Pawns.

The Black steamroller, if unchecked, will continue with ....

P—KB5, setting up a Pawn chain in his turn (P—B3 has usually come in). Then the base of the Pawn chain will be undermined: .... P—KKt4—KKt5. The assault will be strengthened by doubling Rooks on the KKt file, playing the Q to the K-side, and concentrating as many other pieces on the vital points there as he can spare.

Normally, it is not desirable for White to allow such a counter-attack. And he can take out its fangs by answering .... P—KB4 with KP×BP. Then on .... KtP×P, P—KB4, P—K5, will block the Pawns and leave the K-position easily defended (40B). On .... B×P there is no long-range attack possible for Black, so White can pursue his plans.

Yet Black's counter-action has served some purpose, for the White anchor points at K4 and Q5 have had their defenses blunted. Whether the Black threats against the White QP are sufficient compensation for the White play against the QBP cannot be answered in advance; normally they are not. As a result, White should continue to plan for P—B5; once it comes in it will mark the beginning of the end for Black.

40C occurs when White makes the mistake of liquidating the center with QP×KP. As a result White's Q4 is an excellent roost for a Black Kt, while Black's Q4 is impenetrable. Normally favorable for Black.

40D is another case where White omits the strongest line. Unlike 40C, however, he has made no permanent mistake here, since P—K4 may be played at any time. .... KP×QP is again weak for Black, but .... P—KB4 is much more effective because the strongest rejoinder KP×BP is not available. Normally somewhat in Black's favor.

Since 40A and 40B are the best P positions for White he will try to force them. Before he can make up his mind exactly how to develop, however, he must first decide where he wants to post his pieces. His KKt is most useful at K2, though KB3 is not bad. His KB will be most effective on the long diagonal from where it can support White's center Pawns and help defend the King if need be. Thus we get the strongest line for

White to run as follows: 3 Kt—QB3, B—Kt2; 4 P—K4, P—Q3; 5 P—KKt3, O—O; 6 B—Kt2, QKt—Q2; 7 KKt—K2, P—K4; 8 O—O, R—K1; 9 R—K1, P×P (or 9 .... P—QB3; 10 P—Kt3, Q—B2; 11 B—Kt2, Kt—B1; 12 Q—Q2 and Black's counterplay is meaningless since it does not lead to liberation); 10 Kt×P, Kt—B4; 11 P—Kt3, B—Kt5; 12 P—B3, B—Q2 (*Diagram No. 41*) with a clear advantage. Another good line is that which begins with an early P—Q5. E.g., above 8 P—Q5 (instead of 8 O—O), P—QR4; 9 P—QR3, Kt—B4; 10 O—O, Kt—K1; 11 B—K3, P—B4; 12 P×P!, P×P; 13 P—B4 with much the better of it.

One maneuver in the latter variation must be handled correctly by both sides. Black's counterplay is virtually meaningless if he cannot secure a Kt at QB4. To prevent P—QKt4 he therefore tries 8 .... P—QR4 (above). White can now drive the Kt away with P—QKt3, P—QR3 (note the order), P—QKt4. P—QR3 first is often a mistake because the reply .... P—R5 will block White's Pawns. (Compare French Defense, *Diagram No. 14B.*) In this particular variation it makes no difference, but only because White's Kt and Q prevent a P advance.

There are no improvements for Black which need concern us here since he has little or no choice against the strongest lines. That is one of the main drawbacks for Black—the inelasticity of his counterplay. The only point worth mentioning is that often an early .... Kt—QB3 is tried to compel the White QP to advance. White should accept the offer—if he delays Black may be able to retreat to K2 with his Kt rather than Kt1. On P—Q5 at once the variations are essentially the same as those given elsewhere.

Despite the strength of the main line for White there are several alternatives for him which yield an equally lasting advantage. In these variations, however, he must always advance P—Q5 at an early stage. One is that where he develops his Kt at KB3. E.g., in the main line above 7 Kt—B3 (instead of 7 KKt—K2), P—K4; 8 O—O, R—K1; 9 P—Q5 (best), Kt—B4;

10 Kt—K1, P—QR4; 11 P—Kt3 (not 11 P—QR3, P—R5), B—Q2; 12 P—KR3, etc. The essential point is that White holds on the K-side and advances on the Q-side.

Playable and also quite strong is the line where White does not even fianchetto his KB: 3 Kt—QB3, B—Kt2; 4 P—K4, P—Q3; 5 Kt—B3, O—O; 6 B—K2, QKt—Q2; 7 O—O, P—K4; 8 P—Q5, P—QR4; 9 Q—B2, Kt—R4 (immediate counter-attack is the watchword for Black); 10 P—KKt3!, Kt—B4; 11 Kt—K1, B—R6; 12 Kt—Kt2, Kt—B3; 13 P—B4 and White

No. 41

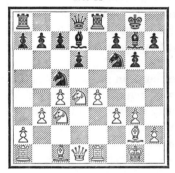

Position after 12 .... B—Q2 in the K-Indian Defense.

No. 42

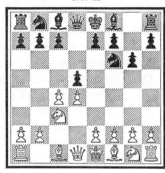

Gruenfeld Defense.

still has the better of it. It is interesting to note that White need not be in a hurry about his attack on the Q-side: that advance can never be stopped (barring a mistake by White) so that time does not matter as long as Black's counter-action on the K-side is blocked. It is even possible for White to build up a K-side attack, e.g., 3 Kt—QB3, B—Kt2; 4 P—K4, P—Q3; 5 Kt—B3, O—O; 6 P—KR3, P—K4; 7 P—Q5, P—KR3; 8 B—K3, K—R2; 9 P—KKt4, Kt—Kt1; 10 Q—Q2, P—Kt3; 11 O—O—O, Kt—R3; 12 B—K2 with the better prospects.

Weak play on White's part can give Black a strong counter-attack—which explains why the K-Indian was popular for such a long time. The major type of mistake which White can make is that of exposing his center too much. This is the case in the famous 4-Pawn attack: 3 Kt—QB3, B—Kt2; 4 P—K4, P—Q3; 5 P—B4, O—O; 6 Kt—B3 and now 6 .... P—B4!; 7 P—Q5 (or 7 P×P, Q—R4!), P—K3; 8 B—Q3, P×P; 9 BP× P, Q—Kt3! with a strong initiative.

The variations with a delayed .... P—Q4 in the K-Indian are really methods of avoiding the Gruenfeld: we shall return to them later.

Gruenfeld Defense: 1 P—Q4, Kt—KB3; 2 P—QB4, P— KKt3; 3 Kt—QB3, P—Q4!

Strictly speaking, the Gruenfeld is a branch of the K-Indian, but the child has already outgrown its parent. While the orthodox variations of the K-Indian have almost disappeared from modern master practise, the Gruenfeld has become one of the most popular defenses.

The main Pawn structures are shown in *Diagrams No. 40E* and *F*. In 40E White has a strong Pawn center, a fruitful middle game possibility, but a minority of Pawns on the Q-side— an endgame disadvantage. As we shall see, this skeleton formation is almost always in Black's favor in the Gruenfeld. Every exchange helps Black since it brings him so much nearer the endgame.

40F is an ideal position for White. This time he has another array of Pawns in the center, but the difference is that Black has an extra P, so that his pieces are cramped. It should never be forgotten that the strength of a P center consists of the fact that it immobilizes enemy pieces. If he exchanges and is not cramped, the P center is useless. In the Gruenfeld this structure is almost always favorable for White.

These two P positions provide a solid framework for all the variations: Black wants the first, White the second. The fight is on to see who will have his way.

The most obvious line was the first tried, historically: 4 P×P, Kt×P; 5 P—K4, Kt×Kt; 6 P×Kt, P—QB4! (necessary at once to prevent B—R3); 7 Kt—B3, B—Kt2; 8 B—QB4 (the exchanges with B—Kt5ch only favor Black, which is in line with our theory), Kt—B3; 9 B—K3, O—O; 10 P—KR3 (to prevent .... B—Kt5), P×P (not essential immediately; Black must however see to it that P—Q5 will never be feasible); 11 P×P and now 11 .... Kt—R4; 12 B—K2, P—Kt3 is the simplest way to make sure of at least complete equality. Black's further play lies on the QB file and the Q-side, White's in the center and on the K-side.

From all this we reach one all-important conclusion: White does wish to set up a strong center (P's at Q4 and K4) but only on condition that there be few or no exchanges. In particular, he is especially anxious to keep Black's QBP on the board. Further, on general principles we can see that if White does get his P's at K4 and Q4 Black must either do a lot of exchanging or break up the enemy center. As in the QGD, ... P—QB4 is the key liberating move for him. If it can be played and followed up properly, Black may well get the better of it—this and the lack of symmetry account for the popularity of the Gruenfeld with aggressive players.

If the obvious will not do, we must turn to the subtle. Here we can easily calculate what the key move for White must be. He wishes to get rid of the Black QP and advance his own KP. To do that he must either compel the exchange .... QP×BP, or prepare for P—K4 anyhow. To prepare for P—K4 requires a lot of time; meanwhile Black will play .... P—QB4 and defeat his purpose. Besides, P—K4 could be answered by .... QP×KP, which might yield an advantage but which is not what White wants. Thus there remains only the plan of forcing Black to exchange .... QP×BP. To compel that, Black unwilling—as should be the case—White must exert pressure on the Black QP. That can be done effectively only with Q—Kt3. The conclusion may be stated as a useful rule: *Q—Kt3 is the key move for all White attacks in the Gruenfeld Defense.*

To this maneuver there are three typical replies for Black: 1)

to hold the center with .... P—QB3 or .... P—K3; 2) to take
.... QP×BP and then seek compensation by a break against
the White center; or 3) to counter-attack with .... P—QB4.

Against the background of these motifs the particular variations of the Gruenfeld are understood easily enough. Though
we should add that the tactical problems are frequently exceedingly complicated; a number are still controversial.

The major continuations for White on his fourth move are 4
P×P (which we have already considered), 4 P—K3 (quick development), 4 B—B4 (double pressure on the QB file), 4 Q—
Kt3 (a speedy decision about the QP), 4 B—Kt5 (compel an
early liquidation of the QP) and 4 Kt—B3 (waiting move,
transposition). Of these, only the second and third—4 B—B4
and 4 Q—Kt3—have retained any measure of popularity, for
reasons which we shall see, though the others may be equally
good from a theoretical point of view.

I. 4 P—K3 is played with a view to getting the pieces out
quickly. Since .... P—QB4 is not thinkable before Black
castles, the normal continuation is 4 .... B—Kt2; 5 Kt—B3,
O—O. Now .... P—QB4 is a distinct positional threat (e.g.,
6 B—Q3, P—B4; 7 QP×P, Q—R4 with at least equality),
so the key move of the attack comes in: 6 Q—Kt3. The
counter-attack 6 .... P—QB4 is not good: Black has no real
compensation for the Pawn after 7 BP×P. To take 6 ....
QP×BP would be pointless: e.g., 7 B×P, QKt—Q2; 8 Kt—
KKt5! (8 P—K4 is also all right), P—K3; 9 B×P, P×B; 10
Kt×KP with advantage. Thus there remains only the defense with 6 .... P—QB3 or 6 .... P—K3. Either one is
good, provided Black works as quickly as possible to get ....
P—QB4 in. The strongest line for White is 7 B—Q2, to speed
up the pressure on the QB file and thereby prevent .... P—
QB4; against accurate play, however, his plan is doomed to
failure. E.g., 7 .... P—Kt3; 8 B—K2, B—Kt2; 9 O—O,
QKt—Q2; 10 KR—Q1, P×P; 11 B×P, Kt—K1!; 12 QR—B1,
Kt—Q3; 13 B—K2, P—QB4 with equality. The maneuver
.... Kt—K1—Q3 is frequently useful for Black.

Since .... P—QB4 cannot be prevented in the long run, two improvements for White suggest themselves: P×P and an early P—K4. E.g., above, 8 P×P (instead of 8 B—K2), P×P; 9 Kt—K5, B—Kt2; 10 B—Kt5 (to weaken the Q-side), P—QR3; 11 B—K2 and now 11 .... Kt—B3!, though 12 P—B4 looks promising for White. This line may have a future; still, in the present stage of theory it need not be feared. 8 B—Q3 (instead of 8 B—K2 or 8 P×P), to force an early P—K4 is also not devoid of merit: on 8 .... B—Kt2; 9 O—O, P—K3; 10 P—K4 is a good try.

We have already mentioned the fact that the Gruenfeld abounds in unsolved tactical problems. It is not our intention to furnish any complete analysis here: that is the purpose of P.C.O. and additions to it. Our suggestions are designed to help the reader understand what has gone before and assist him in striking off on new paths if he so desires.

Without Q—Kt3, Black has no troubles at all. E.g., even where Black voluntarily plays 4 .... P—B3, after 5 Kt—B3, B—Kt2; 6 B—Q3, O—O; 7 O—O, P—Kt3, an early .... P—QB4 is inevitable. Without .... P—B3, ... P—B4 is even easier: 4 .... B—Kt2; 5 Kt—B3, O—O; 6 B—Q3, P—B4; 7 P×BP, Q—R4; 8 O—O, P×P; 9 B×BP, Q×P and Black has every reason to be satisfied.

After an early .... P—QB3 for Black, a maneuver sometimes seen is .... QP×BP, followed by .... P—QKt4, ... B—K3 and a quick attack on the Q-side. Such a plan is strategically unsound since it leaves the QBP backward on an open file. It is usually easily refuted, though Black can sometimes develop violent pressure. However, that is more often the case when White has weakened his Q-side by playing B—KB4.

We see that there are two great difficulties with 4 P—K3: White is unable to exert enough pressure on the QB file to prevent ....¹ P—QB4, and his QB is so much dead wood. This naturally leads to the second branch: 4 B—B4.

II. 4 B—B4 is considered strongest by many masters though, as we shall see, its lustre is fading.

The main ideas have already been mentioned: it develops the QB and increases the pressure on the QB file. There is, however, one great drawback: it weakens the Q-side, as a result of which .... P—QB4 is a far more dangerous counter. In the best lines Black can neither force .... P—QB4 nor permanently prevent P—K4; yet he can simplify to such an extent that the game is even for all practical purposes.

The remark made at the outset that the Gruenfeld has many unsolved problems is peculiarly applicable here: there are a number of controversial questions on which opinion shifts rapidly from one extreme to another.

The main line begins 4 .... B—Kt2; 5 P—K3. Now the QP is defended, so White is threatening to capture the QBP. Black can, if he so desires, give up the P—whether he gets sufficient compensation or not is a matter of dispute. E.g., 5 .... O—O; 6 P×P, Kt×P; 7 Kt×Kt, Q×Kt; 8 B×P, Kt—R3; 9 B×Kt, Q×KtP; 10 Q—B3 and White will have much the better of the ending. Or here 8 .... Kt—B3; 9 Kt—K2, B—Kt5; 10 P—B3, B×P; 11 P×B, Q×BP; 12 R—KKt1, Q×P with a complicated attack. The precise answers to these tactical questions will doubtless be given soon enough; a good deal depends on them. The author inclines to the opinion that the sacrifice is sound.

However, the replies 5 .... P—B3 or 5 .... P—K3 transpose into more regular lines in any case, so that we can still continue to consider 5 .... O—O. Then (if White does not take the P) 6 Q—Kt3 must follow (though 6 R—B1 has been experimented with too). On other moves, such as 6 Kt—B3, P—B4 is too powerful a reply. One illustration will show how the exchanges can lead to a plus for Black: 6 Kt—B3, P—B4; 7 P×QP, Kt×P; 8 B—K5, Kt×Kt; 9 P×Kt, P×P; 10 B×B, K×B; 11 BP×P, Q—R4ch; 12 Q—Q2, Kt—B3; 13 B—K2, R—Q1 and Black has the better ending—the P position is that in 40E.

But after 6 Q—Kt3, P—B4 is no longer strong, for now 7 BP×QP, P×P; 8 P×P, QKt—Q2; 9 B—K2! is powerful, while 7 QP×P, Q—R4; 8 P×P, Kt—K5; 9 Kt—K2 is again controversial, with practise favoring White. So 6 .... P—B3 (or even 6 .... P—K3) is necessary.

Thus we get to a crucial normal line which runs as follows: 4 B—B4, B—Kt2; 5 P—K3, O—O; 6 Q—Kt3, P—B3. Then on 7 Kt—B3 Black need temporize no longer: 7 .... P×P; 8 B×P, QKt—Q2; 9 O—O, Kt—Kt3; 10 B—K2, B—K3 (10 .... B—B4! is also excellent here); 11 Q—B2, QKt—Q4!; 12 B—K5, B—B4 (to prevent P—K4); 13 Q—Kt3, Q—Kt3 with equality. Black has been unable to force .... P—QB4, but the many exchanges suffice to free him. Even here, however, it must be remarked that if White can find some way to preserve the pressure on the QB file and avoid exchanges he should get the better of it because Black's P structure is essentially inferior.

4 B—B4 has been shorn of its terrors because of the weakness of the Q-side which it entails. Consequently, if some move could be found which holds the Q-side, but also exerts pressure on the center and Q-side and keeps the possibility of the development of the B open, it should yield White an advantage. What if we try the key move at once?

III. 4 Q—Kt3 has enjoyed a good deal of popularity in some periods, only to be almost wholly neglected in others. At first sight it appears that 4 .... P×P; 5 Q×BP, B—K3! would give Black enough counterplay, e.g., 6 Q—Kt5ch, Kt—B3!; 7 Kt—B3, Kt—Q4! and White, who can never afford to take the QKtP, will soon be driven back with loss of time. But instead of going after the P with 6 Q—Kt5ch above, White can carry out his basic strategy with 6 Q—Q3 or 6 Q—R4ch, followed by P—K4 in both cases.

Thus 4 .... P—B3 is probably best. Then White can transpose into more routine lines with 5 Kt—B3 or 5 P—K3 or 5 B—B4. But there is an interesting variant available. It is based on the idea of compelling a defense with .... P—K3, which is obviously not so good when White has his QB out. It runs 5 Kt—B3, B—Kt2; 6 P×P, P×P; 7 B—Kt5!, threatening to win the QP. 7 .... Kt—B3 is possible, but on 8 P—K3, P—K3 is best, despite the weakening. In the subsequent play White may try to attack on the K-side or in the center with P—K4 or on the QB file or he may combine several motifs. This line will doubtless be tried more in the future.

While Black's counterplay on the Q-side with .... QP×BP, ... P—QKt4 is strategically unsound because it leaves the QBP backward, it may be quite powerful on occasion because of Black's strong initiative. No general rule can be given: it depends on the peculiarities of each individual case. E.g., after 4 Q—Kt3, P—B3; 5 B—Kt5 can be met by 5 .... P×P; 6 Q×BP, P—QKt4; 7 Q—Q3, B—B4; 8 Q—Q1 (8 P—K4?, Kt×P!; 9 Kt×Kt, Q—Q4), P—Kt5; 9 Kt—R4, Kt—K5 with adequate counterplay.

Alternatives on White's fourth move introduce no new strategical ideas.

IV. 4 Kt—B3 is a waiting move which almost always transposes into other lines, already considered. One variant is 4 .... B—Kt2; 5 P×P, Kt×P; 6 P—KKt3, with the idea of exerting pressure against the Black center and Q-side. Straight development is good enough for Black, though after .... P—QB4 he must be careful not to exchange too early in the center. E.g., 6 .... O—O; 7 B—Kt2, P—QB4; 8 O—O, Kt×Kt; 9 P×Kt and now if 9 .... P×P (9 .... Kt—B3 is best); 10 Kt×P! Black suddenly has a tough job on his hands because he cannot develop normally.

V. 4 B—Kt5 is again inspired by the laudable aim of weakening Black's P position, but fails against 4 .... Kt—K5. E.g., 5 Kt×Kt, P×Kt; 6 Q—Q2 (to develop a quick attack against Black's K), P—QB4! (immediate counter-action is essential); 7 P—Q5, Kt—Q2; 8 P—B3, Q—Kt3!; 9 P×P, B—Kt2; 10 O—O—O, Q—R3 and Black has a powerful attack.

K-Indian Where White Avoids the Gruenfeld Defense

The lines to be discussed here could also be considered irregular variations of the K-Indian but the psychological reason for their choice—at least nowadays—is usually that of preventing the Gruenfeld.

First we have a fairly regular K-Indian where White does not try to force an early P—K4 and where Black reacts with a delayed .... P—Q4. This arises after 1 P—Q4, Kt—KB3; 2 P—QB4, P—KKt3; 3 P—KKt3 (or 3 Kt—KB3), P—Q4 (may also be delayed until White is actually threatening P—K4). The ideas are in no essential respect different from the Gruenfeld: a break with .... P—QB4 is the goal for Black, the advance P—K4 is the goal for White. To allow P—K4 without any immediate counter, however, does not turn out well for Black: 4 B—Kt2, B—Kt2; 5 P×P, Kt×P; 6 P—K4, Kt—Kt5; 7 P—QR3, KKt—B3; 8 P—Q5, Kt—Q5; 9 Kt—K2, B—Kt5; 10 QKt—B3 with advantage. P—K4 must be played early here. To prevent the strong center Black may support his QP with .... P—QB3: 3 P—KKt3, P—QB3; 4 B—Kt2, P—Q4, when he should have no real difficulties. E.g., 5 P×P, P×P; 6 Kt—KB3, B—Kt2; 7 O—O, O—O; 8 Kt—B3, Kt—K5! etc.

After 1 P—Q4, Kt—KB3; 2 P—QB4, P—KKt3; 3 P—B3, to compel an immediate P—K4, is a worthwhile try. One idea behind the move is to hold the center solidly, develop rapidly on the Q-side, and then attack Black's K. E.g., 3 .... B—Kt2; 4 P—K4, P—Q3; 5 Kt—B3, O—O; 6 B—K3, P—K4; 7 P—Q5, P—QR4; 8 B—Q3, Kt—R3; 9 Q—Q2, Kt—B4; 10 B—B2, P—QKt3; 11 O—O—O, followed by P—KKt4, P—KR4, with a strong attack. Black can equalize only by an early break in the center here or an effective .... P—KB4. Somewhat stronger for Black, though more risky, is 3 .... P—Q4; 4 P×P, Kt×P; 5 P—K4, Kt—Kt3; 6 Kt—B3, B—Kt2; 7 B—K3, O—O; 8 P—B4, Kt—B3!; 9 P—Q5, Kt—Kt1; 10 Kt—B3, P—QB3 with vigorous counterplay. The important point to remember is that Black cannot afford to be passive here: he must adopt some kind of systematic counter-action. Thus 3 .... P—B3 has its merits if followed up properly.

When White does not play P—QB4, Black has no theoretical problem (the same thing occurs in the analogous case of the QP opening) because White has omitted the strongest move. Black is at liberty to develop normally; if he uses his liberty he equalizes easily and early.

One line is of some interest as a precursor of a strong defense to the Reti Opening: 1 P—Q4, Kt—KB3; 2 Kt—KB3, P—KKt3; 3 B—B4 (the London System), B—Kt2; 4 P—KR3, P—B4; 5 P—B3, P—Kt3; 6 QKt—Q2, P×P (not essential immediately, but forestalls an early P—K4); 7 P×P, B—Kt2; 8 P—K3, O—O; 9 B—Q3, Kt—B3; 10 O—O, P—Q3; 11 Q—K2, P—QR3 with equality: both sides will be able to effect P—K4.

C. TCHIGORIN'S DEFENSE (OLD INDIAN): 1 P—Q4, Kt—KB3; 2 P—QB4, P—Q3

The only difference between this and the K-Indian is that Black's KB is not fianchettoed. Essentially, however, the ideas are the same: White wishes to force P—K4, hold on the K-side, advance on the Q-side, Black will break with .... P—KB4. The position of Black's KB is of no great importance.

It is important for White to threaten P—K4 early; if he does so his advantage is assured. A typical variation runs 3 Kt—QB3, QKt—Q2; 4 P—K4, P—K4; 5 P—Q5, Kt—B4; 6 P—B3, B—K2; 7 B—K3, O—O; 8 P—QKt4, etc.

Black may develop his QB early here, but it will be equally useless, if not more so, in its new position: 3 Kt—QB3, B—B4; 4 P—KKt3, P—B3; 5 B—Kt2, QKt—Q2; 6 P—K4, B—Kt3; 7 KKt—K2, etc.

There is a slight finesse on White's third move: if 3 Kt—KB3 (instead of 3 Kt—QB3), B—B4 gives Black reasonable prospects of equalizing because a normal P—K4 is no longer possible.

The type position may also arise from the Ruy Lopez (page 34). The frequency with which the Ruy Lopez and the Indian Defenses transpose into one another is one reason why the Ruy remains so refreshingly modern.

D. UNUSUAL ALTERNATIVES AFTER 1 P—Q4, Kt—KB3

While the lines to be discussed here have little theoretical value, they point to many new paths which an enterprising player may enter.

Budapest Defense: 1 P—Q4, Kt—KB3; 2 P—QB4, P—K4.
Though this is technically a defense, it might just as well be called a gambit. There is not too much rhyme or reason to the names of the chess openings!

If we view the opening as a gambit, we will find it much easier to understand because the regular principles for gambit play hold true. First, White takes the Pawn. Then, he does not try to hold on to it at all costs, but returns it in order to secure the better development. In that event White gets the better of it because Black's position will be disorganized. A striking analogy with the KP openings is that traps occur chiefly in the form of plays on White's KB2.

Thus the normal line runs 3 P×P, Kt—Kt5. Now 4 P—KB4?, B—B4 would be bad: Black has all the play. Likewise 4 Kt—KB3, B—B4; 5 P—K3, Kt—QB3 is inferior because his QB is shut in.

Instead, there are two strong continuations. One is 4 P—K4, Kt×KP; 5 P—KB4 (or even, less violently, 5 B—K2 followed by Kt—KB3 with a theoretically superior P position), KKt—B3; 6 B—K3 (or 6 Kt—B3, B—B4; 7 Kt—B3, P—Q3; 8 P—QR3—but it is simpler to block the diagonal), B—Kt5ch; 7 K—B2!, O—O; 8 Kt—KB3, Q—K2; 9 B—Q3, B—B4; 10 R—K1 with much the better of it, since White retains greater freedom for his pieces. This superior mobility is the essential point—White need not worry about his Pawn position as long as he retains it.

The alternative on White's fourth move is 4 B—B4, Kt—QB3; 5 Kt—KB3, B—Kt5ch and now 6 QKt—Q2 will yield him a permanent though slight advantage, while 6 Kt—B3, B×Ktch; 7 P×B, Q—K2; 8 Q—Q5, Q—R6; 9 R—B1, P—B3; 10 P×P, Kt×P (B3); 11 Q—Q2 maintains the Pawn at the cost of weak Pawns—a feasible procedure in this case. Against weak play on White's part Black can develop quickly and start an attack against White's K position.

By and large, however, there are so many ways in which White can get the better of it that the Budapest is practically never seen in games between two equal players.

Blumenfeld Counter Gambit: 1 P—Q4, Kt—KB3; 2 P—QB4, P—K3; 3 Kt—KB3, P—B4; 4 P—Q5, P—QKt4.

The motivating idea of this enterprising gambit is quite similar to that of the Evans: give up a P on the wing in order to secure ideal development and a powerful P center. E.g., 5 P×KP, BP×P; 6 P×P, P—Q4; 7 P—K3, B—Q3; 8 Kt—B3, O—O; 9 B—K2, B—Kt2; 10 P—QKt3, QKt—Q2 and eventually .... P—K4 with a powerful attack.

But if White spurns the gift and plays positionally Black's premature thrusts recoil on him. 5 B—Kt5 provides a thorough refutation, though the main variation is by no means hopeless for Black: 5 .... KP×P (best); 6 P×QP, P—KR3 (again best); 7 B×Kt, Q×B; 8 Q—B2, P—Q3; 9 P—K4, P—R3; 10 P—QR4! (essential to make the square QB4 available), P—Kt5 and now 11 P—R3! preserves White's vital Kt against Black's useless B and gives the first player all the chances in view of his immensely superior Pawn structure.

Minor alternatives offer no significant new ideas: they are easily understood as tactical attempts to get some more out of life.

In general, it is advisable for White to bear in mind that against a wholly passive attitude on Black's part, P—K4 will give him the better of it, while on .... P—QB4 without due preparation, P—Q5 is usually cramping. Black should remember that careless or passive play by White allows an early P—QB4, which should be followed by .... P—Q4 and eventually .... P—K4. Both sides must pay the greatest attention to transposition possibilities.

Benoni Counter Gambit: 1 P—Q4, P—QB4.

An aggressive but unsound counter-attack. With proper

play White secures an iron grip which Black cannot break.

On general principles the reply 2 P—Q5 is best; then 2 ....
P—K4—otherwise Black can have no hopes for counterplay
at all.

There are many ways to crush Black's play here; White has
an embarras de forces. These refutations employ one or more of
four ideas:

1. Get a Kt to QB4 and make it immune against attack with
P—QR4, thus exerting pressure against Black's QP and Q-side.

2. Attack the Pawns on the Q-side with P—QB3, P—QKt4,
or, on occasion, P—QKt4 directly.

3. After P—K4, an early P—KB4 may be played despite the
fact that Black may secure the square K4 for his pieces.

4. Fianchetto of the KB coupled with a general Pawn advance (P—QB4, P—K4, P—KB4)—this is much like cor-
responding variations in the K-Indian. The Q-side break is
facilitated by Black's P at QB4.

For Black the only independent plan is an advance on the
K-side with .... P—KB4 (normal break if White's P is at K4).
Otherwise he must react to what White does.

Two examples will illustrate the execution of these ideas.

2 P—Q5, P—K4; 3 P—K4, P—Q3; 4 B—Q3, P—QR3; 5
P—QR4, Kt—K2; 6 Kt—K2, Kt—Kt3; 7 Kt—R3, B—K2;
8 Kt—QB4, O—O; 9 O—O, Kt—Q2; 10 B—Q2! (prevents
.... Kt—Kt3), P—QKt3; 11 P—QB3 with a clear superiority.

Or 2 P—Q5, P—K4; 3 Kt—KB3, P—Q3; 4 P—KKt3,
P—KKt3; 5 B—Kt2, B—Kt2; 6 Kt—B3, Kt—K2; 7 O—O,
O—O; 8 Kt—Q2, P—B4; 9 Kt—B4, P—QR3; 10 P—QR4,
P—Kt3; 11 B—Kt5, R—R2; 12 Q—Q2 to be followed by P—
B4 or B—R6 with a powerful attack.

Dutch Defense: 1 P—Q4, P—KB4.

Black's main idea here, as we have already mentioned, is to
prevent P—K4 by a flank advance. He thereby reserves the
option of any one of a number of good Pawn configurations in
the center, the main ones being as usual .... P—Q3 and ....
P—K4 or .... P—K3 and .... P—Q4, with .... P—QB4

always useful. White, of course, will not abandon his plan to advance the KP. Thus both sides will bring up reserves, White to prepare P—K4, Black to prevent it or to neutralize it.

As so often in the QP opening, White's play is most effective in the center and on the Q-side, while Black's counter-action will take place on the K-side. Against careless play Black may well build up a strong attack.

The K-fianchetto is the best procedure for White, though it is not immediately obvious why that is so, in view of the fact that there is no Black QB at QKt2 to neutralize. We do know, however, that play will center around White's K4 to a considerable extent, and that Black has hopes of a K-side attack. The easiest K-position to defend in such cases is that with the fianchettoed B (provided it is not exchanged) while the control of the center from a distance is most forceful in all these openings.

While Black can choose one of two or more P configurations, quick development is as usual essential for him. Further, his B is best placed at K2 or Q3 (often it is a good idea to exchange it), so that .... P—K3 will be necessary regardless of which Pawn set-up he chooses.

These points suffice to explain the main line: 2 P—KKt3, Kt—KB3; 3 B—Kt2, P—K3; 4 Kt—KB3, B—K2; 5 P—B4, O—O; 6 O—O (*Diagram No. 43A*).

Now Black must make up his mind about the further course of the game. He has two major alternatives and one minor one: 6 .... P—Q3, 6 .... P—Q4 and 6 .... Kt—K5.

6 .... P—Q3 is inferior because Black cannot compel .... P—K4 under favorable circumstances. On the contrary: White can often force P—Q5 in a position where the reply .... P—K4 is impossible, so that after .... KP×QP by Black, or QP×KP by White, Black's Pawns will be irrevocably split and permanently weak. This is one of the major motifs for White against the Dutch.

After 6 .... P—Q3; 7 Kt—B3, Q—K1 (7 .... Kt—B3 allows 8 P—Q5) there are many ways in which White can get the better of it. All the lines boil down to development plus preparation of P—K4. The simplest is doubtless 8 R—K1, Q—R4; 9 P—K4, P×P; 10 Kt×P, Kt×Kt; 11 R×Kt, Kt—B3; 12 B—B4, B—B3; 13 P—KR4, P—KR3; 14 R—B1!, P—R3; 15 P—B5—note the ingenious way in which Black's Pawns have been hopelessly weakened.

On .... Kt—QB3 by Black at any earlier stage (before P—K4) an immediate P—Q5, to split the Black Pawns is both imperative and positionally crushing.

No. 43A

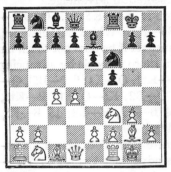

Position after 6 O—O in the Dutch Defense.

No. 43B

Position after 7 .... P—B3 in the Dutch Defense.

From the above variation it is clear that Black cannot develop his Q-side quickly but must bank on play on the other wing. The reason is that .... QKt—Q2 cramps his game too much, while .... Kt—QB3 is always refuted by P—Q5. Consequently the idea of forcing .... P—K4 without the development of the QKt comes to mind. One way to do it is by getting the B to B3. Thus we see the raison d'etre of 6 .... Kt—K5. Unfortunately White can break immediately with 7 P—Q5!, e.g., 7 .... B—B3; 8 Q—B2, and now 8 .... P—K4 is best, though after 9 QKt—Q2, Kt×Kt; 10 Kt×Kt!, P—Q3; 11 P—B5 White retains all the play. This variation, however, has not been analyzed too much.

6 .... P—Q4—the third branch on Black's sixth move (*Diagram No. 43A*)—is by far the best: it blocks P—K4 for a long time to come and by holding the center solid paves the way for play on the K-side. After the further 7 Kt—B3, P—B3, there is no way in which White can get significantly the better of it (*Diagram No. 43B*). He can try to force an early P—K4 by Kt—K5, P—B3, etc. but allows too much blood-letting: 8 Q—Q3, Kt—K5; 9 Kt—K5, Kt—Q2; 10 KKt×Kt, B×Kt; 11 P—B3, Kt×Kt; 12 P×Kt, P×P; 13 Q×QBP, B—Q3 and Black has exchanged sufficiently to get a free game, though White still has a slight theoretical advantage.

Black's counter-attack calls for .... Kt—K5, ... Q—K1—R4, ... P—KKt4, ... R—B3—R3. White can, however, afford to disregard the entire maneuver if he does not touch his K-side. Thus he can touch off a sharp struggle by advancing immediately on the Q-side: 8 R—Kt1, Q—K1; 9 P—B5!, Q—R4; 10 P—QKt4, Kt—K5; 11 Q—B2, Kt—Q2; 12 P—Kt5, B—B3; 13 B—B4, Q—K1!; 14 B—B7, R—B2; 15 B—R5, P—K4! with approximate equality.

Again we have a situation where both sides search for improvements: White because his advantage against .... P—Q4 is too small, Black because he does not secure full freedom.

One most suggestive variant for White is developing the Kt at KR3, for in one of the main lines he must move the Kt away anyhow to prepare P—K4. Then the situation is reversed for Black: .... P—Q4 is inferior, while .... P—Q3 is strong. The reason is that now there is less to prevent .... P—K4. E.g., 2 P—KKt3, Kt—KB3; 3 B—Kt2, P—K3; 4 Kt—KR3 and now 4 .... P—Q4; 5 O—O, B—Q3; 6 P—QB4, P—B3; 7 Kt—B3, QKt—Q2; 8 Q—Q3 (to defend the BP), Kt—K5; 9 P—B3, Kt×Kt; 10 P×Kt, B—K2; 11 P—K4 and White has all the play. But after 4 .... P—Q3 (instead of 4 .... P—Q4); 5 O—O, B—K2; 6 P—QB4, O—O; 7 Kt—B3, Q—K1; 8 Kt—B4, B—Q1; 9 P—K4, P—K4!; 10 P×KP, QP×P; 11 Kt—Q3, P×P; 12 QKt×P, Kt—B3; 13 R—K1, Q—Kt3 Black has a free game and little to fear.

For Black the only important variant is that where he tries to exchange his KB early (compare the Q-Indian). For a long time it was believed that such an exchange was favorable for him. To avoid it White then delayed the advance of the QBP until Black's B has moved. Recent practise, however, indicates that this view is not justified.

After 2 P—QB4, P—K3; 3 P—KKt3, Kt—KB3; 4 B—Kt2, B—Kt5ch; 5 B—Q2 leads to very little after 5 .... B×Bch; 6 Q×B, O—O; 7 Kt—QB3, P—Q4; 8 Kt—B3, Kt—B3!, though the weakness on the Black squares is painful for the defender. However, this time White can avoid the B exchange effectually: 5 Kt—B3 (5 Kt—Q2 is also good), O—O; 6 Kt—R3, P—Q4; 7 O—O, P—B3; 8 Q—Kt3, Kt—R3; 9 Kt—B4, B—Q3; 10 Kt—Q3, Kt—B2; 11 P—B5, B—K2; 12 B—B4 with advantage because of his hold on K5.

The Staunton Gambit, 2 P—K4, is a complicated and promising line for White. Though there is no theoretical refutation known, it is still highly speculative. It is based on the idea of quick development to secure a K-side attack.

2 .... P×P is virtually forced. To regain the P immediately leads to nothing for White: he must attack. Thus he will advance on the K-side. E.g., 3 Kt—QB3, Kt—KB3; 4 B—KKt5, P—KKt3; 5 P—KR4, P—Q3; 6 P—R5 with a strong attack. Best for Black is a delayed support of the center with .... P—QKt3. E.g., 4 B—KKt5 (as above), P—QKt3; 5 B—QB4, P—K3!; 6 B×Kt, Q×B; 7 Kt×P, Q—K2; 8 B—Q3, Kt—B3; 9 P—QB3, B—Kt2 followed by .... O—O—O with good chances.

In virtually all variations White may sooner or later play P—KB3, when Black will have to capture, advance .... P—K6, or defend with .... P—Q4. .... P—K6 is usually good enough to equalize, though White then retains the initiative. .... P×P or .... P—Q4 must be tried if Black wants to refute the gambit.

Chapter VI

RETI AND ENGLISH OPENINGS

RETI OPENING: 1 Kt—KB3, P—Q4

The Reti opening is the quintessence of hypermodernism. It was most popular when the brilliant but erratic masters of that school were on top. Since then (about 1930) it has declined somewhat, though it still remains one of the most important openings.

It is frequently said that White's leading idea in the Reti opening is *control* rather than *occupation* of the center. To a certain limited extent that is true, for White develops his Bishops by fianchetto and does not (normally) advance a center Pawn for six or seven moves. And yet the statement is a deceptive over-simplification. In reality *the basic idea is to occupy the center at a time when it is directly favorable for White*. White's goal is as ever a strong center, but he goes about it *indirectly*. If Black is not aware of what his opponent is driving at, he will assuredly fall into a subtle positional trap; if he is, he should have no trouble.

One of the major weapons which White uses is that of allowing his opponent to occupy the center with his Pawns and *then*, when Black is exposed, to strike at those Pawns and create irremediable weaknesses (mainly "holes"). Again the defender must be careful not to be taken off guard. Essentially the idea is the same as that in Alekhine's Defense or some branches of the Indian; the only difference is that this time White is playing a come-hither-my-darling-and-let-me-snare-you game with Black, instead of the reverse. It is no accident that many masters who are addicted to such defenses for Black also like Reti's for White.

The fianchetto is a characteristic of this opening. There are two ways to deprive such a Bishop of its strength: one is by firmly planting the center with Pawns (rarely feasible for any length of time), the other is by exchanging it (the most usual method).

We have repeatedly had occasion to observe in the QP opening that when White neglects the powerful P—QB4, to increase the pressure on White's center, Black's theoretical troubles are over. Here P—QB4 is played, but P—Q4 is omitted—and the same observation holds true. By sticking to a few fundamental

No. 44   No. 45

Reti opening.   Catalan System.

principles—the ones we have been emphasizing throughout—Black will overcome the inherent difficulties of the opening.

After 1 Kt—KB3, there is only one important independent reply, 1 .... P—Q4. Now P—Q4 is good, of course, but the Reti continuation is 2 P—B4.

There are four possible replies for Black, each based on different ideas. Objectively, there is little to choose among these lines, though each has special advantages and drawbacks. They are:

1. 2 .... P×P avoids complications and prepares the construction of a powerful center with .... P—QB4 and .... P—K4. Its advantage is that normal continuations lead to a con-

siderable superiority for Black; a minor drawback is that White can transpose into the QGA.

2. 2 .... P—Q5 cramps White and sets up a Benoni Counter Gambit with colors reversed. Careless play by White leads to an overwhelming position for his opponent; on the other hand Black's center may collapse or prove terribly weak.

3. 2 .... P—QB3 maintains a Pawn in the center and allows the QB to get out. Its good feature is that it permits free and easy development of all the pieces, its bad one that a delayed advance in the center by White may cramp Black all over again because the natural .... P—QB4 would be out of place.

4. 2 .... P—K3 likewise holds a Pawn in the center, but this time shuts in the QB—it is in reality nothing but the Orthodox Defense applied to the Reti opening. Black's liberating plan is the same: P—QB4 and eventually .... P—K4. It is more solid than any of the others, but less aggressive. Black can at best secure equality here; in the alternatives he can frequently get the better of it.

We shall now consider these alternatives in greater detail.

I. 2 .... *P×P* is undoubtedly simplest for Black, though White can level the game too easily if he so desires.

Of the three ways in which White can recapture the Pawn, only two—3 Kt—R3 and 3 P—K3 have been seriously tested, though 3 Q—R4ch, by analogy with the QGA and the Catalan System, certainly has its merits.

It is rather difficult to explain why 3 Kt—R3 held the stage for such a long time. That it is bizarre and pleased the hypermoderns on principle because it violated the tenets of the classical school surely were weighty psychological factors. But be that as it may, there can be no doubt today that 3 Kt—R3 is a bad move. After the further logical continuation 3 Kt—R3, P—QB4; 4 Kt×P, Kt—QB3; 5 P—QKt3, P—K4; 6 B—Kt2, P—B3!; 7 P—Kt3, KKt—K2; 8 B—Kt2, Kt—B4! (somewhat stronger than 8 .... Kt—Q4); 9 O—O, B—K2; 10 R—B1, B—K3; 11 P—Q3, O—O; 12 KKt—Q2, Q—Q2 Black has a considerable advantage on every count. It should be borne in mind that Black must be careful not to let his QBP be subject to attack before he is fully developed.

The attentive reader may have noticed that the final position here is structurally the same as the variation of the Sicilian Defense (page 90) where White manages to play P—QB4; The colors of course are reversed. In that line Black is reduced to passivity because he has no prospects on the QB file; here the same holds for White. If White maneuvers for an early P—KB4, to get rid of one of Black's major trumps, he may equalize; otherwise he is bound to come off badly.

However, if White avoids the above line, he can equalize without any trouble. Thus instead of 5 P—QKt3, 5 Kt(B4)—K5, Kt×Kt; 6 Kt×Kt, Kt—B3 (not 6 .... P—B3 now because of 7 Q—R4 ch); 7 P—K3, P—K3; 8 P—QKt3, Kt—Q2; 9 B—Kt5, B—Q3 whittles down the wood too much.

Likewise 3 P—K3 is good enough to equalize because it will normally transpose into the QGA. E.g., 3 .... Kt—KB3; 4 B×P, P—K3; 5 P—Q4, P—B4, etc. Both sides may vary from the QGA, though the results are unclear. White must then avoid the natural P—Q4, which bodes ill for his prospects of getting an advantage. Black may try 3 .... Kt—QB3 on 3 P—K3; then 4 B×P, P—K4; 5 Q—Kt3, Kt—R3 leads to wild and woolly complications.

II. 2 .... P—Q5 is the normal reply for White against the Benoni Counter Gambit (which White is playing here with colors reversed and a move in hand), so strong there that it constitutes a thorough refutation. Yet here it is somewhat dubious because of a new factor: the extra move makes it uncertain whether Black can maintain his powerful wedge at Q5 under favorable circumstances or not.

Again, if Black is allowed to reinforce his QP he will secure an overwhelming position. E.g., 3 P—QKt4, P—KB3; 4 B—Kt2, P—K4; 5 P—QR3, P—QB4; 6 P×P, B×P; 7 P—Q3? Kt—B3; 8 QKt—Q2, P—B4!; 9 P—Kt3, Kt—B3; 10 B—Kt2, O—O; 11 O—O, Q—K1 with terrific pressure.

We see why it is essential for White to hammer at the Black

QP early or secure compensation in some other way. For this reason both P—K3 and P—QKt4 must come in. It so happens that 3 P—K3 is best: then a normal line would run 3 . . . . P— QB4, 4 PXP (again 4 P—QKt4, P—B3; 5 PXBP, P—K4 is good for Black), PXP; 5 P—KKt3, Kt—QB3; 6 B—Kt2, P— KKt3; 7 P—Q3, B—Kt2; 8 O—O, P—K4; 9 R—K1, P—B3, 10 P—QKt4! (it is still strong; otherwise Black could consolidate his center), 10 . . . . KtXP (otherwise White's pressure becomes too strong on the Q-side); 11 Q—R4ch, Kt—B3; 12 KtXQP, QXKt; 13 BXKt ch, B—Q2 with equality. It should be noted that White's compensation for Black's strong center consisted of pressure against the Q-side, for which his KB is ideally situated. The attempt to hold Q5 with a piece is also feasible, but after 3 P—K3, Kt—QB3; 4 PXP, KtXP; 5 KtXKt, QXKt; 6 Kt—B3, P—QB3; 7 P—Q3, P—K4! is necessary to hold the White QP.

III. 2 . . . . P—QB3 is played to hold the center and get the QB out. It allows a number of transpositions, chiefly to the Slav Defense with 3 P—Q4. But the major line to be considered here is Reti's old favorite, where both Bishops are fianchettoed.

White's idea in Reti's continuation is to control the center from a distance, then, after development is completed, break at an opportune moment and get the upper hand in the center himself. Passive play on Black's part would allow a crushing bind. A classic instance is the game Reti-Bogoljuboff, New-York, 1924: 3 P—QKt3, Kt—B3; 4 B—Kt2, P—K3; 5 P— Kt3, QKt—Q2; 6 B—Kt2, B—Q3; 7 O—O, O—O; 8 P—Q4, R —K1?; 9 QKt—Q2, Kt—K5; 10 KtXKt!, PXKt; 11 Kt—K5! P—KB4; 12 P—B3!, PXP; 13 BXP, Q—B2; 14 KtXKt, BXKt; 15 P—K4 with an overwhelming position. Note how effective the delayed break in the center has been. But once Black gets his QB out, he will have no such troubles. Then it is essential for White to block the diagonal of the enemy B, which means P—Q3 is to come in rather than P—Q4. This weakens his K5 square, so that Black is at liberty to advance his KP.

Reti hoped that the two Black center Pawns would then prove weak; we know today that his hope was a mirage. Thus a main line here, where both sides carry out their plans, would run as follows: 3 P—KKt3, Kt—B3; 4 B—Kt2, B—B4; 5 P—Kt3, QKt—Q2; 6 B—Kt2, P—K3; 7 O—O, B—Q3; 8 P—Q3, O—O; 9 QKt—Q2 (logical, but 9 Kt—B3 is better), P—K4! (takes advantage of the first good opportunity); 10 P×P (not to exchange would be worse because the diagonal of White's KB would be rendered useless), P×P; 11 R—B1, Q—K2; 12 R—B2, P—QR4! (always strong against this type of forma-tion); 13 P—QR4, P—R3; 14 Q—R1 (still aiming at the Black center), KR—K1 and Black has much the better of it. Al-ternatives for White lead to equality at best unless Black ad-vances his KP prematurely. E.g., above, 8 .... P—K4? (in-stead of 8 .... O—O) would be refuted by 9 P—K4! B—K3; 10 KP×P, BP×P; 11 P—Q4! P—K5; 12 Kt—Kt5, O—O; 13 P× P with a won game. Should White try P—Q4 instead of P—Q3, Black's QB will control a powerful diagonal, while White's B's will do little. Black can then attack on the Q-side with .... P—QR4—R5, B—R6, if possible.

IV. 2 .... P—K3 is solid, but introduces no essentially new ideas. Development is the order of the day for both sides. Black's normal strategy is to play .... P—QB4 early, ... P—K4 too, if possible; White would then have to exchange early to prevent a powerful center. The problems for both sides are much the same as in the previous lines. On the whole, however, this line is most passive and least promising for Black.

From what has been said there is one all-important con-clusion to be drawn: Reti's original thought of provoking a center advance by Black in the conviction that the Pawns would later prove weak has to be discarded because with any kind of reasonably good defense by Black, his center remains as strong as ever. In all the variations where White does nothing about the center in the early stages but try to "control it from the sides," Black gets a clear superiority. If White, however, prevents such a center, or neutralizes it immediately, equality results. On the other hand, if Black ignores his opportunity and does not occupy the center White gets an overwhelming bind.

Yet there can be no doubt that the Reti system and the idea of control of the center from a distance have some merit as is shown, e.g., by the many traps which Black must be careful not to fall into. We are therefore naturally impelled to look for an opening which will have the good feature of the Reti (real control from a distance, effective diagonals for the B's) and avoid the bad ones (enemy center Pawns become too strong, enemy develops too freely). Such a line is the Catalan System, which combines some long-distance control of the center (P—KKt3) with occupation (P—Q4) and has the additional virtue of permitting several favorable transpositions.

CATALAN SYSTEM

There are several forms of this opening, which makes it difficult to set up an exact beginning. Besides, it may arise in a variety of ways, from the Reti, QGA, QGD, or the Queen Pawn Game. All however have one essential unifying idea for White: the combination of P—Q4 and P—KKt3.

No. 46A	No. 46B

Position after 7 .... Kt×P! in the Catalan System.	Position after 7 Kt—B3 in the Catalan System.

One of the first things that strikes us (see *Diagram No. 45*) is that Black has been made to transpose into the .... P—K3 defense to the Reti (page 215) which is, as we saw there, the least promising for the second player.

There are two main transposition traps which Black must sidestep. The first is familiar from the regular Reti: Black must hit at White's center with .... P—QB4. .... P—QB3 instead leaves him with a terribly cramped game, which he might conceivably hold, but which is a long uphill fight at best. The second is more subtle: after .... P—QB4, White may well reply BP×QP. Then, ... KP×QP would suddenly leave Black in a most unfavorable branch of the Tarrasch Defense, the Rubinstein variation (page 126).

As in the regular Reti, one thing is again clear: to get a reasonably good game Black must play aggressively. With this in mind, and to avoid the traps mentioned above, Black can choose one of two defensive ideas: a) an early break with .... P—QB4 coupled with speedy development or b) the exchange .... QP×BP to transpose into a QGA type of position.

.... P—QB4 may be played on the 4th, 5th, or 6th move. It is usually seen on the 6th, though that does not mean that it is necessarily best at that point.

The main line from *Diagram No. 45* runs as follows: 4 .... B—K2; 5 B—Kt2, O—O; 6 O—O, P—B4; 7 P×QP, Kt×P! (*Diagram No. 46A*). Note that 7 .... KP×P here instead of 7 .... Kt×P would transpose into the unfavorable Tarrasch Defense.

In *Diagram No. 46A* the normal 8 P—K4 sets a difficult problem for Black: how to develop adequately without weakening the P position. As it is put, the problem is insoluble: Black must submit to weak Pawns in order to get his pieces out properly. But he can neutralize his weakness by foreseeing his position. Thus, e.g., 8 P—K4, Kt—Kt3; 9 Kt—B3, P×P; 10 Kt×P, B—B3? is weak because of 11 Kt(Q4)—Kt5, Kt—B3; 12 B—K3, Kt—B5; 13 B—B5, Q×Q; 14 QR×Q, R—Q1; 15 R×Rch, B×R; 16 P—Kt3 and Black still has his QR and

QB back where they don't belong. White's main idea here has
been to keep Black's Q-side undeveloped and increase the
pressure against it slowly but surely. But in the above variation, after 8 P—K4, Kt—Kt3; 9 Kt—B3, P×P; 10 Kt×P,
Kt—B3! is sufficient to equalize because on 11 Kt×Kt, P×Kt;
12 Q—K2, P—K4; 13 B—K3, B—K3; 14 KR—Q1, Q—B2
Black's exposed QBP is easily defended and he has adequate
counterplay against White's Q-side Pawns.

The alternative 8 Kt—B3 in *Diagram No. 46A*, to leave the
long diagonal open for the White KB, is harmless against
speedy development: 8 .... Kt×Kt; 9 P×Kt, P×P; 10
P×P, B—Q2!; 11 Kt—K5, Kt—B3! and we have a familiar P
position, favorable for Black (*Diagram No. 40E*).

While these lines are enough for theoretical equality, it is
understandable that Black will want to look for improvements.

.... P—QB4 earlier may transpose into the above main
line, but Black has some fair variants at his disposal.

After 4 .... B—K2 (*Diagram No. 45*); 5 O—O, P—B4 (instead of 5 .... O—O); 6 P×QP, Kt×P; 7 P×P, B×P; 8 Q—
B2 with some pressure is possible: White will try to cash in on
his headstart in development. Other lines lead to nothing for
White.

Better for Black is 4 .... P—B4 (in *Diagram No. 45*) and if
then 5 BP×P, Kt×P; 6 B—Kt2, P×P; 7 O—O, B—B4!, thus
posting the B more aggressively without loss of time. Black
can then equalize easily by straight development.

On the alternative 4 .... QP×BP, which leads to a QGA
type of position, White recaptures his P with Q—R4 ch. It
will be recalled that this is one of the most promising lines of
the QGA. Here too White retains a little pressure in almost all
variations. In *Diagram No. 46A*, after 4 .... P×P; 5 Q—R4
ch, QKt—Q2, it is best for White to delay recapture of the BP
as long as possible, for in that way he keeps Black's game
cramped longest. Thus the main line runs 6 B—Kt2, P—
QR3! (to compel the capture); 7 Kt—B3! (preventing ....
P—QKt4—*Diagram No. 46B*).

Now Black has a choice of three lines: .... R—QKt1, to compel Q×BP and a consequent clarification of the position, ... P—B4, the normal break in such cases, and .... B—K2, to complete his development before undertaking any counter-action. The first two are about equally good; the third is rather passive, though quite playable.

White's major idea is to compel Black to weaken his position in some way in order to develop properly. E.g., on 7 .... P—B4; 8 O—O, B—K2 is necessary, when 9 P×P gains a move, which may well turn out to be of great value: 9 .... B×P; 10 Q×BP, P—QKt4; 11 Q—KR4, B—Kt2; 12 B—Kt5, O—O; 13 QR—Q1, Q—B2; 14 R—B1! with strong pressure.

Perhaps simplest for Black is the forcing 7 .... R—QKt1; 8 Q×BP, P—QKt4; 9 Q—Q3, B—Kt2; 10 O—O, P—B4; 11 P×P, Kt×P; 12 Q×Qch, R×Q; 13 B—B4 and now simply 13 .... B—O3 with approximate equality. 7 .... B—K2 is also good: 8 O—O, O—O; 9 Q×BP, P—QKt4; 10 Q—Q3, B—Kt2 and if 11 P—K4, P—B4 with strong counterplay.

On 5 Q—R4ch (after 4 .... P×P in *Diagram No. 45*) an alternate idea for Black is 5 .... B—Q2; 6 Q×BP, B—B3; 7 B—Kt2, B—Q4; 8 Q—B2, Kt—B3! with good chances.

White may also try the Catalan on his third move: 1 P—Q4, Kt—KB3; 2 P—QB4, P—K3; 3 P—KKt3. In most cases there is no essential difference; Black may, however, vary with 3 .... B—Kt5ch. After 4 B—Q2, B×Bch; 5 Kt×B, Kt—B3!; 6 KKt—B3, P—Q3 with a line analogous to the Zurich in the Nimzoindian defense is best. .... P—Q4 is inferior for Black: it enhances the value of White's KB and gives White play on the QB file.

ENGLISH OPENING: 1 P—QB4

The English is in many respects similar to Reti's. Both are openings which derive their strength largely from transposition possibilities. Both involve complicated positional motifs where knowledge and good judgment are equally essential. Both appeal to players who like to leave the beaten track.

From a theoretical point of view, it is quite easy to see what the analogy is due to. In both White does not occupy the center but hits at it from the side. Consequently Black will place his Pawns in the center, which will, in many cases, lead to familiar openings with colors reversed.

The English may lead into a number of familiar openings directly, as, e.g., with 1 P—QB4, Kt—KB3; 2 P—Q4; here we

No. 47

Position after 3 .... Kt—QB3 in the
English opening.

shall only consider those lines which distinctively belong to this opening.

As in Reti's opening, the natural reply for Black is to place a P in the center with 1 .... P—K4. Then we have a Sicilian Defense with colors reversed and with a move in hand. This extra move creates three important differences from the regular Sicilian. The first is that while .... P—Q4 is normally a great problem there, here it can be played whenever White wishes to do so. The second is the significant feature that White can build up his counterplay on the QB file more quickly in the present case. The third is that P—Q4 by Black (analogue of the strongest for White) is by no means simple. These three differences, in addition to the normal characteristics of the Sicilian, determine the further course of play.

In the main line, both sides first develop their Kt's: **1 ....**

P—K4; 2 Kt—QB3, Kt—KB3; 3 Kt—B3, Kt—B3 (note the order in which the Kt's are developed—it will be commented on later) when we have *Diagram No. 47.*

In *Diagram No. 47* White now has four lines to choose from:

a. 4 P—Q4 is the normal break for Black in the Sicilian. It equalizes there, and here too, but White wants more.

b. 4 P—Q3 leads to the Dragon Variation of the Sicilian with an extra move—the most popular.

c. 4 P—K4 prevents .... P—Q4, envisages transposition into a number of favorable lines, based on the possibility of hitting at Black's KP.

d. 4 P—K3 is passive and unusual, but trappy.

These lines are worth more attention.

I. 4 P—Q4 is played chiefly in the hope that White will be able to set up a favorable Pawn flanking with P—QB4 and P—K4 against a Black Pawn at Q3 (compare page 37 in the Ruy Lopez). E.g., on the passive 4 .... P×P; 5 Kt×P, P—Q3?; 6 P—K4 sets up a familiar positional superiority. Yet 5 .... P—Q4 above would be too loose. An aggressive move is called for which will develop and prepare a center break: here it is 5 .... B—QKt5, the strength of which is derived from the fact that it pins the Kt which controls the two vital central squares, Q4 and K5 (Q5 and K4 for White).

Thus the main line from *Diagram No. 47* is (4 P—Q4), P×P; 5 Kt×P, B—Kt5! There are now two feasible replies to the threat of .... P—Q4: one is 6 Kt×Kt, which simplifies too much, the other is 6 B—Kt5, which maintains the tension. On 6 B—Kt5, the crucial variation is 6 .... P—KR3!; 7 B—R4, B×Ktch; 8 P×B, Kt—K4!; 9 P—K3, P—Q3; 10 B—K2, Kt—Kt3; 11 B—Kt3, Kt—K5; 12 Q—B2, Q—K2; 13 B—Q3 with about even chances: White's superior development and two B's are equalled by Black's better P position.

II. 4 P—Q3 is probably the most promising for White, since the extra move changes a good deal. After 4 .... P—Q4; 5 P×P, Kt×P, 6 P—KKt3 (6 P—K3 is weak, 6 P—K4!? is not impossible) we have the Dragon. Then on 6 .... B—K2; 7

B—Kt2, Kt—Kt3; 8 O—O, O—O; 9 B—K3 Black's best procedure is to be consistent and play as though he were White in the Dragon: 9 .... P—B4! and if 10 Kt—QR4, P—B5!; 11 B—B5, B—Q3! etc. In other words, the extra move compels Black to neglect the Q-side completely and attack on the other wing. Passive play on the other hand will most likely lead to an inferior game because White's counteraction on the QB file gets under way so quickly; Black can also maintain equality by holding the center solid.

III. 4 P—K4 is designed to prevent .... P—Q4 and prepare to remove the Black KP. With a passive defense Black will again be badly off: e.g., 4 .... P—Q3? 5 P—Q4, B—Kt5 (5 .... P×P is familiar); 6 P—Q5, Kt—Q5; 7 B—K2, B×Kt; 8 B×B, B—K2; 9 B—K3, Kt×Bch; 10 Q×Kt and White has a P position which we know to be favorable: he will soon advance on the Q-side (*Diagram No. 360*).

Again Black comes out all right if he develops his KB. E.g., 4 .... B—B4; 5 Kt×P, Kt×Kt; 6 P—Q4, B—Kt5; 7 P×Kt, Kt×P; 8 Q—Q4, P—KB4 with approximate equality.

As long as Black avoids the positional error of giving up his KP without reason he should have no trouble.

IV. 4 P—K3 is a tricky move, played in the hope that a Black advance in the center will prove premature. But as usual normal development is good enough for Black. E.g., 4 .... B—Kt5; 5 Kt—Q5?, P—K5!; 6 Kt×B, Kt×Kt; 7 Kt—Q4, O—O; 8 B—K2, P—Q4 with the better prospects, or above 5 Q—B2, O—O; 6 B—K2, R—K1; 7 O—O, P—Q3; 8 Kt—K1, B—K3, eventually .... P—Q4 with an excellent game. 4 .... P—Q4 may also be played at once, though 5 P×P, Kt×P; 6 B—Kt5 transposes into one of the strongest Sicilian lines for Black with an extra move (page 90).

The main ideas to be remembered in the above lines are, for White, that he can try to get an advantage with P's at QB4 and K4 vs. one at Q3, or with the extra move in the Dragon Variation, for Black, that .... P—Q4 should be played whenever feasible (though there are some traps) and that he should concentrate on quick development, especially of the KB.

We mentioned above that the order of moves is quite important in the early stages. There are two important variants which illustrate this point.

The first is that after 1 P—QB4, P—K4; 2 Kt—KB3 is more than adequately met by 2 .... P—K5!, provided Black takes advantage of the first good opportunity to break with .... P—Q4. Thus: 2 Kt—KB3, P—K5; 3 Kt—Q4, Kt—QB3; 4 Kt—B2, Kt—B3; 5 Kt—B3, B—B4!; 6 P—QKt3, O—O; 7 P—Kt3, P—Q4! and if 8 P×P!, Kt—KKt5! with a strong attack, or even 8 .... Kt—QKt5; 9 Kt×Kt, B×Kt; 10 B—KKt2, R—K1; 11 O—O, B—KB4; 12 B—Kt2, Kt×P with full equality. But 7 .... R—K1 above (instead of 7 .... P—Q4); 8 B—KKt2, P—QR4; 9 O—O, P—Q3; 10 Kt—K3 is in White's favor because the break with .... P—Q4 will never again be possible.

The second major instance where the order of moves can mean a great deal occurs after 1 P—QB4, P—K4; 2 Kt—QB3. Now 2 .... Kt—QB3 (the right move is 2 .... Kt—KB3 for an early .... P—Q4) allows 3 P—KKt3!, when .... P—Q4 at an early stage is out of the question. Consequently Black must develop with .... P—KKt3, which is an inferior line against the Sicilian. White may then get somewhat the better of it by advancing his KBP before getting his Kt out, thus securing good pressure against the enemy center. E.g., 3 P—KKt3, P—KKt3; 4 B—Kt2, B—Kt2; 5 P—Q3, P—Q3; 6 P—B4!, KKt—K2, 7 Kt—B3, B—Kt5; 8 O—O, O—O; 9 P—KR3, B×Kt; 10 B×B, Kt—B4; 11 K—R2, P×P; 12 B×P with the better prospects because of his two B's and stronger center potential.

It should be remembered that the first law for White in the Sicilian is to be aggressive; thus here if Black is passive White will be bound to get the better of it.

Of the many possible alternate defenses, there are only two which merit any consideration.

The first is the symmetrical line with 1 .... P—QB4. Here White can secure a slight advantage with 2 Kt—KB3, Kt—KB3; 3 P—Q4!, for if say 3 .... P×P; 4 Kt×P, P—Q3; 5 Kt—QB3, Kt—B3 6 P—K4! we have a real Sicilian Defense (with the right colors!) in one of the worst variations for Black. Likewise, after 2 Kt—KB3, Kt—KB3; 3 P—Q4, P×P; 4 Kt×P, P—Q4 is refuted by 5 P×P, Kt×P; 6 P—K4. If White omits an early P—Q4 Black can equalize by playing it himself.

In other words, if White plays P—Q4 first he gets the better of it, if Black does, he equalizes.

Thus symmetry is not good for the defender because White can break in the center first and get an advantage.

The other alternative occurs after 1 P—QB4, Kt—KB3; 2 Kt—QB3; P—K3. Here 3 P—Q4 or 3 P—KKt3 is routine, but 3 P—K4! leads to some intriguing complications: 3 .... P—Q4 (the most natural); 4 P—K5, P—Q5! (essential); 5 P× Kt, P×Kt; 6 KtP×P, Q×P; 7 P—Q4, P—QKt3 (7 .... P—B4 is good enough though less promising); 8 Kt—B3, B—Kt2; 9 B—K2!, P—KR3!; 10 Kt—K5!, B—Q3!; 11 Q—R4ch, K—K2! 12 B—B3, B×B; 13 Kt×B, R—Q1; 14 O—O, K—B1; 15 R—K1 with fair attacking chances for his inferior Pawns. That is the central thought of this and related lines: White allows his Pawns to be weakened in order to develop more quickly and build up an attack.

Chapter VII

BIRD'S OPENING AND
NIMZOVITCH'S ATTACK

These two openings have several features in common, the chief of which is that White wishes to settle a Kt at K5 and attack on the K-side. Neither however, has any theoretical value: their chief virtue is variety.

BIRD'S OPENING: 1 P—KB4

This is really (after 1 .... P—Q4) a Dutch Defense with colors reversed, but if played as such it has little force.

After the most natural reply, 1 .... P—Q4, White's ideal

No. 48A	No. 48B

Ideal Positions for White in Bird's   Opening and Nimzovitch's Attack.

position is shown in *Diagram No. 48A*. After Kt—R5 he has a winning attack against the K-side.

Another excellent type of position, though not quite as crushing as that in *Diagram No. 48A*, is that in *48B* where

225

Black's QKt has been exchanged, White's Kt at K5 is unassailable, he again has a strong attack against the enemy K-position, and Black's Pawn structure is weak. The last factor, however, is not essential: White exerts strong pressure even if Black's P is at QKt2 instead of QB3.

But, as usual in such esoteric openings, if the defender is aware of what the ideal position is, and avoids it, he equalizes without any trouble.

After 1 .... P—Q4; 2 P—K3, there are two major alternatives for Black, both satisfactory.

The first is that where he pins the White KKt and prepares an early .... P—K4 (the Schlechter line). White must prevent .... P—K4, which allows other favorable simplification. E.g., 2 .... Kt—KB3; 3 Kt—KB3, B—Kt5; 4 B—K2, B× Kt! (he wishes to prevent Kt—K5 at all costs); 5 B×B, QKt— Q2; 6 P—B4!, P—K3!; 7 P×P, P×P; 8 Kt—B3, P—B3; 9 O—O, B—K2 with equality. White's Bishops mean little because their scope is limited.

The other choice is the K-fianchetto which, as we have seen on a number of occasions, takes the sting out of a White K-side attack. E.g., 2 P—K3, P—KKt3; 3 P—B4, Kt—KB3; 4 Kt—QB3, B—Kt2; 5 Kt—B3, O—O; 6 Q—Kt3, P—B3 with a good game, or 3 Kt—KB3, B—Kt2; 4 P—Q4, Kt—KB3; 5 B—Q3, O—O; 6 QKt—Q2, P—QB4!; 7 P—B3, P—QKt3 with a line analogous to the Colle System, this time in Black's favor —it will be recalled that a fianchetto defense is quite strong against the Colle.

About the only important alternative to 1 .... P—Q4 is 1 .... P—K4, the From Gambit. It is considered unsound. After 2 P×P, P—Q3; 3 P×P, B×P; 4 Kt—KB3, P—KKt4! there are two good lines for White: 5 P—Q4 and 5 P—KKt3. E.g., 5 P—Q4, P—Kt5; 6 Kt—Kt5!, Q—K2; 7 Q—Q3, P— KB4; 8 P—KR3 or 5 P—KKt3, P—KR4; 6 P—Q4, P—Kt5; 7 Kt—R4, B—K2; 8 Kt—Kt2, P—R5; 9 B—B4. In neither case is Black's attack sufficient compensation for the Pawn. Tartakover has won some pretty games with White here.

NIMZOVITCH'S ATTACK: 1 Kt—KB3 IN CONJUNCTION WITH THE Q-FIANCHETTO

It is obvious that this attack must have much in common with Bird's opening. In point of fact, the two ideal positions 48A and 48B may also be secured here. Again the same defensive ideas apply: break the back of the attack either by exchanging White's KKt or a K-fianchetto or an early center advance.

Two illustrations of attack and defense will be sufficient.

Where Black plays too passively, White may post his Kt at K5, solidify its position with P—KB4 and build up an attack against the K-side. E.g., 1 Kt—KB3, P—Q4; 2 P—QKt3, P—QB4; 3 B—Kt2, Kt—QB3; 4 P—K3, Kt—B3; 5 B—Kt5, B—Q2; 6 O—O, P—K3; 7 P—Q3, B—K2; 8 QKt—Q2, O—O; 9 B×Kt!, B×B; 10 Kt—K5, R—B1; 11 P—KB4, Kt—Q2; 12 Q—Kt4 with good attacking chances.

An example of good, though unusual, defensive play is 1 Kt—KB3, P—Q4; 2 P—QKt3, P—QB4; 3 B—Kt2, Kt—QB3; 4 P—K3, Q—B2 (to force .... P—K4); 5 B—Kt5, P—QR3; 6 B×Ktch, Q×B; 7 P—Q3, P—B3; 8 Q—K2, P—K4; 9 P—B4, Kt—K2; 10 O—O, B—Kt5 with excellent prospects.

As long as Black does not allow his opponent to post a Kt at K5 and solidify its position there he should have no trouble.

Chapter VIII

IRREGULAR OPENINGS

There are many players who feel that they can beat a "bookish" opponent by adopting some bizarre opening never before seen on land or sea. On occasion they are successful, chiefly because the flustered "bookworm" feels that anything unorthodox should be defeated in at most ten moves.

The reason why such upsets occur is not that the "books" are wrong, but that they must confine themselves to the refutation of plausible replies. *For really bad moves can always be refuted by general principles.*

The most fundamental general principles are those which teach us to develop and control the center. Where one side is allowed to get all his pieces out while the other moves about aimlessly, or where a crushing Pawn center is permitted, an overwhelming superiority is created. That is the case in these irregular openings.

In a sense irregular openings belong to the middle game rather than to the openings. For once one side sets up Pawns at Q4 and K4, or gets an appreciable lead in development he has a clear advantage and the opening problem is solved. There are however two mistakes frequently seen in such cases: the superior side exposes his Pawns too much, or he attacks prematurely. But with normal care there should be no difficulties. Of course, once a plus in development or center is set up, a well-conducted attack will decide.

A model example of the treatment of a fairly reasonable Irregular opening runs as follows: 1 P—K4, P—KKt3; 2 P—Q4, B—Kt2; 3 Kt—KB3, P—Q3; 4 Kt—B3, Kt—Q2; 5 B—

QB4, P—K3; 6 O—O, Kt—K2; 7 P—QR4, O—O; 8 B—K3,
P—KR3; 9 Q—Q2, K—R2; 10 P—R3, P—QB3; 11 B—B4,
P—Q4; 12 B—Q3, P—R3; 13 B—Q6. Note how White keeps
Black cramped, prepares an attack slowly but surely. In the
future he can proceed on either side—*Diagram No. 49.*

No. 49

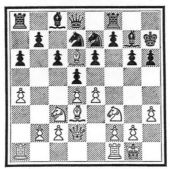

Ideal position for White against an
Irregular Defense.

APPENDIX:

References to PRACTICAL CHESS OPENINGS

PRACTICAL CHESS OPENINGS will be referred to as P.C.O.; the present work as Ideas. Light face page numbers refer to P.C.O., bold face page numbers to Ideas. All columns are in P.C.O.

The major openings are listed alphabetically in P.C.O., topically in Ideas.

Chapter II

1. *Diagram No. 1* is best illustrated in Philidor's Defense, p. 137, column 8, Ruy Lopez, p. 390, column 168, p. 391, column 174 and Scotch Game, p. 403, column 15. Examples of the equalizing force of .... P—Q4 by Black are legion. Ponziani's opening, pp. 140–141, columns 1–7, Scotch Game, p. 401, columns 1–5, especially Two Knights' Defense, p. 456, column 40, are the most striking.

2. *Diagram No. 2* is seen in p. 29, columns 1–5.

3. *Diagram No. 3* is on p. 401, column 3.

4. *Giuoco Piano:* pp. 93–102.

Diagram No. 4 is in column 20.

The Greco line, on **p. 14,** is column 8–9; the alternative 8 .... B×Kt in columns 1–7.

The strong point defense, on **p. 15,** is seen in columns 15–17.

The Canal Variation, on **p. 17,** is in columns 26–30.

5. *Two Knights' Defense:* pp. 443–457.

Diagram No. 5 is seen in columns 1–19.

Pinkus's analysis is in cols. 1–4.

The major line given on p. 19 is column 6. Recent games indicate that White's bind is quite strong.

6. *Ruy Lopez:* pp. 325–399.

Diagram No. 6 is best illustrated in column 156.

The Steinitz Defense is in columns 156–175; column 163 is the first main line. The improvement indicated on **p. 23** is in columns 164–165, and 169–170, especially the latter.

The counter-attack **(p. 23)** is the Berlin Defense, columns 141–155; the main line is given in columns 141–144.

Diagram No. 7 is considered in columns 1–105.

Diagram No. 8 is handled in columns 36–50.

In the strong point system the main line **(p. 26)** is in columns 76–89; the crucial line is column 36. The alternative 8 .... O—O **(p. 27)** is in columns 51–56; Marshall's sacrifice **(p. 28)** in columns 67–69. The Worrall Attack is in columns 76–87.

Diagram No. 9 is treated in columns 1–22.

The alternative 5 .... B—QB4 **(p. 33)** is in columns 91–93.

Diagram No. 10 is in columns 106–133.

In the Steinitz Defense deferred, the normal variation given on **p. 34** is reached by transposition from the Worrall Attack, column 86. Columns 126–127 are analogous.

The fianchetto defense is in columns 121–124.

7. *Diagram No. 11* is seen in pp. 58–61, columns 1–11.

8. *Diagram No. 12* is on pp. 462–463, columns 11–17.

Chapter III

9. *French Defense:* pp. 71–92.

The main line on **p. 70** is in column 7.

Diagram No. 13A is best illustrated in column 7. Analogous positions are those in columns 38, 13, note (j) and 14. Columns 49, note (m) and 50 show why it is important not to allow Black to strengthen his center.

Diagram No. 13B is seen in a normal line with chances for both sides in column 6. White is usually well advised to play QP×BP; the positional continuation with that line is then illustrated in column 9, the combinative (K-side attack) in columns 17–18. Compare also columns 12–14 for another typical attack. Columns 31–33 show what happens when White can strengthen his center, column 34 illustrates some of Black's opportunities.

Diagram No. 13C is almost always a prelude to a later .... P—QB4. See columns 13–14 for some possibilities.

Diagram No. 13D: the strongest version for White is in column 29. Black should play both .... P—QB4 and .... P—KB3, of course, but his problem is to choose the proper moment for the exchange. Columns 18 and 48 (.... P—KB3 will come later here) indicate what the best solution should be. Compare also columns 7, 9, 17 and 37 for suggestive lines.

Diagram No. 13E is not found in any French Defense column because it would lead to a lost position too quickly. The best example of White's possibilities is in Nimzovitch's Defense, p. 128, column 10.

Diagram No. 13F is column 7.

Diagram No. 14A is treated in column 47.

For the general Pawn structure see *Diagrams No. 15B, C* and discussion.

Diagram No. 14B is best seen in column 48; compare also columns 35 and 37.

10. *Caro-Kann Defense*: pp. 16–27.

Diagram No. 15A is in columns 1–3.

Diagram No. 15B is treated in columns 6, note (b), 7, and 10. It is also seen in the French Defense, p. 87, columns 46–47, and pp. 79–80, columns 25–28.

Diagram No. 15C is best illustrated in column 13. The Queen's Gambit Accepted, p. 160, columns 12–13 must be consulted. For the isolated QP for Black see French Defense,

p. 89, columns 52, 54, also Queen's Gambit Declined, p. 191, columns 91–92, Queen Pawn Game, p. 251, column 60.

Diagram No. 15D is handled in columns 24–26.

11. *Sicilian Defense*: pp. 407–438.

Diagram No. 16 is seen in columns 1–26.

Diagram No. 17 is in columns 31–53.

12. *Alekhine's Defense*: pp. 1–7.

Diagram No. 18 is in columns 1–4.

Chapter IV

13. **Queen's Gambit**: pp. 143–221.

Diagram No. 19 is the beginning of all variations of the Queen's Gambit Declined.

Diagram No. 20 is treated in columns 1–27.

Diagram No. 21A is not seen in any of the standard lines because the break . . . . P—K4 is almost always possible and strong. For illustrations of the play when P—B5 is followed by . . . . P—K4 see columns 14 and 20, note (p). An excellent example of how loss of time may permit a powerful P—B5 is seen in column 156.

Diagram No. 21B is best illustrated in column 56. Compare also columns 58, 59, 13 for good defensive ideas.

Diagram No. 21C is not found in exactly the same form in P.C.O. The nearest approach is column 60.

Diagram No. 21D is a variation which may arise in column 17 if Black does not play 14 . . . . Kt—K5.

Diagram No. 21E is most closely approximated in column 52. Inferior defense would lead to the diagram.

Diagram No. 22 is treated in columns 11–14.

Diagram No. 23A is handled in columns 51–59. Column 13 is significant.

Diagram No. 23B is seen in column 60. Compare also columns 172–175, in the Slav Defense.

Diagram No. 23C is not discussed independently.

Columns 37–40, in the Cambridge Springs Defense, are suggestive.

Diagram No. 24 is in columns 31–42.

The lines which avoid the Cambridge Springs are in columns 51–54.

Diagram No. 25 is in columns 43–45.

Diagram No. 26 is handled in columns 61–65. Columns 71–73 are also interesting here.

Diagram No. 27: the unusual variations are treated in columns 71–90.

Diagram No. 28A is seen in columns 91–105.

Diagram No. 28B is in columns 91–94.

The alternatives on **p. 128** are in columns 106–110.

The deviation 3 Kt—KB3, on **p. 130,** is seen in columns 111–120.

Diagram No. 29, the Slav Defense, is in columns 121–175.

Diagram No. 30 is treated in columns 121–131.

Diagram No. 31 is considered in columns 141–153.

Queen's Gambit Accepted: pp. 157–162.

Diagram No. 32 is in columns 1–10.

Diagram No. 33 is treated in columns 12–13. Compare also Caro-Kann Defense, **p. 81,** *Diagram No. 15C.*

Diagram No. 34 is handled in columns 14–16; column 20 is similar. For analogous lines in the Catalan System see p. 316, columns 23–26 and p. 317, columns 26 and 28.

14. *Queen Pawn Game with 1 P—Q4, P—Q4 where White Does Not Play the Queen's Gambit*: pp. 234–238.

Diagram No. 35 is seen in columns 1–9.

Chapter V

15. *The Indian Defenses*: pp. 239–294.

Diagram No. 36A is illustrated in columns 48, 69 and 71–74. Compare also column 81, note (b) and column 76, note (a).

Diagram No. 36B is seen in columns 26–27, and columns 56–57.

Diagram No. 36C is an ideal position which Black usually manages to avoid in these defenses. It is best seen in column 89, note (o). Close approaches to it are in columns 80 and 105. The position as it arises from other openings is well illustrated in p. 288, column 166 and Ruy Lopez, p. 373, column 113. With Black's KKtP at KKt3 it is, of course frequent in the K-Indian Defense.

Diagram No. 36D is another ideal position which appears, so to speak, by omission. Column 43 note (h) shows what happens when White can play P—Q5, but is compelled to abandon P—K4. Compare also column 80. The best example is in Tchigorin's Defense, p. 288, column 167.

Diagram No. 36E is seen chiefly in the Q-Indian Defense, column 87 is the best instance for Black. Columns 93–94 illustrate the dangers of a premature .... P—QB4. Compare also columns 89, 96 and 115. In the Nimzoindian compare columns 33–35 and p. 250, note (b). See also English Opening, p. 45, column 20 for play around a delayed .... P—Q4.

Diagram No. 36F is handled in columns 36–43, (usually with an early .... P—K4 by Black). With White's Pawn at KKt3, it is considered in the Q-Indian Defense, columns 100 (most important), also 81, 99 and 101. The strongest set-up for Black is seen in the Dutch Defense, pp. 299–305, column 201, note (b). Compare also columns 199 and 203 here. An analogous formation for White is to be found in Nimzovitch's attack and Bird's opening **(pp. 225–227).**

Diagram No. 37, the Nimzoindian Defense, is treated in columns 21–79.

Diagram No. 38A is in columns 21–25.

Diagram No. 38B is in columns 36–37.

Diagram No. 38C is handled in columns 51–54.

Diagram No. 38D is best seen in column 75, note (q). Compare also columns 69 and 78.

Diagram No. 38E is most closely approximated in columns 56–57.

Diagram No. 39 is handled in columns 81–88.

Diagram No. 40A is seen in almost all variations of the K-Indian. See especially columns 122–124 and 128. For analogous lines in the Ruy Lopez compare p. 364, columns 86–87 and p. 375, Col. 122, note (d).

Diagram No. 40B is most closely approximated in columns 126, note (b) and column 118.

Diagram No. 40C is best illustrated in column 124, note (i).

Diagram No. 40D appears in column 128; its chief importance there is as an ideal position. See especially note (o).

Diagram No. 40E is seen in columns 141–143. Compare also column 161, and Queen's Gambit, pp. 190, columns 87–89.

Diagram No. 40F is significant in most cases as an ideal position. It is best seen in column 147, note (i). Compare also columns 160 and 133.

Diagram No. 41 is best illustrated in column 120, note (1). See also Column 128.

Diagram No. 42 is in columns 141–165.

16. *Dutch Defense:* pp. 299–305.

Diagram No. 43A is found in columns 199–201.

Diagram No. 43B is in columns 196–198. See also columns 204 and 207. Compare Queen's Gambit, p. 186, column 79.

Chapter VI

17. *Reti Opening:* pp. 306–324.

Diagram No. 44 is handled in columns 1–40, directly and elsewhere by transposition.

Diagram No. 45 is seen in columns 16–26. Analogues in the QG are pointed out in the text.

Diagram No. 46A is treated in columns 16–18. Compare Queen's Gambit, pp. 187–190, columns 84–90.

Diagram No. 46B is found in columns 23–25. Compare the QGA, pp. 160–161, columns 14–17 and column 20.

18. *Diagram No. 47* is in pp. 41–42, columns 1–9. For analogous lines without the extra move compare the Sicilian Defense.

Chapter VII

19. *Bird's Opening:* pp. 8–11.

Diagram No. 48A is taken from the celebrated Lasker-Bauer game. It is most closely approximated (and there only as an ideal) in Nimzovitch's attack, p. 322, col. 42, note (c).

Diagram No. 48B is best seen in column 3, note (g).

Chapter VIII

20. *Diagram No. 49* is taken from p. 104, column 2.

INDEX

(The numbers refer to pages)